"Congregational leaders don't need to be told that the context of Christian ministry has radically changed in our lifetime, nor that, for many of us, these changes continue at a dizzying pace. The contributors to this book are neck deep in these realities, so they're well-positioned to invite us into an important conversation about what it means to be the church in mission today. We would be suspicious if a book like this offered easy answers, but we have much to learn from these stories about hearing the voice of the Spirit in our local contexts as we envision and cultivate missional churches."

Joel B. Green, professor of New Testament, Fuller Theological Seminary

"The essays in this volume rescue the phrase 'missional church' from the kind of indiscriminate use that threatens to make it little more than a slogan or cliché. The editors do not give us a one-size-fits-all strategy for church planting but offer instead a series of accounts about the ways a group of local congregations, as they thought about the ways they would organize their life together and ministries, sought above all to be attentive to ways the Spirit is at work in our rapidly changing world. The result is a book that stimulates the imagination for responding to the unique circumstances of our communities with the good news of Christ."

Barry Harvey, professor of theology in the Honors College, Baylor University

"Nick Warnes is a passionate church planter who reflects well. Mark Lau Branson is an excellent thought leader who has planted and participated in daring missional communities. The two of them have come together with several other engaged missional thinkers and practicing planters to offer compelling stories that will inspire missional leaders to renew local missional communities. Stories (re)create worlds, and this volume is in the business of renewing leaders and communities to shape our local neighborhoods (our worlds) for the gospel."

Kyle J. A. Small, associate academic dean and associate professor of church leadership, Western Theological Seminary, Holland, Michigan

"If you want to learn about and be inspired by missional churches that are gospel-driven, prayer-shaped, and parish- and neighborhood-oriented, this book is for you. The emphases on God as the primary agent in church planting, neighbors as subjects and actors, leadership as plural, and crossing economic and cultural boundaries as crucial make this book refreshing, unique and timely!"

Rick Richardson, director of the masters program in missional church movements, Wheaton College Graduate School

THE **MISSIONAL** NETWORK

A network of leaders across North America and the UK committed to a practical and biblical/theological engagement with the missional conversation in the church.

Missional Perspective

TMN frames its processes, tools, and resources within a robust biblical and theological missional perspective—God's mission in the world and the church's participation in this mission. An organizational understanding of systems is used in relation to these frames to support transformation across local, regional and national church bodies.

Resources for Transformation

TMN offers a variety of well-tested tools and resources that can help church organizations and their leaders engage in intentional processes of missional innovation and transformation. These resources support the consulting/coaching processes TMN makes available for systems change.

Consulting and Coaching

TMN provides both consulting and coaching to support the transformation of church systems at all levels. The consulting is designed to build the capacity of church systems to engage in systemic missional transformation. The coaching is designed to walk alongside leaders in strengthening their skills and capacities for leading in the midst of change.

Publishing

TMN has a Writing/Publishing Team made up of a broad, cooperative table of church leaders—pastors, teachers, and practitioners that produces a book series and other printed resources to deepen the missional conversation while informing system transformation from a biblical and theological perspective.

TMN Associates and Partners

TMN consists of a team of associates and partners who are part of and have a deep understanding of the historical development of denominations as faith traditions and polities. In all its work this team takes seriously the traditions and histories of each church system viewing it as helpful gift to the larger church.

International

TMN is an international organization that works with church leaders in North America, the UK and Europe to understand the particular ways in which the Gospel interacts with the churches and cultures in these locations, with a view towards the transforming of Western cultures.

www.themissionalnetwork.com

EDITED BY

MARK LAU BRANSON
AND NICHOLAS WARNES

LIFE WITH GOD IN
THE NEIGHBORHOOD

FOREWORD BY DAVID E. FITCH
AFTERWORD BY ALAN ROXBURGH

IVP Books

An imprint of InterVarsity Press
Downers Grove, Illinois

InterVarsity Press
P.O. Box 1400, Downers Grove, IL 60515-1426
www.ivpress.com
email@ivpress.com

InterVarsity Press® is the book-publishing division of InterVarsity Christian Fellowship/USA®, a movement of students and faculty active on campus at hundreds of universities, colleges and schools of nursing in the United States of America, and a member movement of the International Fellowship of Evangelical Students. For information about local and regional activities, visit intervarsity.org.

All Scripture quotations, unless otherwise indicated, are taken from the Common English Bible.

While all stories in this book are true, some names and identifying information in this book have been changed to protect the privacy of the individuals involved.

Cover design: David Fassett
Interior design: Beth Hagenberg
Images: © jonathansloane/iStockphoto

ISBN 978-0-8308-4116-5 (print)
ISBN 978-0-8308-9656-1 (digital)

Printed in the United States of America ∞

Library of Congress Cataloging-in-Publication Data
Starting missional churches : life with God in the neighborhood / edited by Mark Lau Branson and Nicholas Warnes.
pages cm
Includes bibliographical references.
ISBN 978-0-8308-4116-5 (pbk. : alk. paper)
1. Church development, New. I. Branson, Mark Lau, editor.
BV652.24.S68 2014
254'.1—dc23

2014013487

P	20	19	18	17	16	15	14	13	12	11	10	9	8	7	6	5	4	3	2
Y	31	30	29	28	27	26	25	24	23	22	21	20	19	18	17				

To those who wrote these stories,

their neighborhoods and their faith communities.

And to Nina and Whitney, forever partners

in this adventure.

CONTENTS

FOREWORD

I received a big surprise recently while sitting in a meeting with a group of denominational leaders. We were discussing church planting when a prominent leader in the room announced, "We will spend no more money on traditional church planting. The failure rate is over ninety percent. No one is willing to give us funds for this kind of effort anymore."

It did not surprise me that this one person would say this. I was stunned, however, to see that almost everyone in the room agreed.

Can it be any clearer? The landscape has changed for church planting.

For years, to expand their reach into new neighborhoods and population groups in North America, denominational groups would send small groups of people into a locale, set up a worship service and provide a list of support services for families. They would announce their arrival with some advertising and then wait for people to gather at a public "launch" service. A new church would be born.

There are now, however, fewer and fewer Christians even remotely interested in another local "franchise" of a church. Once a ready market of Christians eager for these new churches, North America has become a mission field. What used to work in starting new churches now fails. We need a new practice of church planting for the challenges of a post-Christianized society.

The good news is that, beneath the radar of most large church-planting organizations and outside the purview of the "100 largest churches in America" lists, hundreds of new churches are springing up in North America that look very different from the church plants of the past. They begin small and relationally. They live life among their neighborhoods. Viewing the incarnation as the way God works, they go be present *with* people, not offer services *to* people. Inspired by an enlarged view of God's triune work in the world, they seek to discern God at work preveniently where they are living. They are there to join in God's mission. And so a missional movement of churches is now sprouting up all over North America.

Mark Lau Branson and Nick Warnes are two veteran grassroots workers in this movement. In this book they open a window into what God is doing in these churches. Bringing their theological skills and their on-the-ground experience, they give us a way to understand missional and incarnational that helps us reflect on what is happening in church planting—as well as what we're doing in our own church life. Most importantly, they let the stories tell themselves. In so doing, this book funds our imagination for what church planting can be: a renewal of mission for North America.

For hundreds of years God has rebirthed his church through movements. Whether it was the monastic movements, pietist movements or frontier revivals, the church has always been renewed through the forming of new communities that call the rest of us to repentance and renewed commitment to live into the fullness of the gospel for God's mission in world. I believe the missional church movement is one such renewal movement in our time. And there comes a time in all such movements when the stories must be told if we are to learn and grow with them. I believe now is the time for some of these stories to be told. Branson and Warnes have collected some of these stories. They have provided a framework to understand them. They are doing the work here that is so essential for this next leg of the journey that is the missional church.

The only question is, will we go with them? Will we as Christians, disciples of Jesus, leaders and pastors join them in the vast new territories of God's mission in North America and beyond? I pray it be so. I pray that the stories of this book be multiplied a hundred times over.

David Fitch

ORIENTATION AND APPRECIATION

Mark Lau Branson
and Nick Warnes

We would like to provide a brief overview of this book. *Starting Missional Churches* is a collection of stories of new and diverse churches in the United States. The stories are preceded by two opening chapters that frame key issues, and followed by a final chapter that reflects on the stories in light of a set of priorities that we are advancing.

In the opening chapter, Nick Warnes describes some of the social, practical and theological challenges that we face regarding the need for an increased pace of planting. He notes how earlier priorities and methods do not provide opportunities for enough new churches, especially when compared to growth in population densities in the United States. He particularly notes the emphasis on suburban locations, the problems created when new churches come primarily from splits, the misplaced dependence on expert strategies, and assumptions that charismatic leaders are needed to attract new congregations. In chapter two, Mark Lau Branson brings the missional church conversation into an engagement with this church-planting conversation. He focuses on the centrality of discerning God's initiatives in a particular context, a priority on engaging the neighbor as a subject rather than as an object, the need to cross ethnic and economic boundaries, and the importance of plural leadership. These missional priorities are matters of theology and cultural context, with significant implications for how leadership teams begin their work.

The seven stories, told by pastors who lead local teams, provide geographical and denominational diversity. These are not new models to be packaged and transplanted; rather, they give readers insights into the processes and lessons of each specific, concrete, local initiative. Those of us who wrote these chapters—the stories, the frameworks and the reflections—hope that we have provided encouraging, enlightening narratives for others who want to be reflective and active in starting missional churches.

→

We also want to say thank you. Nick and six other church planters took the time to tell their stories. (There are notes on each writer beginning on page 209.) We asked them to be reflective and to provide more than narratives about their successes. We wanted to hear the voices of their leadership teams and of their neighbors. We wanted to know what challenges they faced, how and when they turned corners, what processes they engaged to discern their priorities and steps, and how they were changed by those they met. We are grateful that they decided to work with us, and that they committed time, thoughtfulness and prayer to this work. We are also grateful for the teams and neighbors around them—because the stories would not be worth telling without these numerous participants. We are grateful also to Dave Zimmerman at InterVarsity Press, who was constant with guidance and encouragement, and to David Fitch and Alan Roxburgh for contributing the foreword and afterword, respectively.

Personally, Mark notes how much he learns from students and graduates at Fuller Theological Seminary, which is how he met Nick. In addition, Mark is a senior consultant with The Missional Network (TMN—themissional network.com), and he recognizes the huge benefits of working with that team and being continually involved with churches across the country. This book is part of a new TMN line of books with IVP. The inaugural book in that TMN line, which Mark coauthored with Juan Martínez, addresses matters of leadership and intercultural life in churches. *Churches, Cultures and Leadership* provides numerous theological, social and leadership frameworks for those engaged in these settings of diversity, and the related website offers video clips and other resources (churchesculturesleadership .com). We hope, as a way to further this conversation, that readers will join us through our Twitter handle, @startchurches.

1

SHIFTING PERCEPTIONS ON HOW WE PLANT CHURCHES

Nick Warnes

With every week that passes, a smaller percentage of people are con-nected to the American church. This is the primary ecclesiological issue for us in America as we move through the first quarter of the twenty-first century.

In his book *The American Church in Crisis*, Dave Olson points out that 17.5 percent of people on any given weekend attended a worship service in 2005.[1] This is down from 20.4 percent in 1990 and 18.7 percent in 2000. This trend is notable for those that care about the church and the church's role within the kingdom of God. While attendance in numbers has largely re-mained the same over that time, approximately fifty-one million people per weekend, America has also grown by approximately fifty-one million people during the same period.[2] This is an important factor that is often forgotten, and it explains why the percentage of people connected to a church on any given weekend is shrinking. Regardless of the stats, the bottom line is clear: a significant percentage of the population is not connected with the church.

We believe that an important and effective way for churches to not only keep up with population growth in America but hopefully extend beyond population growth is to plant more churches. It is estimated that this year in America, 3,700 churches will stop functioning. In the same year it is es-timated that 4,000 churches will be planted.[3] This net gain of approximately 300 churches simply cannot keep up with the population growth in America. According to the 2010 census, the population in America grows by approximately three million people per year.[4] In order to keep up with population growth the church needs to plant one church for every fifty already-existing churches. To grow beyond population growth the church will have to plant two or more churches for every fifty already-existing churches.[5]

THE HOWS OF CHURCH PLANTING

We are fortunate to have the luxury of looking back on the past two thousand years of church planting as we begin this book. From Paul's heroic efforts throughout the Eastern Mediterranean to monastic movements that spread across Western Europe in the fifth century; to the Jesuits, Augustinians and Franciscans moving into Asia in the sixteenth and seventeenth centuries; to the series of Great Awakenings in America that created communities of faith as America grew through the eighteenth, nineteenth and twentieth centuries; expressions of church planting have been rich and diverse throughout the course of history. This diversity continues today.

Over the past fifty years an ever-multiplying subcultural landscape in our increasingly globalized world has led to diversified and contextual approaches to church planting. With all of these different expressions of starting new churches in mind, we would like to set a framework for summarizing the landscape of these different expressions through identifying what we have experienced as the four most common preconceived notions of how churches are planted today in the West. (These can be easily remembered through the acronym *SPEC*.)

Suburban sprawl: Shaped by a generation. Many denominations try to replicate the success that they experienced in mid-twentieth-century church planting. This success was largely achieved by initiating new churches in areas where suburban sprawl was extending from city centers. As many people moved farther away from the city after World War II, churches were started in the places where people were moving. These mostly white, mainline denominations—Presbyterians, Lutherans, Methodists and Episcopalians—as well as Baptists and Pentecostals experienced unmatched growth during this time; as recently as the 1950s the growth rate of these denominations equaled or exceeded that of the United States as a whole.[6]

While there were several approaches, a common strategy involved buying a piece of property in a strategic location, building a church building, hiring a pastor and attracting people to join the church based on denominational affiliation. The strength behind this type of strategy was founded on the connection between two institutionally minded generations—the silent generation and baby boomers—and a postindustrial corporate church. Denominational church planting made sense to people who were part of this post–World War II societal expansion.

While this movement was successful in the middle of the twentieth century, times have changed, and there are two obvious weaknesses to using this approach today. First, as we continue to move deeper into a postdenominational landscape, we should not expect migrating families to seek out the local franchise. When a family moved into a new home in 1956, denominational allegiance was common. The family wouldn't take time to look at different churches; they simply asked where the Methodist, Presbyterian or Episcopal church could be found. As mainline denominations continue to decline, there will be fewer people who ask this question. Second, as *Time* magazine reported in July 2013, there are fewer people moving to the suburbs.

> In 2011, for the first time in nearly a hundred years, the rate of urban population growth outpaced suburban growth, reversing a trend that held steady for every decade since the invention of the automobile. In several metropolitan areas, building activity that was once concentrated in the suburban fringe has now shifted to what planners call the "urban core," while demand for large single-family homes that characterize our modern suburbs is dwindling.[7]

With our perspective on transportation shifting further away from the priority on automobiles, this trend will continue into the foreseen future, making this strategy for suburban church less appropriate.

Because the mid-century strategy was rooted in other social habits, there are important theological matters for our attention. During those decades, denominations rooted in Euro-tribal religion were following the US cultural norms of corporations. A "strong center" provided management, strategies, control and imagination. From those centers regional and local franchises were shaped as distribution points for the goods and services of the denomination. So programs, liturgies, mission initiatives, renewal initiatives and leadership development were all delivered along that hub-spoke organization.[8] While this may have benefits for conformity and connections, it tends to shape churches and systems in ways that lessen how well we listen to our neighbors, how well we attend to those who are different and how aware we are of what God in doing in the local and concrete context. If a planting strategy is shaped to deliver predetermined commodities ("we know what they need"), then the winds of the Spirit and the profoundly local expressions of Jesus' love tend to be missed.

Mark and I frequently hear stories of church-planting strategies as we listen to pastors and denominational leaders around the country. For example, in a West Coast metropolitan area, a local judicatory (denominational network) thought it saw a great opportunity. Many people were migrating to "San Lucas" (not its real name) in order to escape the busyness and density of the city. With the guaranteed population growth, mainline denominations prioritized strategies to start new churches in these new developments. As one executive said, it was a "can't miss" opportunity. One denomination heard that another denomination was doing well in the new suburbs, so they decided to join the activity. They poured $500,000 worth of salary and programs into a new San Lucas church. They placed an ordained pastor in a local high school auditorium. They gathered members from other surrounding churches who were willing to leave their own churches to begin the new church.[9] They sent mailers over successive weeks to the surrounding homes and prepared a worship service they believed would be attractive. The new worshiping community launched and had moderate success in gathering people. However, as the activities of the church moved from the high school auditorium to the new facilities, and as they tried to formulate programs, differences in notions about church began to pile up. The mailers were not as effective as forecasting promised, and they learned that denominational allegiance was scarce in the new suburb. The church quickly began to shrink, and the ordained pastor left in disappointment. Another pastor came in to save the day, but it was too late. The trajectory for their deconstruction had been set. In the end the denomination that thought the new suburb was a can't miss opportunity learned that their goods and services could not create a foothold. Obviously, there are large and small churches in suburbs, and some are affiliated with traditional denominations. Some of those churches have found what they believe to be the transferable success package—but we recommend that you not buy it. The earlier suburban strategies of commodities and marketing, of franchises aimed at consumers, are too limited in their capacities to engage contexts in all their twenty-first-century diversity.

Protestant splitting: The DNA of the Reformation. The second type
of church plant that we commonly encounter is the church split. Holding
true to our *Protest*ant history, many new churches begin as they become
dissatisfied with their present church. In fact, by the turn of the twenty-
first century there were more than 33,000 Protestant denominations as
a result of their protesting history, a shocking number all Protestants
should remember.

There are many reasons for a group of people to split from an already-
existing church—dysfunctional leadership, bureaucratic structures, finances, moral failures, unhealthy boundaries, theological disagreements,
power struggles and personality clashes, just to name just a few. In the end
church splits typically have some combination of these different factors,
and more. It is our observation that the most often-named reason is heresy.
For example, one group in the church believes another group has left a
certain theological norm and therefore the first group determines that the
appropriate course of action is to begin a new church that once again is
fully orthodox. The church that split off and started a new church will then
hold strongly to the particular theological position they have taken, and
will work at attracting to their church others who share their view. The
strength of this type of new church is a strong sense of communal belief.
The new church typically has clarity on a particular belief, and they likely
share other conceptual matters regarding the Bible and their traditions.
The weakness is in the foundational discontent that initiates their church.
If a group of people is willing to leave in discontent over a theological issue,
what will keep them from leaving once again when the next theological
disagreement arises?[10]

The Enlightenment priority on certainty, arising from the anxious times
of Europe in the seventeenth and eighteenth centuries, provides impetus
for Protestant churches who make claims that their cause is *right*.[11] This
continues to have an impact on denominations (which continue to split),
but it also sets the DNA for churches. This fosters a mindset that encourages
groups within a congregation to become certain that their beliefs (about
theology or money or programs or music) are correct. This myopia is even
more problematic because churches in the West are also profoundly shaped
by consumerism—so we mistake consumer preferences for righteous causes
(about which we are certain).

A church in Michigan went through a difficult split. The church was from a Baptist tradition and when members disagreed about how the church would worship and how much they would participate in small groups, a split ensued. The older population wanted their songs to be accompanied by the organ, and the younger population wanted to use drums and guitars, which made the older population uncomfortable. The younger population also wanted to make small groups a center of the life of the church, while the older generation appreciated the already-existing events (Sunday potluck, rummage sales, an annual fish fry) for their fellowship. Unable to resolve their differences, the church split into two churches, and both pastors of the churches felt that it was better for their "kingdom witness" to do so. Five years later, the split was less than an ideal manifestation of witness on many levels, two of which should be highlighted.

First, at the core of the historical church is the mission of God. In a lecture to a group of church-planting coaches Darrell Guder, the Henry Winters Luce Professor of Missional and Ecumenical Theology at Princeton Theological Seminary, reminded the group that missional churches need to be identified as missional due to the reality that a church can still exist today without the primary lens of mission. Neither side of the church split in Michigan wore the primary lens of mission. While both sides of this split were somewhat aware of their neighbors as they stood their ground, people outside of the church were not at the forefront of their priorities. Although the older generation thought that the organ would be more attractive for their friends, and the younger generation thought that guitars and drums would be more attractive to their friends, at the center stood a consumer model of church that shapes members to consume something they want for themselves. In the end their claims for the superiority of their consumer preferences led to splitting the church. After the split they both received what they wanted to consume. However, the problems didn't end with the split. This gets to the second point.

The split made local news. Everyone around this small town was talking about what had happened. The younger population in the new church was initially excited about the news, as was the older generation. *Now that we got rid of what was holding us back, we can really move forward as a church,* they both thought. Unfortunately for both churches, the local news didn't help them solve their growth challenge. While the younger group was excited about their new church, their ability to satisfy the appetites of their clients through their products of a hip worship service and savvy small groups faded. They have had trouble creating a local identity in the neighborhood; mission was secondary in their ecclesiology. Thus, earning trust with local people has been challenging, and the local news actually created cynicism in the neighborhoods around the churches. For the originating church, people have continued to enjoy their events and their organ. However, these services did not attract more people, and they soon began to miss the younger families and the kids. Five years have passed and they have gotten older, many of them recently passing away. All these factors have created an imminent sense of despair as they have become increasingly aware that the life of their church is coming to an end.

Too often Protestant splitting is tied (unconsciously) to believing that a church is a set of commodities to be consumed. When churches focus on their own preferences and their assumptions about other shoppers, we fall into deadly traps of our consumer culture and nobody wins—neither the church nor the neighborhood. In the case of this spilt in Michigan, both parties still feel the loss and regularly lament the previous five years on multiple levels. Isaiah 11:6-9 reminds us of the day of the earth being filled of the knowledge of the Lord.

> The wolf shall live with the lamb,
>> the leopard shall lie down with the kid,
> the calf and the lion and the fatling together,
>> and a little child shall lead them.
> The cow and the bear shall graze,
>> their young shall lie down together;
>> and the lion shall eat straw like the ox.
> The nursing child shall play over the hole of the asp,
>> and the weaned child shall put its hand on the adder's den.
> They will not hurt or destroy
>> on all my holy mountain;
> for the earth will be full of the knowledge of the LORD
>> as the waters cover the sea. (NRSV)

In the case of the church from Michigan, and thousands more like it across the world, the lamb can't even live well with the lamb. We all anticipate a better day when the knowledge of the Lord covers us all as the water covers the sea while enjoying an embrace on God's holy mountain. In the meantime the new church and the existing church could not listen to each other. They could not reconcile. They could not prioritize unity over uniformity. It should come as little surprise that neither could effectively do this with their neighbors. Churches rarely split and form new churches because of missiological insights into how to best love their neighbors. It is clear that consumer preferences regularly are prioritized over the practice of God's mission.

Expert strategies: Modernity and its consequences.[12] We have also noticed that as modernity is in transition many have been shaped into thinking that planting new churches is work meant for the experts, and that those experts can shape models that are proven and reliable. We live in an era in which nonprofits have built extensive structures for assessing, training, coaching and resourcing people to plant new churches. We have seen top-heavy denominational systems with power and money to execute the complicated work of beginning new faith communities through appropriate branding and advertising schemes. There are also megachurches with the resources and expert staff to take hundreds (or even thousands) of members to a new part of town to begin a new ministry. The strengths in these models include the importance of understanding some of the complexities of church planting, the value of assessments and the vital role that mentors and connections play. However, the weakness in expert systems is that they assume too much about what can be generalized, what can be repeated from their experiences and what can be managed by their systems. Whether these efforts work through people at the top of such structures or through local mentors, they often miss the unique characteristics of a particular context and how God is already moving among their neighbors. A new church needs to connect with the innovations of a local people (who have seldom been told that they are worth listening to). The unique relational dynamics of a context and the perceptions and capacities of a team and their neighbors can be sidelined by the tools and priorities of experts who typically live outside of the context of the area where the church is being planted. Because they are confident in their approaches, they tend to undermine participation from less experienced people and spoil the possibility of plural leadership. In contrast to experts, *expertise* is brought in by different people to aid the work by shaping a creative and engaged environment.[13] But the people in the context of the new church offer their gifts to create a thriving expression of the Spirit of Christ. The mindset of experts, without the inclusion of people in context, can slow the process of following the Holy Spirit. The expertise of local people, respected by planters and mentors aids in the process of listening, is required for discerning God's initiatives.

An expert strategy recently unfolded in the Northwest. The staff of a large church in a suburban area felt that it was the right time for church planting on another side of town. The already-existing church had abundant resources and felt that it was their job "to bless" another part of the city with what they had to offer as an institution filled with resources. When a church building became available in this other part of town, they hired another person to be the pastor of the new church. They poured money into making the church building look more appealing to outsiders. They did extensive demographic studies electronically. They conceived a brand, built a website and engaged extensive social networking tools. They sent mailers to thousands of people around the neighborhood and prepared for a big launch. For the launch they appealed to people in the already-existing church to attend the new church for six months until they could achieve enough density of local people from the neighborhood to sustain the church. In short, from a distance they employed all of the common expert approaches.

Unfortunately, no one from the distant church—researchers, interested people or the newly hired pastor—actually lived in the context. No one did the work on the ground to listen to neighbors, understand the gifts and challenges of the context, or discern what God was already doing.[14] They acted as if they were going to bring God, as if God was not already present. It was impossible to not know that the event was happening in the neighborhood. Mailers had been sent over the course of successive weeks, ads had been placed in the local newspaper and money was even spent on advertising on Facebook to accomplish the task of niche marketing to reach the targeted area. As the launch day came, the fifty people who were committed to the church for six months couldn't wait to see who would show up. They drove in from the other side of the city to attend the event. When 11 a.m. came, the energy drained from the room as it quickly became clear that the work of the experts didn't achieve what had been so carefully imagined and managed from afar. Only sixty people attended. All the work, time and money invested to attract people from the neighborhood had not worked as promised. While the number grew to seventy-five in the next six months, as soon as it was time for the "members on loan" to head back to the existing church, it was clear that the plan, led by the staff, wasn't going to be sustainable. Only twenty-five people were left, and they felt betrayed by the parent church, which was still managing the project from across town. These are the consequences of the work of the experts.

What was the problem? First, the staff of the megachurch did not engage the new neighborhood, so they did not get to know the people who live there. They led from a distance, as if corporate mindsets would accomplish the task of starting a new church. Bob Logan, the author of *The Missional Journey*, emphasizes the local and concrete: "Jesus didn't teach from afar. He lived personally and relationally among the people he ministered to. Some he knew well: He cried with them, laughed with them, ate with them, traveled with them."[15] This is a drastically different approach. The megachurch staff, in their distant corporate perspectives, viewed people around the location of the new church as potential targets for their new project, not as people with whom to enjoy relationships. In the targeting, people were objectified as consumers who could not assist the parent congregation and their goals. The neighbors could sniff it out with every mailer that entered their mailbox.

The second consequence arises from that objectification—the staff was unable to create ownership among the people who first responded. No doubt the people of the neighborhood have stories, gifts, hopeful ways to meet local needs, and imagination for their environment. Only by listening to others, by dwelling in their contexts, can stories be heard and imaginations followed. Without relationships, outsiders remain outside. So when the local participants were expected to receive the gift of the church and adopt it as their own, they concluded that this was not really their church.

In the end, not only did the people of the neighborhood feel objectified, so did the people of the parent church. They were a gifted group of fifty people fit with diverse gifts and willing to bring some time and resources. But in what was supposed to be a managed transition of excitement and gratitude, many locals believed they had been used and participants from the megachurch were frustrated because their efforts were not welcomed.

Ephesians 4:15-16 reminds us of the roots of love that result when the priesthood of believers—all believers—work with one another.

> But speaking the truth in love, we must grow up in every way into him who is the head, into Christ, from whom the whole body, joined and knit together by every ligament with which it is equipped, as each part is working properly, promotes the body's growth in building itself up in love. (NRSV)

The church and the neighborhood cannot be built up in love when the experts work from a distance or deliver their plans. The body's growth cannot be achieved when the gifts of the local body aren't empowered to function. The expertise of the people actively listening to the prompts of the Holy Spirit enable new churches to follow faithfully in their call.

Charismatic figure: Big personalities. We have also spent time with new churches gathered around a centralized charismatic figure. This final notion of how new churches begin is intimately connected to the E, for expert strategies, in SPEC. A centralized figure is one who will typically have expert plans, but also focuses the beginning of the church on their charismatic personality and vision. This person has typically been positively assessed in his or her church-planting aptitude by a denomination or agency. Other standards for this charismatic figure include a knack for gathering people, for engaging them with a strong presence of preaching and for innovation. This model of church planting has been effective for quickly gathering crowds of people in both urban and suburban settings. The benefit of this type of movement is that it is agile. Churches with a top-down structure led by the charismatic leader should be able to make quick decisions because decisions do not need to go through any boards or leadership committees. The weakness of this type of new church is illustrated well by Ori Brafman and Rod Beckstrum in their book *The Starfish and the Spider*.[16] If a church leans too heavily on the pastor as an agent of attraction—the head of a spider—and the pastor leaves the church, which inevitably happens, the head of the spider is cut off and the whole organism dies. On the other hand, in new churches that prioritize a plural leadership—the many arms of a starfish—if the arm of a starfish is cut off not only does the starfish grow another arm but the arm that has been cut off can also grow into another starfish. So while a centralized figure can function well to gather people and quickly make decisions, the exit of that figure can be supremely disruptive to a new church.

In *Grow Where You're Planted* Dan Steigerwald defines the marks of increasing maturity in new churches. One of the hallmarks is empowering a stable leadership structure that is healthy, diverse and sustainable. He writes, "The community, for its part, empowers its leaders and respects their role in cultivating the growth, interdependence, and protection of the flock."[17] Notice that in this description of a maturing church there are leaders, not a singular leader, and they cultivate growth, interdependence and protection of the church. If a community begins with a single leader, a transition to a diversified group of leaders will always be difficult, leaving less room for time spent on the mission of the church. And if the charismatic leader is known for innovation, others often learn that their creativity and experiments are not as important.[18] Beginning with a plural leadership, while not prioritized in many traditions, is essential to a communal discernment of the Spirit within context. If an empowered leadership, not a centralized figure, is what a new church wants to eventually develop, then beginning with such a structure is important. (Plural leadership will be discussed in chapter two.)

One particular denomination teaches their church planters that they have been given a particular vision for the church. Therefore, they are to be the ones who give tasks, not titles, to people participating in the new church. Again, while the efficiency of such a perspective is appreciated, the wisdom and competencies of the collective body are often missed. A charismatic figure, as the only one with the power to make decisions and attract people to their perspectives, loses out on the collective voice of the whole community. Giving titles may cause inefficiencies in time and effort because the group will assume that those with titles need to be heard. Conflict can arise over the different perspectives, and decisions can be slowed as a result of this conflict. Yet in these various perspectives multiple gifts come forth, gifts that lie outside of the centralized figure, and the body of Christ can be equipped to function as a whole.

Church plants that follow the model of gathering around a charismatic figure are abundant. One example of a charismatically driven church arose in the South as a young preacher emerged in a local church. The lead pastor of the church recognized the gifts of the young pastor and formed an entire worship service for young people around him. The church was thrilled as hundreds of new people were attracted to watch this man preach. He spent hours in his study absorbing the writings of scholars both new and old. He was able to articulate his findings to the masses, connecting good scholarship to a culture in need of such depth. Soon the preacher and some of his friends decided that it was time to start their own church, so they took the group from the new worship service to begin. What started as a small church quickly grew to thousands of people under this man, who effectively branded himself as the leader of this movement. The movement was intoxicating as flocks of people left their churches to be a part of this new church that was much more exciting. The church continued to grow in the coming years, gaining national attention. The pastor became a public figure. He wrote books, spoke at conferences and became a leading figure in the national conversation on Christianity. His fame provided enough of an income that the demands of the local church became less and less consequential. He decided to leave the church to do the work of building his brand. Needless to say, his church was tremendously disappointed and didn't know what to do without their leader. They had been shaped by his personality and were not engaged with their neighborhoods. Church members had been formed to be consumers of preaching and volunteers in church programs (all part of the founder's vision). Slowly they left and went back to their old churches, some still secretly missing the moments of worship in the church that had become a shell of what it once was.

There are two problems in this story. First, as is frequently true of a charismatic leader, he did not develop significant relationship among the people of his community. While the masses appreciated his preaching and his priority on sermon prep, his frequent travels to speak elsewhere kept him away from his congregation and neighbors. The time that it took to manage travel, write books, participate in interviews and engage national matters demanded increasing attention. These demands left little room for his work in the local church. When it became clear that it was time for him to leave, many in the church were ready for the change. They knew that the deconstruction of their church would follow his exit, but they welcomed the transition because they knew they had a price to pay for making a person other than Christ central. They wanted a more hands-on approach to shaping the future of the church, changing their roles as program volunteers to that of being neighbors among their neighborhoods.

The second problem is in the church's inability to decentralize their leadership. A plural leadership would have provided the glue that would have better held together the church after the exit of their first pastor. Every new church struggles with the transition from their first pastor, especially when the leadership of the church hasn't been well distributed. In the case of this church, while extreme, the leadership was poorly distributed. As a remnant of people in the church struggled to define power structures, conflict increased to new levels. Even with aspirations of listening to the people of the neighborhood and working at developing meaningful relationships with those outside of the church, this essential task was soon disregarded. The next pastor was quickly fired because his preaching did not match that of the first pastor, and while the third pastor has held his job, the church is still in decline.

Both Mark and I receive calls from pastors who have been hired after a founding pastor leaves. Even though those transitions might be cautiously planned and less traumatic, in churches that have focused on a charismatic pastor who was not able to shape plural leadership and create habits that fired the imagination of others, decline is not only normal but is very difficult to reverse.

The time of a pastor in a new church is best spent in relationship with his or her neighbors and the people committed to founding the church. There is sure to be a time when a more attractive preacher or music program or programmatic mindset of a nearby church better caters to people who want to consume such products. When the priority is building relationships and equipping others to build relationships, a solid foundation is built for an effective witness. Time spent in these activities builds trust and is imperative for leading a new church in following the direction of God's call. The time and demands of a charismatic figure are often pulled in too many directions to spend time with people who are interested in the local expression of the church. Building relationships with people and equipping them to do the same with others is the most important asset not just for the pastor but for everyone in a new church. When the pastor of the church has different values, the day that the head of the spider is cut off is sure to be difficult.

We need to expand our vision of church planting beyond the four narratives we are currently working with. The seven stories that we have gathered, while still containing elements of SPEC, prioritize different values than those found in SPEC. The stories we have gathered come from different contexts and different locations across the United States. One thing ties them all together: the priority they give to fostering missionally minded churches.

This missional mindset has roots within the metaphors of Leslie New-bigin, which have become central to the missional church conversation. His ecclesiology reminds us that the church is the sign, foretaste, in-strument and witness of the kingdom of God.[19] The church is the primary means through which God loves the world. We believe this and have en-joyed compiling how these seven churches have courageously lived into this type of ecclesiology. They are continuing to watch and listen as the Holy Spirit shapes men and women to engage this changing American environment as a mission field, paying attention to neighbors and neigh-borhoods, to injustices and wounds, to creativity and goodness. In these emerging missional relationships we are encouraged by their continuous experiments in church formation suitable to specific contexts.[20] We hope that this collection of stories will move you in this direction. We pray that the narratives will create motivation and imagination, while providing some corrective elements beyond SPEC, in order that more people will be able to participate in this two-millennia-old practice of beginning new churches. We have engaged these topics through story, and through story we have been encouraged as we have seen theory and praxis come together. We will begin presenting them in just a moment. But first let's take a look at some different priorities that extend beyond the reach of SPEC.

2

PERSPECTIVES FROM THE MISSIONAL CONVERSATION

Mark Lau Branson

We chose to shape this book at the intersection of church planting and the missional church conversation. Not long ago I was asked for a list of books about church planting, but because I had explored this literature only sporadically I had to do more reading. I became aware that creativity and commitments are notable, but modernist cultural assumptions and habits that shape other churches are also dominant in the literature on church planting. Even many who claim to be postmodern have the managed, controlling and marketing traits of late modernity.[1] So while these books provided valuable stories and perspectives on the challenges of church planting, we decided to focus on the assets that have been developing among the children of Lesslie Newbigin.

If we accept the Newbigin framework that the West is a mission field, then, like the best of missionaries, we need to become reflective participants in the context.[2] We need habits of listening, observing, participating and discerning, all in the hope that we will be part of the widening learning community that attends to God's initiatives. Church planters are both insiders and outsiders when they engage a context. They are usually outsiders in that they did not previously live in the neighborhood—they are not known, they cannot assume they have a voice, and the Christian story they carry is probably known only through media fragments and fading memories. They don't know the people, the social fabric, the stories, the beauty, the pains or the challenges. But they are also insiders in a shared culture—usually shaped by unreflective modern consumer capitalism and romantic individualism. These modern forces are also interacting with a profound pluralism—multiple, diverse stories regarding gods and worldviews and politics and values. This means that Westerners tend to live unreflectively in a world that gives priority to personal consumer choice, affective transactions and strategies of persuasion. Western culture focuses on commodification—we package and market everything, so churches (and church plants) struggle to provide the goods and services that can be "sold" to those who are not "us." The vibe of the music, the relational feelings of groups and gatherings, and the attitudes of acceptance or cynicism are shaped as products. Newbigin would have us become aware, be participants, while also being people of a counter narrative.

THIS CULTURAL CONTEXT

In my own work on church transformation, which has not only shaped my church involvement but also my work as a teacher and consultant, I repeatedly encounter misplaced confidence in strategic planning, programmatic solutions, the marketing of commodities and the work of experts. These frameworks arise from various convictions of modernity—that we can predict and control outcomes, that we can create generic products or programs that will work in diverse contexts, and that specialists can give us magic bullets for our challenges. Alan Roxburgh writes,

> Leaders are comfortable talking about the maps of modernity but resist examining the implications of those maps on their leadership practices. Never is this more evident than when I suggest that the process of strategic planning in the church is structured by modernity's map and argue that the ways it is practiced actually undermine what God is about in the world.[3]

When leaders work with these approaches, they may create organizations that function for a while, but there are significant limits on adaptability, genuine participation and capacities to discern and participate in God's missional activities. I have frequent conversations with these pastors and planters as they face discouragement, when the people exhibit dissipation and as they look for another strategy to meet their challenges. Modernity has given us these habits of thinking, feeling and acting, and such habits are not just in older churches—

citizens of Western culture have been shaped by these characteristics, so they are present in neighborhoods and among church planters.

In an important way the West is a profoundly different mission field than the Mediterranean world of Paul's first-century initiatives or the foreign lands of the foreign missionary movement of the last four centuries. Unlike those contexts, the United States has institutions, narratives, cultures and locations where various permutations of the Christian story still exist. Churches and Christian-based agencies are there or have been there, and their beliefs and practices are already at play. So most residents of the United States have been to a church, have heard parts of the Christian story or are aware of the hospitals, universities, food banks and homeless shelters that have roots in the Christian narrative. Various media feature stories of Christians engaged in works of justice and economic provision, or in protests against abortion or the death penalty. There is no consistent story—it is fragmented and contradictory. There are Tea Party activists, church-based community organizers and monasteries that become retreat centers for corporations. Those fragments of the Christian narrative are in our contexts.

Not long ago I was having a beer with my friend and colleague Bill Pannell. We were planning a consultation for pastors concerning different leadership practices that are required in our urban contexts. A man at the next table turned his chair and (politely) interrupted us, "Are you guys Jesuits? I've never heard people talk about faith like that except Jesuits." I claim my doctoral studies among Jesuits at the University of San Francisco and the Jesuit School of Theology at Berkeley. Bill couldn't blame Jesuits— he had always fronted a gospel of justice and biblical narratives and cultural engagement. I said that we were professors at Fuller Seminary— which brought an affirming comment, something like, "I appreciate Fuller; we need more evangelicals who think outside the box." When I said that I was often dismayed about how the media focused on Christians behaving badly, he said, "Yeah, but many of us know the difference. We don't lump all Christians together." We learned of overlapping professional interests in urban research and various matters of justice so I've been able to continue our conversations and introduce him to other Fuller colleagues. I have also found it easy to engage nonbelievers during demonstrations for racial or economic justice, and my Jesus-rooted reasons for being there are a welcome part of the conversation. I have discussed movies and music, or politics and policies, in so-called secular settings, and find that a meaningful conversation that includes Christian perspectives is a respected element of the interaction.

I also know that the behaviors and opinions of believers and churches create antibodies to Christian witness—we have sown pain and injustice, and have espoused prejudice and nonsense. Our churches and agencies may be disconnected from any obvious expression of God's love—and from the actual work of the Spirit in a place and among a people. We frequently look more like self-serving social clubs, hierarchical and hoarding corporations, and retirement centers protecting themselves from their neighborhoods. I am actually energized when I get to work with those churches. I honestly believe, as do others in the missional church conversation, that God is among the everyday believers in all kinds of churches. As Alan Roxburgh and Fred Romanuk write, "If the Spirit has been poured out in the church—the church as it is, not some ideal type—then we are compelled to believe that the Spirit of God is at work and alive among the congregations of America."[4] Most of my speaking, consulting and writing, and my own church life, focuses on how these churches can come to believe and engage God's vocation for us.

I am not naive—this shift of imagination and practices is profound and difficult.[5] Along the journey we will need to listen to Scripture in ways that let God's initiatives take precedence over our consumer wants, cultural biases and institutional habits. Our definitions and practices of spirituality will focus on personal and church transformation as we learn how to major on discerning God's grace in our own communities and among our neighbors.[6] We will work on new patterns of leadership as the men and women and youth of these churches learn how to experiment our way into participating in what God is doing in our own contexts. That means that we will adopt the practices and experiments that can reengage our neighbors and our networks.[7] It also means that we will plant new churches.

In a recent conversation with a denominational exec I said that I was beginning to see that the lessons I was learning about the transformation of churches—matters of theology and leadership and practices—have significant parallels with the work of church planting. He was surprised; he said that he had assumed these were dissimilar activities. As we talked through a cluster of priorities and practices, the similarities became even more focused. This sense of similarities has been deepened in conversations with church planters—especially those with whom I stay in conversation around Los Angeles: Josh Smith, Nick Warnes, Kevin Doi and Kevin Haah. Their experiences and priorities are often overlapping what Alan Roxburgh and I teach in our doctor of ministry courses on missional leadership. These priorities can provide a framework for engaging the stories of this book. We don't want the themes we have chosen to be a grading rubric for the authors of our chapters; rather, we want to look for related traits in the stories, and to see if they provide guidance for those of us who are tracking with new imagination and practices for planting.

PROCESSES FOR MISSIONAL ENGAGEMENT

We are aware that the four preconceived notions in chapter one, concerning how church planting is often done, indicate some of the challenges we face. For example, they largely leave everyday people out of the narrative. It is too often assumed that we need experts with official plans or, alternatively, that we are just pawns who are caught in another round of church splits. Our hope is that church planting can be a more common expression of discipleship in the lives of everyday people in everyday churches across America. So we would like to invite churches, boards and students into an imagination that is shaped by the following four lenses, which are not just theoretical or regulatory claims but ways of seeing and engaging real on-the-ground stories. This is our way of bringing together some resources of the missional church conversation with the creativity and energy of those who are experimenting with diverse planting activities and practices across the United States.

Each of these traits is both theological and practical. In fact, we don't believe that those two adjectives are distinct types of activities. The work of "doing theology" is a reflective process that engages our biblical, creedal and historic texts while we are engaged by the Spirit of God in our daily lives.[8] The word *praxis* encompasses this—it describes the constant movement from engagement and action, then to study and reflection, and back to further actions (see fig. 2.1).[9] We read the Bible differently when we are engaging our neighbors. We see things in the text that we had not seen, and the text can shape us to listen and engage our neighbors in different ways.

This is also how we engage the praxis cycle concerning church history and the theology of earlier centuries. When we are participating with neighbors concerning polluted water or limiting our energy consumption, and we recite, "We believe in God the Father Almighty, Maker of heaven and earth," the creed energizes and interprets our experience, and those activities provide meaning to the text. This is how we learn; this is how creativity happens; this is how theology is shaped and lived out.[10]

Figure 2.1. Praxis

Throughout these stories there are numerous times that this praxis cycle is obvious (even though that group may not have called their process "praxis" or their conversations might not have been scheduled as "theological reflection"). We are especially interested in how church planting engages some of the theological frameworks of the missional church conversation whether or not participants used that term. There are numerous uses of the term *missional church*, and the following priorities indicate some elements that we think are important. We want to avoid several common meanings—that it is just about a church becoming more "external" or that churches should adopt some romantic ideals from "ancient churches" or that some strategic plan or reliable formula will give them a missional church.

Alan Roxburgh developed the "Missional Change Process" as a way to frame the work of existing churches who want to be reshaped in light of changing cultural realities and the initiatives of God in their neighborhoods (see fig. 2.2).[11] These five steps are also useful for church-planting teams: awareness, understanding, evaluation, experiments, and commitments. The process assumes that we are constantly learning, making mistakes, listening and attending to the Spirit, and becoming different people.

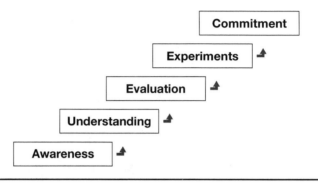

Figure 2.2. Missional change process

Awareness. **Awareness** is about neighbors and neighborhoods, the shifts in our sociocultural environment, the team that is exploring a new church initiative, and the previous and current initiatives of God in this context. In order to become aware we need to shape the space, the conversations and the language for what we are observing and experiencing. Roxburgh and Boren write,

> The role of the leader is to cultivate these safe spaces and assist the people in finding (but not provide) the means whereby they can name what is happening. People need time and opportunity to work through their feelings to the place of a new awareness, and they need the space to discover language for what is happening in their rapidly changing world.[12]

They note that if the pastor provides all the language, then the power of discovery and innovation among the people is diminished.[13]

Understanding. As awareness grows the participants need to pursue a deeper **understanding**, which requires additional listening and re-flection. This step "is focused on people talking among themselves about what they are learning, seeing, and experiencing in the new space." Leaders can shape formal and informal opportunities for conversations, listening prayer, and new efforts "to frame meaningful explanations for the changes they are experiencing."[14] The tendencies to make assumptions about what others believe or to jump to planning need to be re-sisted. Using an illustration about a tree, which has visible branches, foliage and fruit above ground but also massive roots below ground, Roxburgh and Romanuk note,

> if we too quickly assume we know what is happening in the lives of our people or the larger community in which the church is located and hasten on to plans and solutions, we are only addressing the tree we see above ground. We're missing almost all of what is actually happening to people, and our action will tend to be misdirected.[15]

This work leads to thicker interpretive resources about the current situation, including its causes and dynamics, and deepens the capacities of participants to engage in innovation.

Evaluation. **Evaluation** connects this accumulating set of experiences, knowledge and reflection with a hope that we become more faithful and competent as God's people in this setting. When we look at this set of circumstances, including our context, God's initiatives and ourselves, what new social imaginary might shape our future in this place? In an existing church this is the step for looking at current priorities, activities and competencies, plus the opportunities and challenges of our context. In a church plant the same basic conversations are pursued. Craig Van Gelder's questions—What is God doing? and What does God want to do?—shape the process.[16] These questions shape discernment, wisdom and planning. So participants ask, What competencies do we have? What new capacities do we need to develop? What do we need to learn? What stories do we hear from our neighbors? What groups, activities and dreams are alive in our context, and how do we come alongside them? What challenges exist in the community, who is involved, and how can we take steps to learn and engage? This step includes looking at the church's resources in Scripture, history, personal narratives and networks. Roxburgh and Boren write, "It is in this space that people are ready to risk dreaming a little about what God might be calling the church to be in their neighborhoods."[17]

Experiments. Rooted in an imagination that is being formed through the first three steps, participants then shape some **experiments** that help them check their read of the circumstances and their discernment of the Spirit as they seek to enter into what God is doing on the ground. Roxburgh and Boren write,

This is about inviting people to dream in ways that can give them some early wins after taking risks. This is a big transition for most churches since the default is to assume plans and proposals come from leaders and are put into action by the people. Here we reverse that process in order to invite people into different habits and imaginations.[18]

Instead of being limited by the vision of a charismatic leader, the initiatives are shaped by the people—those in the planting team and the neighbors they are meeting. These experiments, in the context of continued prayer, conversations and evaluation, continuously call participants to additional learning and more faithful imaginations.

Commitments. Finally, based on what we learn from the experiments, we make **commitments** to some experiments. When experiments are initiated, success is not the primary goal. The priority is on shaping an environment of risk—which means lots of failures. So this cycle (awareness, understanding, evaluation, experiments, commitments) is reengaged as participants get a sense of what happened with the experiment. Effective leaders will provide an environment of encouragement and learning. Sometimes the experiments will have effects that we want to continue, which means we will provide time and resources so that those activities can endure for a longer period of time. Roxburgh and Boren, writing to existing congregations, emphasize,

> It is at this point, in the midst of growing experiments, that people realize that they have discovered for themselves a way of being church that isn't dependent on outside programs, gurus, or even ordained clergy. Tangible, measurable, and observable actions occur. This is the point at which a local church tips over to a place from which it can't go back to the old ways of being passive recipients of religious goods and services.[19]

The following chapters will often exhibit these steps even though different language and sequences will be apparent. Even though these steps are listed in a linear fashion, and initially that sequence is important, the process becomes more like loops and braids as the participants continually moving back and forth among the steps.

MISSIONAL PRIORITIES FOR STARTING CHURCHES

These steps have been shaped and tried in hundreds of churches. The following priorities are our way of naming a few themes that are embedded in those steps and have traction in the missional church conversation. These descriptions are intended to prompt observation, understanding and discernment as readers engage the following chapters.

1. Priority on discerning God's initiatives. If God is living and active, then church life, including church planting, should attend to discerning God's initiatives in their lives and context. This is not just a process of finding biblical commands and doing them—rather it requires that we engage the living Trinity now, on the ground, in the mission that is around us and ahead of us. Jürgen Moltmann writes, "It is not the church that has a mission of salvation to fulfill to the world; it is the mission of the Son and the Spirit through the Father that includes the church, creating a church as it goes on its way."[20] This is an important theological conviction—that God is on the ground in neighborhoods and communities. There are diverse ways this is articulated in various theological traditions, all rooted in God's active love for the world: the Holy Spirit is (actively, continuously) bringing healing and justice and salvation, and we are to participate in the Spirit; Jesus is in and among men and women, bringing peace and salvation, and we can discern and participate in his presence and actions; the Father loves the world, intervening with specific and timely graces, and we are called to be receptive and to "be about our Father's business" as agents of that love; the gospel is the announcement of the present and coming reign of God. God is the primary agent, and our agency is to be that of participating with the Trinity.[21] These theological affirmations lead us to place a priority on discernment—that a church, continually shaped and resourced by leaders, gains the needed capacities and courage to discern what God is doing in their context and in their own lives, and then to participate in those initiatives (graces) of God. This is an alternative to seeing our work in functionalist, consumerist categories that deal in niche markets, the development of goods and services, and an emphasis on prediction, management, and control. Rather, we attend to what God is doing and enter into God's life and work around us.[22]

The work of discernment, then, requires that practices and processes be developed for the planting team and incipient church. I will provide a more thorough process in our concluding chapter, but Roxburgh's five-step Missional Change Process is an excellent overview. Inside the MCP are numerous activities like conversations, research, Bible study, listening prayer,

testing ideas and monitoring the relationship between actions and consequences. Further, discernment is rooted in personal and corporate practices
like personal Bible reading and prayer, loving our neighbors, giving ourselves to hospitality (as guests and as hosts), worship, generosity, and corporate attention to Scripture. These activities are symbiotic with the personal and corporate characteristics needed for a planting group to be
vulnerable to God, sensitive to the Spirit's initiatives, constantly reflecting
and learning, and ready to be engaged in God's initiatives. These are basic
traits of holiness and righteousness, and discernment is less likely if these
characteristics are not being nourished. Alan Roxburgh and I, in consulting
work and in teaching a doctor of ministry series, spend significant time
providing a mirror for leaders, along with processes for developing the
habits and practices and traits needed for church leadership.[23] Roxburgh
writes, "In our situation, the way this discernment develops is through corporate practices and . . . rhythms of life. The learning of the church through
the centuries is in the recognition that in such practices lies the possibility
of unmasking our enmeshments and forming ourselves as a parallel society."[24] If we are to discern and participate in God's continual initiatives, we
need to be able to name how we are malformed (from without and within),
how our cultures provoke both brokenness and beauty, and how our
neighbors and we experience true and false narratives. Church planters
need to engage the practices that tune our lives to God.

2. *Priority on the neighbor as subject.* Too often churches assume that
we know what our neighbors need and we will deliver our version of the
gospel's provisions to them. So we listen briefly to determine our next steps
(or we just presume that we already know), and we assume our main job is
to provide the goods and services and knowledge, based on what we have
and what we determine. But our first priority, to discern what God is doing,
helps us remember that God creates our neighbors and us as subjects or
actors, rather than as objects. We often assume (or at least our actions
belie) that *we* are subjects—agents of ministry—but that our *neighbors* are
objects. Daniel Anderson notes this common approach and the contrast of
missional modes:

> The modern approach to context asked how the church could be in ministry
> *to* the context. Demographic studies of neighborhoods led to defining target
> audiences, identifying the needs of those audiences, and developing programs

and ministries to meet those needs. . . . However, . . . other emerging ministries are taking different approaches to context. . . . These emerging ministries hold what is essentially a subject-to-subject rather than a subject-to-object relationship of engagement with their community.[25]

So while our initial priority affirms that God is the primary agent, human agency also needs to be affirmed, especially the agency of our neighbors.[26] The biblical narratives repeatedly tell of the risk God takes in not shaping humans like robots, and even though we are often wayward, God refuses to reduce us to commodities or targets.

If we believe that our neighbor is a subject, then our behaviors and expectations shift. We listen. Roxburgh writes, in reflecting on the Luke 10 account of Jesus sending the Seventy, "Like strangers in need of hospitality who have left their baggage behind, enter the neighborhoods and communities where you live. Sit at the table of the other, and there you may begin to hear what God is doing."[27] In this way we dispense with our tendencies to maintain power and to treat neighbors as those to whom we deliver our products, programs and truths. Rather, we come alongside our neighbors— we pay attention, we work, we eat, we converse, we cry, we laugh, we hope.

When we are shaped by other priorities—collecting data, developing programs, using our gifts, forming institutions, prioritizing numerical growth— we easily miss the important stories *and* how God is already involved.[28] We have been shaped to classify the stranger as a distraction or a problem, or as someone who might require a change that we prefer to avoid. "We create more and more ways to safeguard ourselves from the stranger," Roxburgh writes, "which does nothing to strengthen our sense of belonging or community."[29] But hospitality is the practice, according to Roxburgh, that brings us into a missional engagement that we cannot control. These genuine, human encounters, which are always life-on-life, are the times in which we find ourselves engaged in God's initiatives that bring new healing, love, beauty, justice and salvation. So for those engaging a context for the sake of the gospel, relating to the neighbor as a subject is critical; this is the vital connection that is needed to know how God is present, what opportunities exist for partnerships, and how a church can participate in healing, beauty, trust-building, belonging and witness.

3. Priority on boundary crossing. Most humans have a tendency toward security that favors what is familiar. While we may push out toward new experiences in limited ways (especially in travel and aesthetics), we want to control those encounters so that we always have the power to retreat to our own habits and preferences. Even when we want to claim that God loves those who are different from us, we want to keep those differences adequately fenced. But the border-crossing love of God doesn't give us that kind of consumer option. If we are to know God's love of the world, we need to be carried by that love, and that means we will be changed by those who are different. There is real discomfort here—and we find that challenge acknowledged in biblical narratives. When Jesus provided a sermon in Nazareth, concerning God's care for Gentiles, his hometown worshipers coalesced in rage (Luke 4:14-30). Also, throughout Acts the Holy Spirit made clear that ethnic boundaries were to be crossed. In his work on the Acts, Roxburgh writes,

> This boundary-breaking work of the Spirit creates conflict, consternation, and confusion. It leaves people struggling to figure out how the things they thought normative to the gospel fit into this shifting of boundaries, which at one time seemed so clear and well-defined. The reason for this boundary-breaking work of the Spirit is that God is about something in the world that is far bigger than the confines of an ethnotribal religion even if that ethnotribal religion is the Judaism of the Scriptures. There is a cosmic scope to this gospel, and the Spirit will not leave the church forever sitting inside its well-defined boxes that try to determine what God can do in this world. Hence, in these early days the boundaries are crossed, the assumptions are broken, and the church is set on a whole new journey as the agents of God's future.[30]

So boundary crossing is not just a matter of determining a workable strategy; it is key to participation with God.

Dwight Zscheile, writing about spiritual formation and missional ecclesiology, emphasizes,

> Life "in Christ" means the decentering of the self in a reordering of identity in which our relationship with God is primary. This decentering allows for relationships with others to flourish, for it makes space for them. . . . In the power of the Spirit, new relationships of mutuality and equality become possible.[31]

The specifics concerning boundary crossing will be shaped by the local context, but we can name some common factors: generations, ethnicity and socioeconomic differences. We need to be especially alert to our own provincial habits, and we get the privilege and work of engaging neighbors who are different, who may give us eyes that we don't want, and who actually reshape us in the encounter.[32]

4. Priority on plural leadership that shapes an environment. We have been shaped by cultural forces that emphasize individualism and that delegate to leaders the work of providing directions. Our priority on plural leadership counters those assumptions. Our cultural norms set us up to look for the visionary, the CEO, the charismatic leader, the rugged pioneer and the entrepreneur. The metaphor of a coach often assumes an all-wise authority who provides the plays. The biblical word *apostle* is misunderstood in our context as one who has final authority and the only clear channel from God. When we challenge these cultural habits about leadership, we want to be clear that we do not believe leadership should be eliminated. However, we want to emphasize that as God is shaping a people (a church), the Spirit is inspiring, forming, motivating and teaching a cluster of people who are to provide leadership on the ground. As Van Gelder and Zscheile write, "[Leaders] must not seek primarily to satisfy the hungers of spiritual consumers (as in the professional paradigm) but rather to create the conditions under which people can come together in shared life to discover their participation in God's mission."[33] Roxburgh and Romanuk clarify the work of leadership as "the cultivation of an environment that releases the missional imagination of God's ordinary people."[34] This environment includes relationships, imagination, resources, questions, actions, learning, hope and holiness. Again in reference to Jesus sending the Seventy in Luke 10, Roxburgh notes how the Spirit works:

> In the nameless seventy, Luke is saying something about how the gospel indwells a time and a place as well as the nature of the community and its tasks. It is among ordinary men and women, whose names will not be recorded or remembered, that God shapes a future. Contrary to the way we set everything up in the modern West, it will not be from the stars and professionals, the so-called great leaders and gurus, that the direction of God's future is discovered. . . . It is through the ordinary people of God, the nameless people who never stand on stages or get their photo in the newspaper, that the gospel will indwell their space.[35]

So, within the planting group, while an individual may be aware of his or her personal inspiration, ideas and observations, there needs to be an awareness that others are also having such experiences. God will prompt and inform and provide hope though various people.

God uses the diverse perceptions, strengths and gifts that are present among the leadership team and throughout the entire group. There are various ways to notice and engage such resources—using tools like Strengths Finder (strengthsfinder.com) and Myers-Briggs (myersbriggs .org). Leaders will help a group learn how to talk about such inventories, helping participants learn from them while not becoming either entitled ("I have this gift so I need to use it") or restricted ("Since that is not my strength I will disengage").

The New Testament frequently lists various gifts, character traits and practices that are relevant for leadership teams. Meditation, storytelling and noting observations about each other in light of these texts can encourage better leadership. However, if interpreted as permanent, prescriptive models, such texts can be misleading. At times, churches have created standards based on particular practices (like travel) or certain gifts (like tongues), and diversity, nuances, and contextual factors get lost. I want to pay attention to the fact that these New Testament lists (gifts, character-istics, activities) vary from letter to letter (or city to city). There is no standard model. Also, there is no claim that gifts are permanent. So, based on how the Holy Spirit works, we can assume that gifts can shift depending on circumstances. In churches and classrooms I have often engaged study and meditation in Ephesians 4, which brings together clarity on the church's vocation, a focus on unity and reconciliation, some gifts of Christ, and the trajectories of a church that engages its context in ways that transform persons and the whole group.[36] When I lead these discussions, participants frequently find that the leadership tasks are not what they had assumed. Usually they quickly see that the goal is not just to identify skills and clarify jobs, but that gifts increase capacities throughout the church as members are shaped to embody these gifts. So, for example, a prophet is not just to be an authority on God's voice (which always needs the discernment of the group) but has the work of increasing the church's availability to God's voice, and nurture ways in which others increasingly discern and articulate what God is initiating. So a prophet asks, *How can I create an environment in which listening to each other and to God is increased, and our discernment competencies mature?* Of course, this means that a prophet also gives voice to the Spirit's promptings, but maturity would slow if that were all a prophet did. When a group realizes this shift in the role of gifts, they usually re-engage the specifics of the gifts that are listed.[37] This is usually easy for me since I get to ask questions; here is how this unfolded in a recent classroom:

MARK	What is an apostle? What does the word mean?
PARTICIPANT 1	Aren't they the authorities?
PARTICIPANT 2	Doesn't the word mean "sent"?
PARTICIPANT 3	But when the church was scattered in Acts, didn't the apostles just stay in Jerusalem?
PARTICIPANT 2	They eventually left, as the Romans increasingly made it unsafe. That seems different than being sent. But Paul was sent. Peter was sent to bring back a report.
PARTICIPANT 3	I think the New Testament names the Twelve (with one replacement), then eight others. Those eight were extending the mission—crossing boundaries.
MARK	So let's work with that—their work went beyond their initial context, so they helped cross boundaries, and that eventually meant they were sent to new contexts. What about prophets?
PARTICIPANT 2	We learned that two words describe the work of a prophet—fore-telling ("here is what will happen if we continue in this trajectory") and forth-telling (expounding on God's Word and how God is working with us).
PARTICIPANT 4	Don't they focus on connecting the church with what matters to God? Old Testament prophets spoke about inconsistencies—like when leaders and the people kept up with their worship activities but did not attend to widows, orphans and immigrants.
PARTICIPANT 3	So prophets connect God's Word and priorities with us and our context? Mary sounds like a prophet when she describes Jesus' birth as af-

	fecting political powers, wealth and the coming blessing of the poor.
PARTICIPANT 4	And Agabus warned Paul that he would be arrested by Rome. Some thought that meant he should not go to Jerusalem, but Paul understood it in another way to be engaged!
MARK	So both apostles and prophets have significant work in connecting churches to their contexts. What about evangelists?
PARTICIPANT 2	They are messengers. They announce good news.
PARTICIPANT 1	Wasn't this a contest with Rome? Didn't Rome have its evangelism regarding kings and military victories?
PARTICIPANT 4	So the evangelists are proclaiming a message that counters Caesar while clarifying why Jesus is good news? That means that they also understand and engage a context.
MARK	What is the work of a pastor? Since this is a metaphor, start with the basic work of a shepherd.
PARTICIPANT 2	Shepherds hang out with sheep—usually in fields and hills.
PARTICIPANT 3	They have jobs related to resources, protection and healing.
PARTICIPANT 1	Sometimes they bring sheep to a corral—but I guess they are usually out in the hills with the sheep.
MARK	That's enough for now—like other terms, there are important Old Testament precursors regarding leaders and shepherds that will need study, but how about teachers?
PARTICIPANT 4	That's easy—they provide information and explanations that people need—usually about a particular set of knowledge.

MARK	And in Ephesus, where do you think they worked? [I offered some help here with a picture of the ruins in Ephesus.]
PARTICIPANT 4	Maybe in synagogues, at least until they had to leave. Then they went to houses.
PARTICIPANT 1	You mean they weren't in classrooms? Where were the classrooms?
PARTICIPANT 3	In Greco-Roman cities, weren't teachers in amphitheaters?
PARTICIPANT 2	And in the market?
PARTICIPANT 3	So their work was also in public, in the midst of the ideas and ethics and politics of the cities.
PARTICIPANT 1	So all five leadership gifts were about engaging the church's context—they worked directly and indirectly to help the Ephesian church deal with the specific, concrete realities of how God connects to the world they lived in.

These discussions usually lasted an hour—because I would ask for stories about where and when they had experienced these kinds of activities, both in the world and in a church's engagement with the context. As is obvious, this conversation challenges the common references to APEST, which too frequently turns gifts inward and makes them into offices. There is a significant adventure here as a whole church, with leaders as models and partners, becomes imaginative and articulate in the neighborhoods and civic environments around us.

The overall dynamic of wisdom and faithfulness is strengthened when a group surfaces, articulates and works with all of these voices and experiences. When one participant learns something from texts or contexts, or when there is a sense of God's guidance, that information is placed into the group's corporate conversations and discernment. If one person's experiences and voice becomes too normative, others pull back their full gifts and insights (even though they might continue to participate).[38] So we want to note unique personal actions and roles while we call attention to the whole of God's work in shaping teams.[39] This is why Roxburgh emphasizes that the work of leadership "involves creating safe spaces where ordinary people engage in more and more conversations about what is happening in their lives and what God might be up to in their neighborhoods."[40] In his work with the metaphor of mapmaking, Roxburgh emphasizes that "the map-makers are in our local churches; they are ordinary people in whom the Spirit is gestating all kinds of unanticipated futures for the kingdom. Mission-shaped leaders create environments of permission-giving and experimenting in which these ordinary dreams might be birthed."[41] This is a priority for those who are planting new gospel expressions in our communities.

CULTURAL DEAD ENDS VERSUS CONTEXTUAL OPPORTUNITIES

Many books and speakers who use the missional language are shaped by strategic modes of modernity and the longings of Romantic idealism.[42] So *missional* is wrongly used to indicate ramping up programs for the neighborhood or adopting an idealized approach to worship or seeking effective "community." The impulses behind such approaches may come from dissatisfaction or even cynicism concerning previous church experiences. If those problems were judged to be the result of structures, then the new attempt will be more "organic." If there was frustration across generational differences then the new initiative will focus on younger people "like us." There are also initiatives from denominations or other agencies that want to target a specific type of people (rooted in the perspectives of the church growth movement), so "studies" lead to marketing approaches designed around what they believe about that clientele. These are all a misdirection. I am not discounting important avenues of organized engagement—I am frequently involved in various forms of community development, community organizing and initiatives aimed at social justice and peacemaking, and I encourage churches to engage these activities. I also engage Christian men and women concerning how businesses or government or schools can better serve their communities. But these approaches are usually developmental or traditional missions and do not necessarily express the key theological and praxis turns that are central to the missional conversation. Alan Roxburgh and Fred Romanuk key in on questions that are essential for a missional church:

> Missional communities . . . are learning they need to listen and discern again what is happening to people in the congregation and in the community, and then ask these questions: What is happening to people? What might God be

saying in the stories and narratives of the people in a congregation, if we would listen to them and give them voice? In what ways might God already be ahead of us and present among people in our community? How might we join with God in what is already happening?[43]

These four priorities—God is the primary agent, neighbors are subjects, boundary crossing is essential, and leadership is plural—are intended to shape perceptions, raise questions and encourage the imagination of those who are planting churches. As we previously noted, we do not intend this chapter to be used as a list of strategic goals for the churches and authors in this book. They are all working in specific contexts with unique histories and are learning how their lives can be engaged in God's mission. As we had hoped, they feature significant diversity in their approaches, strengths and challenges. We are encouraged by the stories that follow, and we are confident that conversations among churches of varying ages and places can lead to mutual learning about missional life. We hope that these stories and our comments will inspire others into the practices of missional church planting.

BALANCING LOCATION AND RELATIONSHIPS

EPIC CHURCH

Kevin Doi

EPIC CHURCH

Location: Fullerton, California
Denomination: American Baptist Church
Year of Foundation: 1998
Regular Participants in the Life of the Church: 200
Website: www.epicchurch.net

In the story of Epic Church you will find a church's struggle in balancing location and relationships. Written by Pastor Kevin Doi, this chapter is helpful for those exploring intercultural relationships and how people of different backgrounds grow together within the context of a church. Epic's story is the oldest of all the stories written about in *Starting Missional Churches*, having been in existence for twelve years. Be sure to notice how the church moves and changes with time as God leads them toward an ever-growing missional vigor.

Epic means "grand narrative," and so it follows that the primary shaper of our church is story. As Stanley Hauerwas reminds us, "The primary social task of the church is to be itself—that is, a people who have been formed by a story . . . to form their community consistent with their conviction that the story of Christ is a truthful account of our existence."[1]

There are two stories in particular that have been meaningful and describe how we understand God's ministry with us. These stories, or parables, are set in the agricultural world of farming that surrounded Jesus in the first century. In the first parable, Mark 4:1-20, Jesus tells us that God is like a farmer who sows seed (the Word) indiscriminately and generously. He does so knowing not all his seed will germinate, but some will, depending on where it lands. Jesus goes on to explain the meaning of the parable, this time from the vantage point of the soils (people). How people respond to the Word reveals the kind of soil they are; how they respond to God determines the fate of the seed. In the second parable, Mark 4:26-29, a farmer sows seed; day and night the seed sprouts and grows, though the farmer doesn't know how. Mysteriously the soil produces a ripened crop ready for harvest. This too, Jesus says, is what the kingdom of God is like.

In the same way, we understand that Epic exists as a kind of parable. We are a community of sowers and soils gathered to discern where the kingdom of God is taking root and growing—hoping that one of those places is in us and in the community around us. We understand our purpose to be intentionally serendipitous, attempting to sow faithfully the seeds of the kingdom, realizing that the harvest will appear in ways we may not expect or understand, and certainly cannot control.[2]

An Unconventional Beginning

The origins of Epic Church began just prior to 1998, when nascent whispers of the Spirit came together rather unexpectedly. Four years earlier, I had been sent out with a group of other young adults to cofound Gateway Christian Church, the first church plant of Evergreen Baptist Church near Los Angeles. Subsequently, I was brought back to Evergreen for the purpose of piloting their second church plant, what would become Epic Church.

At the time I was itching to try something new and different. I had been profoundly influenced and shaped by Professor Ray Anderson at Fuller Seminary, who taught a Christo-praxis, trinitarian, incarnational theology of the church, where "the nature of the church is determined in its existence as the mission of God to the world. The church's nature as well as mission and ministry have their source in the life of the triune God: Father, Son and

Holy Spirit."[3] Because God is inherently social and missional, church is ultimately about relationship and connection, where the community is the apologetic of faith witnessed through love for one another.[4]

Part of me was longing to see if God was gathering some friends to help nurture a faith community whose life would be informed by these kinds of theological insights. I was also sensing that God was providing vision for a more culturally inclusive congregation with a heart for justice. As a third-generation American of Japanese descent (Sansei), my ethnic heritage has played a key role in my awareness of justice. Following Japan's attack on Pearl Harbor at the outset of World War II, an estimated 120,000 Japanese Americans living on the West Coast were removed from their homes and relocated to internment camps, even though many were American citizens. Among these were my parents and their families. After becoming a Christian during college and later as a young pastor, one of the discoveries I made in Scripture was God's overwhelming heart for the poor, his desire for justice and mercy, and his love for all tribes, nations and tongues—including my own.

It was with these aspirations that in 1998 I was privileged, along with twenty-two other people, to follow God's Spirit in launching Evergreen South Coast as a new church in connection with Evergreen San Gabriel Valley and Gateway Christian Church.

From the get-go we started unconventionally—certainly not the way the church-planting conferences and workbooks said we should plant a church, and probably not the way I would recommend again. Though we didn't know much, we did want to appeal to people like ourselves, people who could be described as urban and postmodern. This new church initially took root in Orange County, California, with a vision of becoming "a different kind of church community attractive to a postmodern generation of seekers." In 1998 it was typical to plant by sending a lead pastor who would gather a planting team. This is what we did. Some of the people came from Gateway (my former church), a few from Evergreen San Gabriel Valley (our mother church) and churched or dechurched friends from other places who were interested in the vision of this new work. The way we looked at it, we weren't the traditional church simply starting a ministry to reach a new generation, we *were* the new generation trying to create a community that we felt didn't exist.

From its genesis this meant the church was focused more on ministry to a certain type of *person* than it was mission to a geographical *location*. From the beginning this caused a dissonance for us because we desired to be a community—incarnational and practicing justice—but finding it difficult by starting as a commuter church plant in a suburban location. The irony, of course, is that in attempting to appeal to postmoderns, we used a completely modernist paradigm grounded in many of the same church-growth principles I often derided. The result was that from the start, in our own way, this new church—by focusing on a type of person rather than a geographical location—perpetuated the typical modernist assumption that place does not matter.

Nevertheless, God was gracious in allowing some seeds to be sown and finding good soil. One of those was in the area of healing. In the desire to create a safe place for people to be transparent and vulnerable in their brokenness, the experience of God's grace and acceptance through one another became a visible sign of the kingdom. It was a foretaste of the therapeutic community Ray Anderson taught was possible when the body of Christ mediates the real presence of Jesus as a source of hope and healing. "The kingdom of God is a therapeutic context that offers, as Jesus claimed, 'the way the truth, and the life' (John 14:6). This life relates the individual to the community of faith and hope, a community extending beyond, yet including, this present existence with its suffering and sorrow."[5]

In those early days we made a point of communicating that none of us "had it all together," beginning with the pastor. I, for one, needed this kind of community. I didn't grow up in the church, and though I later became a pastor, I never quite felt at home in either Christian culture or the traditional evangelical church. There seemed to be few models among churches of the kind of vulnerability we were seeking for ours. Having come from a broken family myself, I carried my own journey of healing and certainly had my own share of doubts when it came to my faith. Maybe more than anyone, I needed a place to be real and accepted, even as God allowed me to provide leadership to this new community.

One of the people who found our new church to be a safe haven was Sunny. She came to the church as a college student. Her birth mother was absent most of Sunny's life and her stepmother was sometimes abusive, forcing Sunny to shoplift and steal. A gifted artist and musician, her senior art project featured her as a child holding up a milk carton with pictures of her parents under the caption, "Have you seen them?" As we got to know Sunny, she began to open up about her painful upbringing and about harmful behaviors she used to cope. With the support of God's community, she was able to seek healing for hurt and shame—experiencing God's love in new and deeper ways.

THE 427 BUILDING

Our biggest change up to that point was a geographical one. In 2001 God moved us from South to North Orange County, some twenty-five miles up the freeway. Though we had attracted a number of people from South County—among them students from the University of California at Irvine— and had invested ourselves in transitional shelters and motels in the area, our mission mostly existed independent of context.[6] On one hand, we decided to move for purely practical reasons: it was more centrally located for a majority of our members, and it also seemed like a better fit for us, with different needs and less suburban than our former locations.[7] Most important, we got a sense that God was leading us there. So after much discussion and prayer with the staff and congregation, we said goodbye to South County and hello to Fullerton.[8]

We ended up at what we now fondly refer to as the 427 Building, a converted retail space next to a Jack in the Box restaurant. At first we leased the space in the afternoon from another church that was present on Sunday mornings, but soon were the primary tenants 24-7. Decorated with sofas, café tables, and funky colors, it was the first place we could design ourselves. So we created the space intentionally to foster community and the arts during our worship gatherings: we ate there and people could walk around, easily get into groups, dance, paint, kneel at the cross and worship freely.

Though we never closed our doors during this transition, we really became a different church in many ways. One of the consequences of not initially committing to place was that some of our members naturally evaluated the move based on whether it made their commute longer or shorter—less on call or mission. Understandably then, many of those who lived farther south decided not to make the trip. This was a loss we had to grieve. But with the change in address there were also new things to welcome and celebrate: we inhabited a new name (Epic Church), a new city

(Fullerton) and attracted new people too. Many of those who found us here didn't fit into existing evangelical churches or were typically people with church backgrounds but who had stopped going to church for a variety of reasons. In some respects these changes signaled a fresh start without starting all over again.

The move was enough of a geographical shift that we sensed a greater commitment to the area than we had in previous locations. Because we continued to stress being a community as the way of being the church, people began to make renewed choices to put Epic at the center of their lives. For example, one of our key leaders, Rick, lived close to work but far from our meeting place prior to the move. After we moved to Fullerton, he and another leader, Carlos, decided to room together and open their apartment for ministry. This meant Rick would live in the area but commute more than an hour to work. This is what he chose because of his value for community. Others followed suit, like James and Diane, who after getting married decided to settle in the Fullerton area even though both their jobs still remained in South County—again to be closer to the center of community. Families like Janice and Garret, who have led our kids' ministry from day one, remained faithful to our small but growing kids' ministry, understanding that our size and network of vested "aunties and uncles" could be advantageous in the way we approached the discipleship of children through relationship more than program.

During this time too, among God's more significant seeds germinating and taking root were our values—which were developing and gaining clarity as "community, justice, and healing." Two message series were particularly shaping: "The Wild Kingdom" and "Life in the Gray." The former was a twelve-week invitation to live in the kingdom of God, realizing we were ones who desperately needed Jesus' healing (Matthew 9), while also pursuing the call to justice as a nonoptional aspect of discipleship (Luke 16). "Life in the Gray" occurred after the 9/11 attacks and spoke to the reality of living in a world of uncertainty and change, but also ripe with opportunity.

While this value shaping was taking place at the level of the larger gatherings, we also began taking fifteen to twenty leaders at a time through a class called "Groundswell." It was high commitment with the purpose of wrestling with "kingdom things" and attempting to live them together. Our early morning Saturday classes involved reading articles, studying Scripture and sharing our stories. Each week our group was challenged by what life in the kingdom might mean for us.[9]

As in the parable of the sower, we began to notice the effects of the messages and the class—like seed sprouting from good soil in new ways. One of the areas of growth was the increased conviction about serving among the poor. Though we had previously been involved in hotel ministry, shelters for abused women and children, and the rescue mission when farther south, relocating to Fullerton meant not knowing exactly where to invest.

At first we took a shotgun approach of trying different things to discern what God was already doing here.[10] Locally, we began to serve at a soup kitchen. We also got involved with an organization called Solidarity and the after school program they ran for high-risk children. Globally, after a scouting trip to sub-Saharan Africa, we sent two teams to Uganda to serve among street girls. And we also began taking teams of forty people on a regular basis to the El Sauzal Orphanage in Mexico and to a marginalized tribe of Mixtec Indians. These were things we could do together, and it helped shape many of our hearts toward the poor. As we used to say, "One day in Mexico was better than a year's worth of sermons."

Andrew's story is an example of the kind of transformation that took place in people's lives. Andrew grew up in the area and is an engineer for an aerospace company. Though reluctant at first about Epic and the orphanage, he began to make the trips to Mexico at the urging of his brother. Before long Andrew developed an affinity and bond with the kids at the orphanage. Soon he began to take a lead on the larger trips for the church but also planned more frequent excursions for weekends at a time. Though the orphanage children had many needs, sometimes just for basic food and staples, Andrew's love for them developed into a call and sense of passion. Ten years later Epic has been able to enjoy God's ongoing ministry with the orphanage because of Andrew's commitment and love.

Within our community this also marked the season that the Spirit led us to experiment turning our chairs around into groups of twos and threes during parts of the sermon. It became a running joke as well as hallmark: "As is our custom at Epic, turn and get into groups of twos or threes, introduce yourselves to one another, and here's a question to discuss . . ." Not everybody was comfortable doing this, but a byproduct of facing one another is that it fostered a greater sense of togetherness. These abbreviated

Interview Q&A 1

Editors: Members of Epic are constantly living in this context and being prompted by God to be engaged with the Spirit's initiatives. This leads to various relationships and activities. How do you process these prompts so that you discern next steps?

Kevin Doi: Generally speaking, prompts of the Spirit that develop into ministry at Epic—everything from reading groups to non-profits—tend to follow a similar process:

Conviction. We assume God speaks and places wonderful ideas and convictions on our hearts. These convictions come to us in different ways—in response to Scripture, needs around us, our own stories. Through these, God gives us a desire to see certain things happen.

Permission. We teach that being a disciple means acting on the convictions God gives to us. In an Asian American context, however, we find that people need permission to pursue those convictions. So at Epic we want our people to know that this is *your* church—you can do something here. And we'll help you.

Discernment. Not all ideas reach actuality. First an idea gets tossed around the person's community to test whether it is worth exploring. If the idea will not be an officially Epic-sanctioned ministry, people are free to run with it as they feel led. If the participants want Epic to stand behind the ministry, then a proposal (usually just a simple email) goes to the staff. The staff's role is to further clarify the idea and to help provide feedback and assistance for the participants. This is part of the discernment process.

Ownership. If an idea is a go, we offer support in any way we can. At a minimum this usually entails creating space at our worship services for the person(s) to share about the new ministry. This is where we affirm the ministry and ministers publicly and invite others to participate. Feedback, fruitfulness and reflection become part of the discernment process once the ministry has launched. As the congregation recognizes the value of the ministry, it can become part of our yearly budget.

discussions around the sermon topic became a way to process and go deeper. They also led directly to inviting strangers or the unconnected out to lunch or to a small group. The effect was that rarely did any person leave our worship services without having a significant conversation with others. We are grateful that many of these "mixers" have led to deep friendships. Again, this grew out of our conviction of what church is and creating the space for God's serendipity. Peter Block describes simply but poignantly what we discovered by accident: "The key to transformative community is to see the power in the small but important elements of being with others. The shift we seek needs to be embodied in each invitation we make, each relationship we encounter, and each meeting we attend. . . . Social fabric is created one room at a time."[11]

Though the change during this season was necessary, exciting and often fruitful, it also was not easy. Some original members of Epic felt uneasy with our renewed emphasis on justice and the poor. Some staff members left. Several relationships became increasingly strained and broken as we wrestled with priorities and how to love one another in our differences. Reconciliation was difficult and in some cases unsuccessful. It seemed like the best of times and the worst of times.

At this key juncture in our story, the hiring of Erin Hamilton as associate pastor was a godsend. Erin came as a former campus staff worker with InterVarsity Christian Fellowship who also studied under Ray Anderson at Fuller Seminary. In many ways we were fortunate to find another pastor with similar theological leanings and who deeply understood the nuances and complexities of ministry in a post-Christendom, multicultural context. In this somewhat turbulent time, Erin brought a steady hand, keen discernment and solid teaching that served us especially well in that season and into the season to come.[12]

EMBRACING A PLACE

Having been in Fullerton for a few years, place and particularity began to mean something more. It was around 2004 that I began to meet with Chris, a young pastor who was hoping to launch a new church in Long Beach, California. Initially Chris wanted to glean from my experience as an Asian American church planter, but the more I met with Chris the more I realized I was probably benefitting more than he was. Chris would talk about his knowledge of and love for Long Beach in ways that I never talked about Fullerton. Through these conversations I sensed God's Spirit speaking: I recognized that Epic needed to make a shift from simply reaching a type of person to embracing a *place*.[13]

Because we were already in Fullerton it was an easy decision to focus our love here. We prepared the congregation by tracing God's mission from Eden to the Great City in Revelation and by explaining how in Jesus the gospel was incarnated and the good news socially located. We began to ask, "Is it possible that God has led Epic specifically to Fullerton?" My sense of call as pastor of Epic and to the city was solidified when we began to pray that God would move us from the *periphery* (which we were at the time) to the *center* of the city.

For this to happen, several amazing and serendipitous events had to occur. First, the congregation voted to break our lease on the 427 Building before we had another place lined up. That happened on a Sunday afternoon. It was a tremendous step for the congregation, one that will forever be a testament to their faith and maturity and sense of adventure.

The next day David, one of our board members, called to tell me we had an appointment with the facility manager at Fullerton College, blocks from downtown. The facility manager informed us that there had been another church meeting in the auditorium but had ended their stay just days before. Because we were the first group to inquire, it was ours. And so we moved to Fullerton College in June of 2005.

A few months into our stay I struck up a friendship with Kirk Mackie, senior pastor of First Baptist Fullerton, a historic downtown church a year older than the city itself. One day I felt the Spirit stirring in me to ask Kirk if we could meet on his campus. Unbeknown to me, his church was hoping to start a preschool in the fall but wondered where the additional funds would come from. We came to understand that our two churches were an answer to the other's prayers. And so a partnership was born.

Exactly one year after moving to Fullerton College, we journeyed down the street into our new facility on the corner of Wilshire and Pomona Avenues. It felt like home. Now as we look out our office windows we see the Fullerton Plaza and are reminded of how God moved us downtown to *the very center of the city*. It is our promised land story. For this reason we believe God has given Epic a specific call to love the city of Fullerton.

RELATIONSHIP AS THE GOAL

While a board member of Oasis USA, I had the privilege of serving with Andy Matheson, the international director of Oasis Global. Andy had spent ten years working in India among the poorest of the poor. I had asked Andy to help me understand the connection between proximity and ministry. He shared with me that proximity was important and definitely had its advantages, but the goal was ultimately relationship. From his experience, proximity was certainly helpful but not always a guarantee of relationship. If you could build long-term friendships, however, even without the benefit of close geographical proximity, real change was still possible. "In many ways, the projects and programs Oasis set up were really only vehicles for creating relationships among those we served. For it is only ever through relationship that transformation begins to take place. . . . [P]rojects and programs on their own never bring transformation. Only people do that."[14]

The fact that God led Epic downtown helped immensely with the issue of proximity. All of a sudden within a block radius of us were an urban park, the train depot, the Fullerton Museum, transitional shelters, restaurants, schools and art galleries. The question facing us now was how were we going to build long-term relationships here?

Initially we frequented and got to know owners of restaurants in the area, many of them becoming supporters of our nonprofit organizations and events. One of the unexpected things that occurred was the number of people who began to walk to Epic. Neighbors literally helped us become neighbors to other people. For instance, just a few weeks after attending Epic, Brice and Sandee got up in front of the congregation and invited everyone to their house up the street for lunch. Over eighty people showed up.

Brian and Kristy and their two sons were other neighbors who came to Epic on foot. Brian is a graphic artist and Kristy a schoolteacher in Fullerton. (Kristy became our children's director for a year.) They saw our banner on the side of the building with the values of community, justice and healing, and were curious. We ended up being the kind of church they were hoping for (a church that loved Fullerton), and we were grateful to have the kind of people we discovered them to be. A year later Brian and Kristy opened PÄS, now a popular gallery in the downtown arts colony, while also pioneering the Fullerton Art Walk each month. Members of Epic have been involved in exhibiting art, providing music and supporting Brian and Kristy with this burgeoning space and movement.

Jim is another neighbor who became a friend and new member at Epic. Jim is the night resident supervisor at the transitional shelter nearby—assisting men and women facing the issue of homelessness find work and permanent housing. Jim—homeless himself—began to attend Epic when we learned of his story. Since then Jim has become an ambassador to the shelter, introducing his friends to Epic—some who are now part of our community.

As a result of being committed to place, we also began reflecting more and more the people who live here—becoming increasingly multicultural—ethnically and socioeconomically.[15] We could no longer make the same assumptions about race, income or lifestyle. For example, we could no longer assume people could afford to eat out after worship service, which was our custom each week. Instead we increased the church's budget for food and celebrations, and began to bring lunch in to share together. We also began to study the seminal work by Gert Jan Hofstede about cultural differences, especially those related to "power-distance" ratios, which his studies indicate contribute to differences in communication styles between ethnic groups and varying perceptions of authority and hierarchy.[16]

Reflecting back, starting as a community did not make us completely incongruous to mission, but it did make us more vulnerable to homogeneity. Being sent to inhabit a place has made hospitality more than coffee and donuts; rather, it concerns our willingness to let others different from ourselves change the way we live—something we continue to be challenged by and eager to be transformed by.[17]

Certainly one of the things we have learned in this season was how to better discern the movement of the Spirit among the entire congregation, believing assets already present in our church community were waiting to be recognized, encouraged and empowered. This has meant affirming, releasing and supporting the passions and convictions of the body. This has been especially important when individuals or groups of individuals discern God's movement in the needs and opportunities around them and want to do something about it. The result has been that the church is no longer simply my vision but *our* vision.

As we sought to love our city, God was good to provide one opportunity after another. An example of this was the creation of JOYA Scholars. Several of us had already been serving with Solidarity, a community-development organization in the Garnet neighborhood of Fullerton created to help the church live out its faith among the poor. Valeria, one of the Garnet's junior high school students had earned a spot in a Princeton University summer program. Epic was one of the organizations that helped raise money for her to attend. When she returned, Valeria shared with us her doubt that she could ever attend a school like Princeton because of where she is from. Her friends at Solidarity convinced her otherwise.

After Valeria's experience we realized there hadn't been a college graduate from the Garnet neighborhood in over a decade. By then Epic had already begun asking the Lord how we might serve the community with our educational gifts. When the need at Garnet surfaced, we could see the intersection between our world and Valeria's. We asked if there were other students and families here who wanted to attend college? And so with Valeria as our inspiration, Epic member Carey Jeu and I gathered a team of teachers, guidance counselors, social workers and community development staff from Epic and the community and founded JOYA Scholars. Our organization inspires and prepares students in Fullerton toward higher education through long-term mentoring, tutoring, college-prep workshops and campus tours. Now in our third school year, we are assisting bright and motivated students toward fulfilling their dreams of a college education. Earlier this year Valeria became the neighborhood's first four-year university student.[18]

Another ministry we are excited about is Abeni, founded by Meg Muñoz, one of our members. When I met Meg and her husband, Tony, they already had four children and were living in Fullerton. Meg had grown up in a strong disciplinary household from which she eventually rebelled as a young adult. Having gotten into the drug scene, she began to work in the adult entertainment industry to support her habit. When she finally hit bottom, Meg discovered Jesus and also met Tony and turned her life around. When Meg came to Epic and told me her story, she shared her conviction that God would eventually send her back to help other women trapped in similar circumstances. Today, Meg and her ministry team reach out to the adult entertainment industry in Orange County by visiting the adult clubs, caring for and coming alongside women, bringing dignity and love. God has blessed and empowered Meg

Interview Q&A 2

Editors: You note the gifts and complexities of cultural and economic diversity as you live in Fullerton and participate in life with neighbors. What are you learning about boundary crossing, and how are you gaining competencies to hear God's voice through these neighbors?

Kevin Doi: One of the lessons we are learning in our context about boundary crossing is simply the importance of being aware of ourselves. We have to understand that everything is interpreted, that we can only see the world through our own lenses. At best we see only partially. In a multicultural setting this has meant being cognizant of our own biases and assumptions, aware of existing power dynamics, aware of our own agendas. Sustaining such a posture is not easy, but it is central to maintaining openness to others, to valuing difference and creating the possibility for change—beginning with ourselves.

A second lesson about boundary crossing we are learning is the belief that everyone has something valuable to contribute. This is the philosophy behind asset-based community development. What we are learning from our neighbors is that God is here and that there are wonderful assets and dreams in the community already present in the lives of its people. This guards us from taking the stance of doing something *for* others and instead being there *with* others, where we are moving toward increasing levels of mutuality. At Epic this has looked like convening cultural roundtables where we can have conversations with the diverse voices in our community about their needs and hopes. At JOYA Scholars, it has meant inviting students and parents from the neighborhood to be part of our advisory team rather than making assumptions on their behalf. In both cases it goes beyond ensuring a diversity of perspectives at the table, which in itself is of incredible value. It is also about creating the possibility for real relationship. It is about empowering friends and neighbors to shape the contours and content of their own—and our—future together.

in assisting trafficking survivors, escorts and dancers to transition from the clubs to healthier, stable and more hopeful futures.

Being part of the fabric of the city has also meant more partnership and less independence. A few years ago the city faced budget cuts to its summer school programs, prompting some of the neighborhood community groups to inquire about starting their own. Practicing asset-based community development—a worldwide movement founded by John McKnight that postulates that if we want to make communities stronger we should study their assets, gifts, resources and talents rather than their deficiencies[19]—Tommy Nixon, the executive director of Solidarity and member of the Fullerton Collaborative, brought the idea from the community to this committee of civic leaders. With the blessing of the Collaborative, Tommy turned to the church and especially to the pastors of Sojourners, Newsong North Orange County, Rock Harbor Fullerton, and Epic. Because none of these lead congregations occupied buildings during the week, they were forced to bring church to the streets. The result was SOLFUL (Summer of Love Fullerton) in which hundreds of children and volunteers now participate in programs offered in three economically challenged neighborhoods. This has actually aided and coalesced a sense of mission among our churches, with an appreciation for partnership, friendship and interdependence. In a very real way, God has given us opportunity to serve as the church in Fullerton.

THE POWER OF COMMUNITY

As we became more vested in Fullerton, God simultaneously stressed in us the importance of being a community together.[20] Our house churches began to flourish and became more than Bible studies but also centers of community. Eating together on a weekly basis became a sacramental act of hospitality and connection that we enjoyed together.[21]

In this season we also recognized Sunday gatherings as our liturgy, a way for us to practice what it means to live together in the kingdom of God. In this way we remained attractional, but not in the usual sense of the term. Attraction can be an end in itself, a way of building something. But we were trying to be a community whose own life together bore witness to our faith. We still hoped to be attractive in the way a true representation as the body of Christ has the ability to include and connect people to one another and to God.

As part of our liturgy, Communion continued to be a pivotal invitation each week. At the Lord's Table, Jesus stands at the center inviting all of us to consider and respond to the good news of life in his kingdom.[22] The sacraments become space where the goal is connection—with Jesus, with self, with the body of Christ. During our worship services we rehearse the story of the gospel and call people to live in it. As such, we confess the tradition's creeds, listen for the Word of God, partake of food and drink, and spend a significant time on "mingle"—a freestyle space of conversation and connection that makes church "what we decide to do with the space between us." Like the parable of the sower, we see our time together as a time to sow and enjoy what God is doing among us.

Kathy is a good example of someone who experienced real community initially through our gathering. She came to us a stranger, having found us through our website. When we met Kathy, she was unemployed, going through a divorce and a single parent to two young children. Our congregation got to know her through our worship services, where Kathy began benefitting from prayer ministry and connecting with house church. Before long she had a network of support. As Kathy received God's healing and found greater stability in her life, she decided to go back to school to become a nurse. Diane and others occasionally provided babysitting so she could study and attend classes. Sarah and Dan offered a place at their home for her and the kids to enjoy for eighteen months. And the church board invested thousands of dollars for childcare and tuition to make it all possible. Today, we are proud to say that Kathy, who graduated from nursing school as valedictorian of her class, is now gainfully employed and doing well. And some people at Epic, anonymous to Kathy, continue to support her financially by making payments on her car loan.

Rika stands as another example of the power of community. Rika was a Japanese national in America on a student visa. Estranged from her family in Japan, Rika came to Epic when her landlord brought her to one of our house churches. Though she wasn't a Christian, Rika found the people genuine and generous. After many months Rika began to attend our Sunday services even with her limited ability to understand or speak English. Over a three-year span Rika began to feel more comfortable sharing her doubts and questions, and had developed good friendships with many people in the church who cared for her. Because she was welcomed into the arms of Epic and had found community with God's people, she received much healing and also eventually made a decision for Christ and was baptized. Rika was allowed to take her time, accepting the community that was offered, a community that became family and the evidence of God's love for her.

FURTHER SOWING

As I look back on Epic's story, there are two lessons that stand out and are worth mentioning: One is how long it has taken for God's shaping to develop. Many ideals we had at the beginning simply took years to germinate and bear fruit. On average it seems that key decisions could take years to see some significant effect. Factors like the number of children in our kids' ministry, a sense of place, the diversity of people, our value for justice, the ministry of the whole body, a flourishing of the arts—all these took time to evolve and ripen, and continue to require attention and nurturing. The process has necessitated patience, hope and faithfulness. Like the farmer who sows seed and cannot see the growth beneath the surface, but one day is surprised to find a plant sprouting, this has been the story of Epic attempting to follow God's Spirit. It is comforting to know that Jesus says this is how the kingdom works.

Second, I realize that though the stories chronicled here have been significant and certainly representative of the whole, they are not the only narratives that God has used to shape of our community. If culture is the cumulative effect of the Spirit's involvement in the conversations and habits of a people over time, then it can be said that the culture of Epic has been shaped profoundly by hundreds of people making thousands of little decisions for the kingdom of God each and every week—leading to the church we enjoy today. In reality, everyone's story belongs here.

Which brings us to now. As we look to the next chapter in our story, we see two related movements happening simultaneously—mission and community. If God has led us to Fullerton, how will we further be a church for the city? What will this look like? What will be the connection between our context and our ability to make disciples? If the kingdom of God is indeed in our midst, how will we see God's reign further expressed in the convictions of his people—at Epic and among the other Christ followers in the city?

Likewise, how will we extend ourselves to one another as we pursue God's mission together? As we become increasingly diverse in ethnicity, age and socioeconomics, how will we foster an environment that encourages strangers to become friends? If there is no such thing as a neutral multiculturalism, how do we appreciate our call as a particularly Asian American multicultural community while extending inclusion to all? How will we commit to a shared life together shaped around Jesus and his way of life? What practices will be key?

These are just some of the questions and conversations that we discern the Spirit inviting us to ask and pursue as we look to our future.

At Epic we have attempted to live true to our name by inhabiting and valuing story—God's story—however inadequately we may have done so. As we used to tell visiting classes from a local Christian university: "Do not copy us, it is not a mapped out program." Though we could not and still cannot always articulate the uniquely organic nature of what the Spirit is doing at Epic, we can't help but think that God is up to something here— even if that something is never fully formed, never quite there yet, always filled with a bit of surprise and serendipity.

Like seed falling on good soil.

4

GATHERING NEIGHBORS
CITY CHURCH OF EAST NASHVILLE

Craig Brown

CITY CHURCH OF EAST NASHVILLE

Location: Nashville
Denomination: Presbyterian Church in America
Year of Foundation: 2004
Regular Participants in the Life of the Church: 375
Website: www.citychurcheast.org

City Church of East Nashville is a wonderful example of gathering neighbors to listen to one another for how an indigenous expression of faith might look in a particular context. Pastor Craig Brown's leadership fostered an environment for a new church to sprout in a diverse (economics and ethnicities) setting in urban Nashville. Look for a buffet of stories that have emerged out of the congregation pertaining to God's work among the people in the neighborhood.

I slammed the door shut on that cold winter morning because I was cutting it close to getting to a small breakfast being hosted by the mayor of Nashville. Someone sat up from among the bags of leaves next to the house. "You startled me!" he said. "I startled *you*? Rico, what are you doing out here? It's freezing, and you're sleeping in between bags of leaves!" Jana and I had known Rico for several years. He was caught in a continuous cycle of living on and off the streets. We got Rico situated in our downstairs makeshift "apartment" (the unfinished side of our basement had heat and a twin bed). I could still make the breakfast without being *too* late.

Housing the homeless and meeting with the mayor in the same day! The simplicity and complexity of ministry in an urban neighborhood has continued to shock us along the way. Our journey started with questions like, Is it possible to live in a place where loving your (proximate, geographical) neighbors could mean loving "the high up, the low down and the far out"?[1] and Is it true that if followers of Jesus lived in urban cores of American cities that those cities could actually begin to look more like the city of God?[2] After considering various urban environments, we found that the heart of Nashville could serve as a greenhouse to experiment with just such questions.

East Nashville was the "old money" of Nashville—right across the river from downtown. After a major flood and fire devastated the community during the first several decades of the 1900s, East Nashville began the downward socioeconomic spiral that affected many urban neighborhoods during the period that followed. The downward spiral became a fast slide after World War II with the Urban Renewal program.[3] In the 1980s and 1990s East Nashville experienced gentrification in some of its neighborhoods. The result was 63,000 people living in the area inside a horseshoe formed by the Cumberland River. By the year 2000 the area was made up of professional and blue-collar workers, educators, artists, government officials and those living in government-subsidized housing.[4] Ethnically and racially, East Nashville was 54 percent Anglo, 39 percent African American, a small but growing Hispanic population, as well as a consistent refugee population.[5] A constant tension existed of *haves* (people with assets) and *have-nots* (those living below the poverty line) living in close proximity. This was and is our community, our neighborhood, our people, our parish—a place where "the high up, the low down and the far out" live together. Our church, Christ Community Church, under the direction of the presbytery, sent us as missionary church planters to East Nashville. That was the spring of 2003.[6]

Vision to Reality

Jana and I had been captivated by the images and the descriptions of the kingdom of God consummating in an urban reality as found in Revelation

21–22. We had also been challenged by our friends in leadership at World Harvest Mission to pray, "Our Father . . . your kingdom come, your will be done, on earth as it is in heaven" with faith.[7] What would it look like for the invisible kingdom to become a visible reality in our city? What would it look like to "do church" or "be a community" that lived our lives based on *this* vision? We soon realized that it was about being located in a specific place and with specific people.[8] To actually love God and love our neighbors, we knew we had to *be* neighbors. We actually had to incarnate the love of Christ.

We struggled—a lot—through our own insecurities, fear and pride. We found repentant faith to be life-giving and began to believe that all things becoming new meant that God had to dwell with us, that we lived with a deep awareness that we were his beloved people, and that we actually had the power through Jesus to be agents of reconciliation (2 Corinthians 5:11-21). With this in mind, I began to prayer walk the community. At first, I walked and prayed by myself. Later, Jana and my friend John joined me. We walked in pairs or triads, believing that to pray nearer was to pray clearer. The spiritual insights into the community that we gained during this season proved invaluable.

I also began to "knitwork" (networking with people and their relational connections) at this time. The purpose of this was to meet as many people as possible, to learn the story of East Nashville from the inside. In many ways, anecdotal information was the most difficult to obtain because I had to immerse myself into a new culture as an outsider and a learner. In this process we began to sow small seeds of vision, hoping some would take root. A typical knitworking request would be "Hi, my name is Craig Brown. I just moved into East Nashville to begin a new church, and my learning curve is about 90 degrees. Would you be willing to meet with me and give me your insights into the neighborhood? I am not selling anything or recruiting members. I am just trying to better understand the lay of the land." During the appointments I asked three basic questions: (1) What can you tell me about East Nashville? (2) What do you think a church that was really committed to East Nashville would look like? and (3) Who else would you recommend I talk to?

After months of prayer walking and knitworking, along with some follow-up appointments with people who wanted to talk more specifically about spiritual questions they had, we began a vision study. During twenty weeks of winter and spring 2004, grassroots momentum began to build as almost two hundred people came through the weekly word-of-mouth study held in the home of some East Nashville friends. The Spirit of God was actually infusing the vision into a group of people for a "gospel-driven, city-directed" church community in East Nashville. Two empty-nest elders and their wives from our sending church, after originally saying they would not participate, joined the work. People, excited about Jesus and the vision, took name ideas out to their neighbors. "Whether you would ever attend or not—what name would you like best for a new church community in this neighborhood?" Out of twenty or so names, City Church of East Nashville was far and away the most selected answer. We thought it was appropriate that our neighbors actually chose the name of the church!

Of the two hundred who came to the study, twenty-three people committed to be a part of the launch team, to put time and energy into prayer, gospeling (telling others of the good news of Jesus),[9] networking, meeting together, solidifying the vision and carrying out the numerous details connected to launching the essential elements of facilities, worship, neighborhood groups, children and hospitality.[10] The launch team shared a meal together each week in our house as we planned the launch.

Because neighbors were such a focus of the ministry from the start, the members of the launch team also formed three neighborhood groups—geographically formed weekly gatherings meeting with the purpose of "experiencing Christ together" through prayer, worship, Bible study and care for neighbors.[11] Neighborhood groups became and continue to be the primary venues for renewal, care, ministry and shepherding, so it was intentional to have them operational by the time City Church launched public worship services. On September 12, 2004, City Church of East Nashville (CCEN) held its first public worship service at the Y-CAP Building.[12] The majority of the 120 adults who attended were from the neighborhoods of East Nashville!

VALUES

We gathered a team composed of a few friends from East Nashville and a few people who had served in church leadership capacities to identify the core values that would guide our church vision and practice. We knew that our core values would be the underlying shapers of everything we would be and do. We listed seven core values for the first several years of CCEN, but eventually locked on to three defining core values.

Gospel driven. We believe that God has intervened in our world to restore all things to their rightful order through the power of the gospel, that is the teaching and historical reality of the life, death, resurrection and ascension of Jesus of Nazareth. The righting of the relationships between God and humanity, humanity and humanity and humanity and creation comes from God through Jesus Christ. Therefore, the person and work of Jesus Christ must fuel all our relationships and ministries.

Prayer dependent. We believe the gospel secures our access to God so we can enjoy communion with him. Prayer is that communion and is our first and continual resort and not just a last resort, as the Spirit of God leads us into praise, repentance, thanksgiving and requests. We pray for God's kingdom to come and will to be done in our neighborhood and city. Therefore, we are committed to and dependent upon bold, specific, concerted and continual prayer.

Parish directed. We believe that through a gospel culture, the Spirit of God creates a new community of transformed lives through geographic and relational proximity. God values and loves uniting diversity into his family more than we ever will. We believe that we are in East Nashville to promote the beauty, prosperity, justice, and overall well-being of our neighborhood and, through that, the city of Nashville. We are committed to sacrificially give of ourselves and our resources for our neighborhood and city.

If a ministry is not permeated by these values, we will not (or at least, should not) be a part of resourcing or participating in it.

MINISTRY MAP

If you come to a new city and have to find your way around, you need a map. Likewise, we knew that people who had not been involved in church or in this type of missional community before would need a map. We sought to "lower the bar of how church is done and raise the bar of what it means to be a disciple."[13] In other words, getting connected to the community of Jesus followers should be simplified. Going "higher up and further in" to being an authentic follower or disciple of Jesus requires a much higher level of commitment.

Over time our leadership team drew out a simplex map of CCEN.[14] In the way it functions for CCEN the beauty of this classic map is that people can begin at any point in their journey of life (see fig. 4.1).

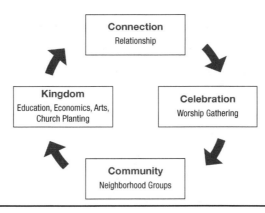

Figure 4.1.

Let's take a closer look at how each of these key developmental markers actually take place.

Connection. As followers of Jesus our leadership team knew that our neighborhood (and the world) is both beautiful and broken. We believe that God made the world and everything in it good, right and beautiful—diversity working in harmony, dominion without domination, the universal flourishing of all things. This understanding is captured in the Hebrew word *shalom*. *Shalom* is "the webbing together of God, humans, and all creation in fulfillment . . . a universal flourishing, wholeness, and delight—in other words, the way things ought to be."[15] We believe that humans have been made in the image of God, to reflect that goodness, glory and beauty in the world as representatives over all creation.

But we also knew—and all too well—that things are not the way they ought to be. There were and are personal, social and ecological crises every day, everywhere. How can this reality be explained from a Christian perspective? As Christians we believe that humanity, in our earliest stages, decided we would rule ourselves and the world without giving heed to divine directive. In the greatest irony of all time, when humanity sought to *gain* control of everything, we *lost* control of everything. As a result, and as Bob Dylan rightly sings, "Everything's broken."[16] So, from a Christian perspective this world is both beautiful (God created it good) and broken (we have spoiled it).

As humans go, so all creation goes. Humans, as God's representatives in this world, were created beautiful but are now corrupt to the core. This does not mean that we are all as bad as we could possibly be. It does mean that every fiber of our being is corrupt. Likewise, our world was created beautiful but is now corrupt.

This sounds pretty negative. Why stress such a negative perspective? The English missionary to Madras, India, Lesslie Newbigin, once was asked in an interview whether as a Christian he was an optimist or a pessimist wisely replied: "I am neither an optimist nor a pessimist. . . . Jesus the Christ is risen from the dead."[17] For a Christian the beautiful-but-broken perspective is not about being positive or negative; it is simply realistic.

One of the implications of this reality is that all people—all people—are worthy of both commendation and condemnation simultaneously. As C. S. Lewis's Aslan informs his human friends in *Prince Caspian*, "You come of the Lord Adam and the Lady Eve . . . and that is both honour enough to erect the head of the poorest beggar, and shame enough to bow the shoulders of the greatest emperor in earth."[18]

As followers of Jesus we look at ourselves, our neighborhood, our city and our world and share a unique diagnosis of problems—humanity and all creation is beautiful but broken. We all desperately need harmonious relationship with God and others. The first step of entrance into CCEN's community is basic relational connection.

This connection has been Noah's experience. He has found that his life has become richer by being in relationship with the "poorest of these."

City Church sends us out every week to enjoy and display Christ in our neighborhood. We are a people on a mission to bring the hope of Jesus and his kingdom to the people around us. I have found power and courage to begin genuine friendships with people who are not like me. The Burchas, a family of Congolese refugees, live in a housing project down the street from my house. I met their three sons at a soccer game in the park and soon I was invited to their home for dinner. They needed rides to the grocery store, to the DMV, to the immigration office and home from school. I had a car.

Today we are pretty much like family. In many ways it's like we come from different planets, and yet God has woven our lives together in a way I could never have imagined. We share happy things like food, music, laughing and traveling. We share difficult things like being broke, language barriers, injustice and the crime that is pervasive in our neighborhood. Do we have some detailed plan for how we are to fix each other's lives? No, we just enjoy our time together. I am certain however, that God is transforming us into a different kind of community where love triumphs over temporary comfort.

Interview Q&A 1

Editors: You were constantly considering ministries and priorities. How did this discernment happen? What process was important to you as you made decisions about your life in the community?

Aaron Sands (CCEN elder):   From day one as a church plant we aimed to keep the number and frequency of official church meetings to a minimum. We wanted to have the right amount of opportunities for gathering and equipping without hindering our engagement in the community, whether in work, play, school or relationships. Rather than assuming we should have ministry A, ministry B and ministry C, which might be typical in many churches today, our first question is, What is already established in the community to address those needs? For some issues and ideas this question gives us an immediate redirect to gain understanding about existing ministries and programs in our neighborhoods rather than assuming we must create, staff and manage our own. A second question to someone asking about addressing a certain need or planning an event is, Who are you going to enlist to help you make it happen? Ideas are not cheap, and great ideas require vision, commitment and usually some sweat. As those in CCEN and our neighborhoods are motivated by the gospel, they are convicted by what they know and excited about opportunities to bring about change. As this happens, because we have a bottom-up environment, we can mobilize more quickly and sustain for longer periods of time as we engage initiatives like economics, the arts and education.

Likewise, the Burchas describe their experience of coming to America and becoming a part of another family through relational connection with Noah.

We had been in a refugee camp. We received permission to come to the United States. We landed in Nashville knowing very little English. The boys played soccer and met friends. Noah began to come over and take us places. He is like a son to us. Noah began taking us to church. Even though we don't understand everything yet, we know God meets our needs through Jesus, Noah and City Church.

We frequent neighborhood businesses as much as possible in order to build the local economy of East Nashville. One of the benefits of this is also relational connection. We have found experientially what others have now studied: that many unchurched people actually believe that Christianity is irrelevant and implausible and that Christians hate them.[19]

Donna and a group of friends from her neighborhood group began the habit of meeting at a local pub after their weekly group meeting. After a month or so, Paula, the tattooed owner, came over to their table. Donna describes it like this:

> Using many superlatives, Paula gruffly asked who we were and why we had become such "regulars." We explained that we were part of a new church community in the neighborhood and that every Thursday evening we got together and studied the Bible and then we came there. "You mean, every week you have a Bible study and then you come here to drink beer?" Paula bellowed in disbelief. "Hey, Johnny!" she gleefully hollered to the bartender, "we got ourselves a table full of f***ing Christians!" The friendship began there.

These people and their stories serve as samples of relational connections that occur daily in the lives of members of our community. From these connections, the next touch point is a CCEN Sunday Evening Celebration.

Celebration. It wasn't long before Paula came to Donna and asked about "seeing what you all are all about." Donna related the experience of Paula moving from connection to celebration.

> "Okay, I'm just curious. What's this church of yours like? Can I come? Will you pick me up?" A little dumbfounded, I muttered, "Uh, yes, of course." Paula was visibly uncomfortable through most of the service. But afterward she said she was impressed that she felt so welcomed by people she normally would have nothing to do with. Next thing we knew she was telling all her friends about her "new church" and telling them they should "check it out."

The root of the Old English word *worship* means "to ascribe worth." CCEN gathers every week to ascribe ultimate worth to Jesus as Lord and Savior. We unashamedly worship Jesus, but we are always aware that those in various places of spiritual belief and journey are present whenever we meet. Therefore, we always attempt to explain why we are doing what we are doing. In so doing, all in attendance—both followers of Jesus and those who are not—benefit. We describe this to our leaders as contextualized or coherent worship, and train them to speak in such a manner.

The CCEN model of worship can be described as "Reformed contemporary worship,"[20] utilizing and combining historic elements of Christian worship with more contemporary language and music.[21] Every service seeks to follow the basic shape of a gospel reenactment.[22]

We originally met on Sunday evenings because we had more options of places to meet. Fairly quickly, however, it became part of the culture of CCEN. We met for the first several years in the Y-CAP Building until we outgrew it. Then we moved to an old church that had been renovated into a school. After several years in that facility we moved into a still larger facility, which is our current Sunday location, East Literature High School. All these partnerships have been very positive.

David Peterson's description of a worship gathering in the epilogue of *Engaging with God* is a picture that we hope to this day describes the feel of CCEN's Sunday gatherings.

> *Anyone could tell from the way the members of this congregation related to one another that their Sunday gathering was an expression of genuine Christian community. It was clearly a high point in their week, but not the only time when most of them met together or engaged in ministry together. Their conversation, their prayers and their contributions during the service reflected an obvious concern for one another in a whole range of situations. This was no spiritual ghetto, since it was clear that members desired to welcome strangers and to minister to the needs of those outside their fellowship. Many seemed to be actively involved in evangelism, pastoral care, or social action groups in the wider community.[23]*

As people move from relational connection into the worship celebration, what do they experience? Teresa tells what happened to her when she attended her first CCEN worship service:

> *"We don't do church. We are the church." After the sermon and before the Lord's Supper, Pastor Craig stood at the front of a packed room and spoke that phrase with gentle authority. Those are the words that changed my mind and my heart almost five years ago. I had not given up on Christ, but I had willfully left the church a few years prior to this first visit to City Church of East Nashville. That night in that room, there was a sober excitement and, for the first time in years, I longed to be a part of it. I wanted to believe in this church he professed.*
>
> *Up until that moment, I had years worth of reasons (excuses, really) of why*

I didn't like the church. In one sentence Pastor Craig shook them all. Without any more detail, he defined the distance that I had placed between myself and the truth. "People, like me, are the church!" I had arrived at City Church feeling broken and cynical. Somewhere during the middle of that service, I started feeling like I was not alone and that in such a condition maybe this was the exact place to be. By the end I wanted to believe in more than just myself. I felt called to repent and place my hope in Jesus. I was invited to keep showing up. And by showing up, and believing in Christ, I was the church.

Today, Teresa and her husband are embarking on planting a daughter church out of CCEN. She recently confessed, "I would have never dreamed of such change happening in our lives." Another member of our community, Rachel, learned that Jesus ministers in spite of her, as she saw God moving a neighbor from relational connection into the worship experience.

As I got to know my neighbor Marla better, she said that she had never heard anyone talk about God and church in the way I did. She said she wanted to attend a gathering at City Church. After two weeks of being on the road (we are touring musicians), I met Marla for coffee. She informed me: "I went to City Church while you were out of town. I heard about who Jesus was and what he did for us to be in relationship with God. Suddenly, it all made sense. This is what I have been missing, what I had been looking for, a relationship with God." I thought it was Marla who needed an encounter with God. Instead, I encountered Jesus as I saw him draw Marla to himself when I wasn't even in town to make it happen!

As CCEN gathers every week to ascribe worth to Jesus as Lord and Savior, we have experienced the whole gambit of life, all the way from having fights break out during singing to people being "delivered . . . from the domain of darkness and transferred . . . to the kingdom of his beloved Son, in whom we have redemption, the forgiveness of sins" (Colossians 1:13-14 ESV). What a wonderful picture of God's grace breaking in through Jesus!

Community. Experiencing the "one another" commands of Scripture cannot take place in a weekly large group gathering. Therefore, people who desire to have a fuller experience of Christianity are encouraged to be a part of a neighborhood group. In many ways our neighborhood groups are the natural extension of the overall vision. Strategically located based on geography, each group meets to experience Christ together through five primary means: Bible study, prayer, service, various means of worship and fellowship. When these elements are engaged on a regular basis, our people start to change and in turn start to change their neighborhood. When we are asking in our neighborhood groups "what it would like to help usher in the kingdom on this particular street?" theory meets action and knees meet the ground. There is nothing so humbling as realizing that we do not have the perfect answer to solve complicated problems like high recidivism and a crumbling public school system. Given our urban context the problems are many and require utter dependence on Christ.

Our neighborhood groups also help us to identify (and take down) our walls. *Community* is such a buzzword in our society, and in Christianity it is often regarded as something that happens naturally. We have found that is not the case. Real community, actual common unity in Christ, is supernatural. The servant leaders of a church can plant a gospel culture, but only the Spirit of God can grow a gospel-missional community. When twelve people start sharing their lives together and being honest enough to talk about hard things, we find out that we might not be as interested in community as we thought! So we learn how to ask forgiveness, how to listen well, how to point each other to Christ. We ask for supernatural help to make these natural relationships actually something lasting and real.

Ron and Renae really began to experience Christ in their neighborhood through their neighborhood group.

> *Imagine life just beginning to get interesting at the age of sixty! Ron had bought a house in the neighborhood of East Nashville. It was a fixer-upper, an investment for us really. Little did we know that we would be living in that house in a few short months and the investment would be greater than a piece of real estate. At first we thought our involvement with CCEN would be from afar as elders to this congregation of young people. But the Lord began to show us that in order to fully experience the community we would need to live in the community. Several years ago we were faced with a financial peril that threatened to take everything Ron and I had worked for all our married lives. Not knowing if a group of twenty- to thirty-year-olds would even begin to grasp the seriousness of our situation, we decided to tell our neighborhood group nonetheless. For weeks upon weeks, they faithfully prayed for us and watched as the Lord rescued us. I have never experienced anything quite like it! We are convinced that being connected to our neighborhood group is an essential element of our spiritual growth.*

Charles tells of the nature of change he has experienced through being a part of a weekly neighborhood group.

I've been a part of the community called City Church of East Nashville for just over five years now. I've seen my own heart, calcified with bitterness and anger, softened overnight—some miracle of God's mercy that I certainly didn't instigate. I've seen a covenant community share life with a family who was homeless and in poverty, and the difference that this has made in a thirteen-year-old girl's life as she grows up in the church. I've seen people (myself included) recognizing more of our own sin and rejoicing in a Savior even more. I've seen people grow in prayer and repentance as a community; grow in love and service and interdependence; grow as a gospel community.

I've also seen, though, that the dividing boundaries of "us" and "them" persist. I've seen racial divisions remain instead of being broken down. I've seen marriages and divorces, births and deaths, people coming in and moving on. I guess that's part of being in it for the long haul. Even in my struggles and frustrations, I find myself in a community that reminds me that Jesus is real. And that is a huge change for me—living in community instead of isolation, even when life is tough.

Jackson, once overwhelmed by life and death, shares the new hope and life he knows in Christian community.

My wife lost her mother and we lost our first child in the same month. We had just moved to Nashville, and I could not find a job. I would like to say that this was the hardest season in our life, but we were just getting warmed up. My wife had to spend six weeks on bed rest in the hospital during late pregnancy. That child had to have surgery shortly after her birth. Two years later, after struggling for some time with depression, anxiety and multiple addictions, including alcohol, drugs and pornography (just to name a few), I spent three months in a treatment center, leaving my wife to care for our two young children alone. During the months I was in treatment, our neighborhood group and others from CCEN rallied around my family and served and loved us through it. One guy mowed our lawn every week for the whole summer. Several people babysat our children on a weekly basis. Still others provided meals and friendship.

After treatment, my wife and I separated for six months. Our group—and the church as a whole—continued to care for my family as they had throughout treatment. Since that time, Pastor Tom has met with us weekly for six months to help us build trust, hope and love in our home. He consistently points us away from ourselves and to Christ, the only hope we have for restoring our marriage. Our neighborhood group and many church friends walked with us through this time and prayed for us consistently. Though many people knew we were separated, there was no gossip or judgment. What we did experience was that we were part of a community who grieved with us but also had great hope in a God who could restore us. God has restored us and is continuing to do so! We now have tools to handle life's challenges. My wife and I are now growing closer to God and each other. We now serve others even as they have served us.

On the first Tuesday of the month, all our neighborhood groups gather for a prayer meeting. Our leadership team looks at these prayer meetings as a real litmus test of the overall spiritual health of CCEN. We are constantly amazed how God meets us during these gatherings, taking us deeper into a community of those being transformed by Jesus in our midst. This time is broken into sections of song, Scripture reading, praise, repentance and kingdom prayers. It is a time for broken people to be broken together and let the Spirit minister to us. It is consistently a time of great rejoicing. We often hear that people have had their bitter and hardened hearts replaced on these nights. The Holy Spirit has been so gracious in these meetings, and you can almost tangibly see people walking out with a lighter burden on their shoulders.

The prayer meeting used to be rather small. A handful of the hard core members of our community would be there. So we started praying for our prayer meetings. We asked the Lord to change our hearts and make us a praying people. He has been merciful in answering. As many as one hundred people now give up their Tuesday nights and actually find they couldn't be doing anything better!

In our weakness he is made strong. Perhaps the prayer meeting is the time when we see this played out most consistently. Someone who appears to have it all together comes in. They might even be scowling a bit. In the course of the next two hours, as they listen to the prayers of the saints humbly seeking the Lord, they break down. They might cry; they might cry out. But they turn to the Lord and confess to something that has been weighing them down for many seasons. Christ is made strong in their weakness and that burden is gone.

Anthony describes the freedom he found to confess addiction and find healing through the prayer ministry.

I had been attending City Church for about five months, maintaining a safe distance, not wanting to get too involved or engaged in the church community. A friend of mine had been going to the monthly prayer meeting. For some reason I really felt like I should go.

I was completely overwhelmed by the openness and intimacy of this gathering. During the time of confession I was struck by the brutal honesty and genuine struggle and crying out to God that I was hearing. During the time of testimony I was overcome by the real ways that God was at work in people's lives! It was truly one of the most beautiful things I had ever been a part of. I was literally shaking in my chair. That night I was still too ashamed of my own unrepentant sin and addictions that I was allowing to destroy me. I was too afraid to join this beautiful manifestation of the community of Christ, but I knew that I wanted this genuineness and honesty to mark my own life. God was drawing me to himself, inviting me out of isolation into community. The very next day I confessed to my family—for the first time—a decade of shame, hidden sin and addiction. I am now in the beautiful and difficult process of being healed and restored. The gospel of Christ has become a reality in my life for the first time!

When we pray that "the earth shall be full of the knowledge of the glory of the Lord as the waters cover the seas" (Isaiah 11:9; Habakkuk 2:14 ESV) and "your kingdom come, your will be done, on earth as it is in heaven" (Matthew 6:10; Luke 11:2), we are engaged in one of the most powerful means of grace God has given us. When we replace earth with "East Nashville," we are praying God's kingdom realities into our parish and experience a fuller reality of Christ in our lives. When we gather in the name of Jesus throughout the neighborhood and throughout the week, it is our prayer that the community of disciples will be

> strengthened with power through his Spirit in your inner being, so that Christ may dwell in your hearts through faith—that you, being rooted and grounded in love, may have strength to comprehend with all the saints what is the breadth and length and height and depth, and to know the love of Christ that surpasses knowledge, that you may be filled with all the fullness of God. (Ephesians 3:16-19 ESV)

Kingdom. Commitment to social justice and caring for the poor is not a merit-earning good deed or just *the right thing to do* for followers of Jesus. Instead, sacrificial social commitment is a response to God's amazing generosity toward us in Jesus. When the church in Jerusalem was experiencing material need, the churches of Macedonia, out of their "abundance of joy and their extreme poverty . . . overflowed in a wealth of generosity on their part" because they knew "the grace of the Lord Jesus Christ, that though he was rich, yet for your sake he became poor, so that you by his poverty might become rich" (2 Corinthians 8:2, 9 ESV).

Jesus taught his followers that they were to love and serve others sacrificially since they had been ultimately loved and served sacrificially by him. Such a lifestyle represents the in-breaking of the kingdom of God.

Amazingly, God actually enlists us as agents in the extension of *shalom*. As the early Jesus movement grew, even the leaders of the Roman Empire recognized the impact of the Christians' care for the poor and needy. The Roman Emperor Julian remarked, "The impious Galileans [Christians] support not only their poor, but ours as well, everyone can see that our people lack aid from us."[24]

In East Nashville engaging in deeds of *shalom* must include a commitment to hospitality, relief (mercy) and community development (justice) as we battle issues such as poverty, homelessness, addiction and economic and educational inequality.[25]

When CCEN first began, we made a splash at the street level through a strong ministry of *relief*. Relief can be defined as "the urgent and temporary provision of emergency aid to reduce immediate suffering."[26] We had scheduled times when members would meet with anyone in need from the several zip codes in our parish and determine if and how we might be able to help. However, our desire all along has been to be a part of making the city of Nashville look more like the city of God. Therefore, we knew that *development* was essential. Development is "a process of ongoing change that moves all the people involved—both the 'helpers' and the 'helped'— closer to being in right relationship with God, self, others, and the rest of creation."[27] We made a major shift over the last four years toward asset-based community development. Cedric appreciates the development approach to poverty because it avoids paternalism and provides tools for lasting impact.

I have personally been affected by City Church's approach to poverty. The approach that has been presented by our leadership has been both transformational for me in my own thinking as well as to some of our members practically.

*City Church has adopted a developmental approach to issues of poverty in-
stead of a relief model. This model of development entails first forming relationships with those in poverty, second assessing assets contained within a
community and third providing any necessary training that moves toward
further development. The relationship serves both as a means of accountability
and more importantly focuses on developing work skills and interpersonal
strengths that begin to remove the individual from the web of entanglements
that keep them in poverty. I have seen that paternalism in any form is never
acceptable if real transformation is to begin.*

Our benevolence team often asks, "What can we do in the next six to
twelve months that will play a part in holistically developing East Nashville
for the next six to twelve years?" As we asked this question for many years,
the Spirit has revealed through answers of prayer, the needs in the community and the gifts of the people in CCEN, four major areas in which we
now invest our resources: education, economics, arts and church planting.

As a result of relationships developed in the neighborhood, several public
schools actually contacted CCEN to see "if the rumor is true" that we would
actually provide tutors for students. Every week, dozens of CCEN members
meet with students from KIPP Academy, East Literature Junior High and
the YMCA to help them with academics, but even more important, to serve
as an adult who can be trusted in life.

CCEN realizes that poverty must be addressed and attacked at multiple
levels. People of God Organized began as different religious organizations
committed to work together under principles of community organizing to
address the needs of East Nashville.[28] One of the needs prevalent in East
Nashville is childcare and relational connection between mothers. Monique
gives and finds loving support and honesty through the International
MOMS Club.

*God has shaped my story in life as I have grown in friendship with many people
from various walks of life in the neighborhood. My involvement in the neighborhood naturally evolved as I had children and then joined a group called
International MOMS Club, a group that primarily seeks to offer daytime
support to moms who are at home with children. I've watched as Jesus has put
himself out there when I least expected it, using me to be his hands and feet.*

*I know how Jesus has loved me and sought me and probed my heart. I want
to love others this same way. I have found through having deep friendships with*

Interview Q&A 2

Editors: You note significant energy and engagement by lots of the church's participants as you grew and engaged your neighborhood. How did this shape the overall leadership (formal and informal)? How did God use members to help the church see, imagine and engage your context?

Aaron Sands   We use the phrase *belonging before becoming* often in CCEN in
(CCEN elder):   relationship to membership and leadership. Our simplex structure reinforces hands-on functioning of people in and around CCEN. In many cases their organic service into the body reveals and validates their functions and roles within the body. We've found that this promotes incarnational relationships and service throughout our entire body—no one is above or below any ministry function. This tends to uncover and unleash energy within CCEN that overflows into our neighbors and neighborhoods.

While we have a very clear vision and set of values, we try not to perpetuate a divide between leadership and service. We welcome questions and ideas to help bring more fullness to the vision that we have yet to imagine or see. Questions about our vision aren't threatening, because a vision is inherently directed ahead, unrealized to the fuller degree. We emphasize that the life of a follower of Christ is immersed in tensions tied to the "already" and the "not yet" of the kingdom of God. Our vision and values are framed within those tensions. One of the more prominent tensions is merging leadership with service—for followers of Christ they must go hand in hand.

our neighbors, nonbelievers are often willing to talk about suffering and longing and disappointments even more readily than believers, and this has transformed the way I think about what it means to be one of God's people. I have been changed into someone who is increasingly honest with my suffering, longing and disappointments and, as a result, know the intimacy of God in my life in a whole new way.

Offering alternating Jobs for Life classes, biblically based classes that train men, women and teenagers to seek, find and maintain jobs, and Red to Black classes, financial literacy training seminars, provide necessary tools of which we pray more and more people in the community will continue to take advantage. CCEN can assist graduates of these classes in setting up individual development accounts (IDAs), which are matching grant accounts set up for those who want to invest toward assets to help alleviate the cycle of economic poverty. Elroy found friends, spiritual encouragement and work through Jobs for Life.

> *I wasted a lot of years drinking and drugging. Spent some years behind bars. Now I believe my best years are still ahead of me! I heard about the Jobs for Life class that City Church offered. I attended the class every Monday and Wednesday evening for two months. Never missed a class. Looks like I'm starting a new job soon and will be getting new housing soon. God has changed my life. I'm staying clean, praying, reading and memorizing the Bible, and making friends with good people. I thank Jesus for all he has done for me.*

YOUR KINGDOM COME

The relationships formed throughout this cycle of connection, celebration, community and kingdom continue to raise up more and more neighbors and disciples who seek the peace of our community. We continue to wrestle through questions: What does it mean to love your neighbor as yourself? What if that neighbor is a drug dealer? What does it look like to be a church of haves and have-nots, where no one is sitting at the rich man's feet? What does community look like when people get close enough to realize that this is messy, that we can't even get relationships with other Christians right? What we know now, in part, is that it looks like learning how to go to Jesus together.

This theme of gospel-driven life and relationships, woven through the stories of East Nashville, our parish, enables us to be prayer dependent. Over and over again we must go to our knees, alone and together, to admit that we just can't do it. We don't have the chops, the mountains are too high and, to be honest, we are often afraid. But we don't stay there. We look to the cross of Christ and know that because he is "with us always," his kingdom is indeed breaking in. This breaking in happens in often difficult lives lived in the trenches of an urban community. The transformations are frequently slow and hard fought, and sometimes the fruit cannot be measured in bushels but rather in seeds. Even as the simplicity and complexity of ministry in an urban neighborhood has continued to startle us all along the way, we remind ourselves regularly, as Richard Lovelace rightly exhorts, "Do not pray only for your own spiritual renewal. Pray for a springtime of the Spirit which will enrich the church and the world, an awakening for which all earlier renewal movements have been only rehearsals."[29]

A BEAUTIFUL COMMUNITY OF DIVERSITY

NEW CITY CHURCH

Kevin Haah

NEW CITY CHURCH

Location: Los Angeles (downtown)
Denomination: Nondenominational
Year of Foundation: 2008
Regular Participants in the Life of the Church: 450
Website: www.newcitychurchla.com

In the story of New City Church you will find a beautiful community of diversity. Pastor Kevin Haah shares the tale of great intentionality in forming a church that is now a national example of creating diversity within the people of God. At New City Church you will find not only diversity in ethnicity but also in socioeconomics: many people from areas around skid row and those living in the downtown lofts have had an active role in forming the church. In the midst of the frequent segregation of Sunday mornings, New City Church is leading the way for missionally minded church plants that value creating community for people of different backgrounds.

A Call to Plant

I felt a sense of God's call into pastoral ministry for a long time, but I had no corresponding desire to heed that call. After college, when I was trying to decide whether I should go to law school or seminary, my parents, who were faithful yet financially minded Christians, pitched this to me: "If you enter into ministry and change your mind later, that will not glorify God, but if you pursue law and decide later to enter into ministry, that will glorify God. So, if you are not sure, why don't you go to law school?" The logic resonated with me, and so I chose to go to law school.

After law school my life consisted of big firms, trying to make partner and generating business. About eight years into practicing law my parents made a tearful confession. They said that God convicted them that they had wrongly discouraged me from going into ministry, and they had been repenting. My mom said, "If you still have a sense of call into ministry, we want to fully encourage you to pursue it." Of course, I had taken full responsibility for my own decisions, but their encouragement made a big impact on me. Six months later Mom suddenly died. I was too busy practicing law at this time to consider going into ministry. But while two more years passed and I made partner at my firm, I felt a renewed sense of calling into full-time pastoral ministry. God gave me a deep and abiding passion for the lost. After about eight months of prayer and discernment, my wife, Grace, and I decided that I should leave law and pursue full-time ministry.

After finally getting my MDiv at Fuller Theological Seminary I was hired as an associate pastor in charge of urban ministries at Young Nak Celebration Church, an English-speaking Korean American church I had been attending for over twelve years. One of my responsibilities was LoveLA, an outreach ministry in the parking lot of Union Rescue Mission, in the heart of skid row, downtown Los Angeles. We held an outdoor revival-like worship service every Sunday afternoon, which 200-300 homeless people regularly attended. I cut my teeth preaching there. Young Nak had started this ministry in the early 1990s and faithfully continued it every Sunday. I started to see an issue with it, though. Through a survey I found that although we thought of the ministry simply as a tool to connect people to a neighborhood church, the majority of those who attended thought they were actually coming to church. I began feeling that we might be doing them a disservice by potentially taking them away from a church where they could grow and find community, and drawing them instead to LoveLA, which had no small groups, Bible study, discipleship, communion and so on. Although there was a strong sense of the movement of the Holy Spirit, and many people gave their lives to the Lord, I didn't see the long-term transformation that happens in the context of a church community. I started struggling with this issue.

Around the same time, I was in my office when an anonymous caller asked, "You guys are a church near downtown, right? Have you heard about what's going on in downtown?" He began to talk about how downtown was growing and people were moving there. Then he asked, "What are you doing to reach out to all the new residents of downtown?" I remember wondering why this guy was calling a Korean church to ask about reaching people in downtown. We had a polite conversation. But for some reason this question started to resonate in my soul. I started to ask myself, *What are we doing to reach out to all these new residents of downtown LA?* I had never seriously considered what was going on in downtown LA until then. I started to Yahoo clip (Google was not as big then) all articles related to downtown LA development and found out that there was a major boom going on. In 2003 the Los Angeles city council had passed Adaptive Reuse Ordinance, an ordinance allowing old office and commercial buildings to be converted into mixed-use commercial-residential buildings. Most of the old buildings started to be converted into lofts. In 2000 the population of downtown was about 16,000; by 2005 it had doubled. Downtown was being revitalized.

Soon afterward, at a LoveLA volunteer dinner (with about forty people in the room), I shared about the struggle I was having with LoveLA. Then, I suddenly stopped, and I said something to the group that *I* heard for the very first time *as* it was coming out of my mouth: "What if we planted a multiethnic, multisocioeconomic church in downtown that reaches out to both the skid row residents and the new loft dwellers?" I remember absolute silence after I said this. A few seconds later I remember saying, "Yeah, but that would never work." Everyone, including me, laughed and went on. I shoved the idea to the back of my mind, but it never left me. From time to time, when I shared the idea with someone, I started to tear up. I wondered why I was always so moved. That's when Grace and I decided that maybe God was trying to tell us something, so we started to pray about it.

Fast-forward a few years. There was a senior pastor transition at Young Nak. After the new senior pastor was installed, I felt that it was time to explore the possibility of church planting in downtown. I had no idea how to plant a church and I had never been a part of a church plant or even seen a church plant happen. When someone forwarded me an email about Exponential Conference in Orlando, Florida, Grace and I felt like we should go and learn. It was billed as the world's largest gathering of church planters. When we went we discovered a whole world of church planters. We learned about the importance of assessment, coaching, launch teams, training and a lot of the best practices of church planting. I started devouring information and books about church planting.

Grace and I came to realize that we needed to go through a church planter assessment. Several people said that assessment was one of the most important things to do when a person felt called to plant. Several books argued that one of the most common reasons for church plant failure was that the planter was not qualified, but no one had assessed him or her beforehand. We were convinced. Grace and I wanted to make sure that we got a reality check. Did we have what it took to be multiethnic, multisocioeconomic church planters?

I submitted an application more than an inch thick to a church-planting assessment service from a brochure that I picked up at Exponential. It was called Church Planters Assessment Center. (I didn't know it at the time, but it was related to the organizers of the Exponential Conference.) Grace and I spent three nights and four days in assessment at Emmanuel Seminary in Tennessee. As we were leaving the center after the first full day of assessment, I remember Grace breaking down and crying, "I never felt so naked in my life!" It was a rigorous process of evaluation. At the end we were given the highest recommendation to be lead planters and encouraged to pursue our vision of planting a multiethnic, multisocioeconomic church in downtown LA. On our flight back Grace and I began to openly envision a church in downtown. Tears streamed down our cheeks as we prayed and saw a church coming together. We started feeling like it was a real possibility.

Discernment, Location and Leadership

Our next step was to seek confirmation of the vision from Pastor Michael Lee, the senior pastor of Young Nak, and the session, the governing body.

When I presented the vision of planting a church in downtown and what happened at the assessment, Pastor Michael was very excited and encouraging. I made a presentation to the session, showing the data regarding the growth of downtown and presenting the vision of planting a multiethnic, multisocioeconomic church. The session confirmed our call and decided to commission Grace and me to plant this church and to contribute $100,000 for our first year. They also allowed me to transition out of my pastoral duties and become a church planter in residence for a few months. This was in September 2007.

Core group development. Pastor Michael asked how many people I wanted to take with me for the church plant. He encouraged me to take at least fifty to one hundred people with me; he was very kingdom minded, but I declined. My target was to reach the residents in downtown, and I didn't want to start with a core group dominated by Korean Americans. I asked his permission to recruit anyone from church that I thought I needed, but I asked him not to encourage people to go with us. With that understanding I started to recruit the core team, the first few people who were to become the core of the church.

The recruitment of the first twenty people was an amazing journey of God's providence and guidance right from the beginning. Although I had specifically intended to recruit a core team that represented the diversity of downtown LA, I frankly wondered how it was going to happen. But God had divine appointments in mind. I asked two couples from Young Nak— John and Lauren, a couple fairly new to faith, and David and Janet, former missionaries. They joined. At a wedding I bumped into Leo, a Latino friend I had not seen for a long time, and felt led to share the vision and invite him. He said he had felt that God was going to lead him to something but had not figured out what it was. He told me later that he couldn't sleep that night because he was so excited about the vision. He joined. I met Akiliah, an African American woman who works at Union Rescue Mission. She was passionate about reaching downtown with the gospel. She joined. I talked to a friend who introduced me to Aric and Booyeon, and when I met them, it was clear that God had put us together to pursue this vision together. They joined. Aric ended up becoming the church's first intern. I shared the vision with Rocky, a man passionate about discipling men, and Carlo, and they joined as well. I invited Ronald and Eugene, whom I had discipled at skid row, and they joined. I asked John, a thriving Korean American worship leader to help us lead worship, and he joined.

I spent most of October 2007 to February 2008 meeting with people and pitching the vision of a multiethnic, multisocioeconomic gospel-centered church. As people joined we met together on Sunday evenings getting to know each other, talking about the whys and the hows of church planting. We also spent this time coming up with a name, vision/mission statement and core values of the church. I probably made around fifty to one hundred pitches of the vision to various people God led me to. It was amazing who God led me to share the vision with, and how the first twenty people came together. They were about as diverse as our church is now.

Getting to know downtown. During the core group development process and continuing into the first year of the church, our core team members spent many hours in downtown talking to whoever we could by asking if they were willing to participate in a survey. We started hanging out at Starbucks, but ended up more at Lost Souls Café (a fitting name) and Pete's Café, a popular bar and hangout. We learned much by just hanging out and listening to people. It was amazing how willing some people were to give their opinions on what they thought of church, why they didn't go to church and what kind of church they might be interesting in going to.

Our goal was to be a neighborhood church for downtown, and so it was important that we spend time listening to the people and discovering what God was already doing here. We also spent a significant amount of time prayer walking through downtown, taking the time to notice every building, every business, every corner and every person. I was very familiar with skid row, but I wanted to make sure I got to know the loft dwellers as well. We met with existing pastors and community leaders and asked them for their wisdom. We went to neighborhood council meetings to get a feel for the neighborhood issues. We devoured the downtown demographic studies done by Downtown Business Improvement District.

Word got around to a reporter of *Downtown News* that we were seeking to plant a church downtown. They ran a front-page article about our plans. The angle was that churches coming back to the neighborhood was yet another sign of downtown revitalization.

Formulating the vision. During the core group development process, I researched and talked to several different denominations and networks about the possibility of joining them as a church planter. For many, I was too advanced in the process to join as a church planter, and some were too narrow in terms of required doctrines. We decided to link with Stadia (stadia.cc) for training, coaching, initial oversight and some startup funding.

When our core team was about ten to twelve people, we started formulating a vision. We all shared the raw vision of planting a multiethnic, multisocioeconomic church in downtown LA. But we needed to refine and test the vision. I was taught at a church planters boot camp that churches grow fastest when there is a common bond outside of spirituality. They called this the homogeneous unit principle (HUP). So they told us to study our target. At one core group meeting we were brainstorming our target, which we called "Downtown Dude."[1] We started to brainstorm what we knew about a typical downtown dude: socially liberal, young, artsy, educated, relativistic, sometimes likes Jesus but definitely doesn't like the church, gay or gay friendly, and so forth. After this meeting I felt a sense of unease. Something was off. Was HUP really right? I could not avoid the logical conclusion that if HUP was right, building a multiethnic, multisocioeconomic church would not work.

As I thought about it, the multiethnic element was a slam dunk. Downtown was already multiethnic; people worked and went to school in a multiethnic context. The question then became, Would a multisocioeconomic church work? Skid row residents and loft dwellers were extreme in their economic differences. A typical skid row resident lived in a mission, single room occupancy (SRO) hotel or low-income housing. He or she received $221 from General Relief (LA county's welfare of last resort to single individuals) plus a few dollars in food stamps. On the other hand, according to research done by Downtown Business Improvement District (BID), the typical annual household income of a loft dweller was about $100,000. We wondered how to create a community out of skid row residents and loft dwellers.

This struggle was highlighted when Akiliah, one of our core leaders, and I met with Scott Chamberlain, the person who planted Central City Community Church of the Nazarene, a vibrant church of primarily skid row residents in the heart of skid row. He said that his intention had been to be multisocioeconomic, but people who were not from there dropped out. He thought it was very difficult to create a multisocioeconomic church in downtown. I was very discouraged. Akiliah had more faith and encouraged me to pursue it. Grace and I kept on praying about this. The only model of a multisocioeconomic church I could find was Times Square Church in New York. I saw a few other churches that crossed some socioeconomic lines—maybe working class and professionals together—but rarely homeless people with well-off people. I began wondering if we needed to be realistic and target just one socioeconomic segment. Maybe we had to target the loft dwellers and serve the skid row residents. Maybe the homogeneous unit principle was correct.

Then, one day, God spoke clearly to Grace and me. We were on a breakfast date at Starbucks. I shared with her about a tape I had listened to from a church-planting seminar.[2] The speaker said something that struck me: The definition of success is not what happens, not the result—that is God's issue. Instead, the definition of success is figuring out what God wants us to do and doing it. I shared with Grace that maybe we shouldn't be overly concerned about whether the multisocioeconomic model was going to work. That was God's problem. We had to discern whether it was God's call to be multisocioeconomic. And given the demographic data and the vision that God had given us, it was very clear that he was calling us to plant a church that was not only multiethnic but also multisocioeconomic. Maybe our posture simply was to obey and leave the results to God.

Grace then said something really interesting. She said that the previous night she had been wondering how Ralph Winter, whom she had worked under at William Carey Library, was doing. He was one of the most influential missiologists of our time. So she Googled him and ran across his autobiography. Something in his autobiography struck her, and she wanted to share it with me. So, we went online and read that portion together. It said,

> After we made the decision to leave Fuller we did not at any point in the next thirteen years, during which we paid off the campus, feel that God had promised us success. We only felt that the value of the goal was sufficient justification to go all out, sink or swim. I coined the phrase, "You do not evaluate a risk by the probability of success but by the worthiness of the goal." We were willing to fail because the goal we sensed was so urgent and strategic.[3]

The statement "'You do not evaluate a risk by the probability of success but by the worthiness of the goal'" struck us, just like the definition of success is not the result but the doing of God's will. Grace and I felt like God was speaking the same message to each of us. When we came to that realization, we both cried, prayed together and submitted the vision to God.

We then shared our conversation with the core group. There was immediate consensus that this was the right path. So, we decided to pursue full throttle the vision of a multiethnic and multisocioeconomic church, and decided *against* following the homogeneous unit principle.

The core group worked through our vision/mission statement and core values when we were meeting for prayer and discussion on Sunday nights. After a few weeks of discussions we felt a sense that God was giving us his vision statement. Our vision statement is: "The vision of New City Church of LA is to become an inclusive gospel-centered community of lovers of Jesus Christ who connect people to God, grow together, serve the city, and extend God's kingdom."

Our vision statement was the mission statement, and each word in it was our core value. There are two parts to the vision statement: (1) what we want to *be,* and (2) what we are called to *do.*

First, we want to *be* an inclusive gospel-centered community of lovers of Jesus Christ. At the heart of New City, we are *gospel-centered.* This means that we are a bunch of messed-up people living in God's grace. Therefore, we are *inclusive.* When we know we are messed up, we know we don't have the right to judge anyone; God's grace makes us inclusive. We are also a *community,* not only on Sundays but also in small groups. We do life together, grow together, learn together and serve together in small groups. We want to be *lovers of Jesus Christ,* to love him and be loved by him.

The second part of the vision is what we want to *do*: connect people to God, grow together, serve the city and extend God's kingdom. We are passionate about *connecting* people to a relationship with God. It's about evangelism. We also want people to *grow together* and *serve the city.* Growing together is about living in the Spirit, which we believe means (1) building a gospel-centered foundation, (2) developing spiritual disciplines, (3) being empowered by the Holy Spirit, (4) all in the context of community. *Serving the city* means being *for* the city by loving and serving the city. We have groups that are focused on growing together and serving the city. We are also passionate about *extending God's kingdom* through church planting.

Beginning Public Worship

Grace and I, with our entire core team, were commissioned to plant New City Church of LA by Young Nak Celebration Church in late January 2008. We started to hold Sunday worship gatherings on the second Sunday of February 2008. About twenty-five of us met at an Italian restaurant in downtown. We tried to use the worship as a vehicle for core group development.

A reporter for the *Los Angeles Times* ran across the *Downtown News* article about us and asked us if she could come by and do a story about us. It was amazing to get the *Times* to do a story about a start-up church of twenty-five people. Our church was incredibly diverse even at that time. We were multiethnic and multisocioeconomic. The story was very positive and provided some encouragement for the group.

Soft launch. We soon had to find another venue and moved to another restaurant, e3rd, in the Arts District. The owner was very gracious. He charged us minimal rent to use his restaurant, which was closed Sunday mornings. This restaurant was very trendy and hip. The ambiance changed immediately. We invited as many people as we could to our Easter service and ended up with about seventy people. This was *not* our official public launch or "hard" launch of the church. We considered this our official "soft" launch, sort of like opening the worship service but not officially promoting it as a grand opening. We started doing the Alpha Course, an introduction to Christianity, as our Sunday worship gathering program. We met for breakfast first, had a casual singing time and then I gave a talk. We had small group time afterward. After the Alpha Course we launched about five community groups, where we did Bible study, shared and prayed together.

We used what some people call a dual launch strategy—a soft launch to get things going and an official grand opening, a hard launch, to pump things up.

The grand opening—hard launch—at Club 740. By June our core group had grown to forty to fifty people. We decided it was time to have an official grand opening of the church, a hard launch.[4] We moved to a nightclub to accommodate the number we were hoping for. It was called Club 740. We didn't move there to be a hip nightclub church but because the owner offered it to us free. He wanted to serve the church and the community. Actually, I insisted on paying $200 per week, just to create more of an obligation on his part to accommodate us even when it was not the most convenient for him. Before it was turned into a nightclub it was a historic

Shakespearean-type theater built in the 1920s. Each Sunday many hands, many hours and many prayers went into preparing the place for worship. The main floor was surrounded by three bars, but we converted it into a worship space with several small tables and groups of chairs. Although the club closed at 3 a.m., the cleaning crew was still working when we walked in, and it still reeked of alcohol and sweat, which we had to air out. Even after cleaning, the floor often was sticky with beer. But the real problem was the space for our children's ministry. It was like a dungeon. There were no windows and it was filthy, but the children's ministry team did an amazing job cleaning it up and trying to create a fun environment.

We did a lot of things to get the word out and invite people to the grand opening. We sent blog releases to downtown bloggers. Downtown loft dwellers were very connected via a dozen key bloggers, so we tried to get them to write about us. We generated buzz by serving in the community, going to downtown events and handing out flyers and invite cards everywhere. We used Facebook invites to create additional buzz, asking core team members to invite their friends. We also invested a significant amount of money sending four sets of direct mail to every resident, one per week leading up to the grand opening. The direct mail focused on us being an inclusive gospel-centered community, although we didn't use the term *gospel centered*.

Finally, the grand opening came on September 14, 2008. We had about two hundred people join us for the grand opening worship service: about one hundred new people from downtown and about fifty well-wishers who came out to support us, in addition to about fifty launch team members. There was a lot of energy. As we expected, the next few Sundays took us down to ninety to one hundred people, meaning that about half of the newcomers stuck. Most were unchurched, and a significant portion was gay. For me, it is very important that we reach out to the GLBTQs because about 25 percent of downtown loft dwellers fall into that category. Although we didn't get everyone to stick, we doubled our size through the hard-launch process. It was a solid start, and from there we started to grow steadily to about 350 in attendance by the beginning of 2012.

Club 740's "dungeon" proved too much for our children's ministry. A few months after our grand opening, Los Angeles Theatre Center, the venue that we had been praying for, became available to us at a price we could afford—an answer to our prayers. It was a beautiful and clean multiplex live-stage theater in the heart of the historic core. They also had large open rehearsal rooms we used for our kids ministries. They didn't use the facility on Sunday mornings, and they needed some additional revenue, so the arrangement worked out well for both parties. We joyfully and thankfully moved to that venue.

God's provisions. Around this time we also moved into a historic office building right across the street from LATC. One of the first things we did was to offer the Alpha Course in our office. The building owner came to the Alpha Course with his pastor because his pastor was interested in offering it at his church. The building owner liked what we were about and offered us the use of pretty much any space in the building without charge. He had an 8,000 square foot, high ceiling, beautiful space on the first floor of the building that was not leased out, so we used it for fellowship, Good Friday services, baptism parties and other events. Later, he offered us a 2,800 square foot office space at a fraction of the market rate. And he gave us permission to use for free a 2,000 square feet conference room right next to the office, where we have our worship team rehearsals, prayer meetings, small group meetings and fellowship events. These have been incredible provisions of God.

Following the Stadia model, we were on a three-year schedule of declining balance of support from outside, from both individual supporters and churches. During our first year, 2008, about 75 percent of our income came from outside sources. During 2009 half came from outside, and during 2010 about a quarter came from outside. In 2011 we budgeted for 10 percent of our income to come from outside sources (although we ended up receiving more). We had originally planned for outside support to be at zero in 2012, but we decided to ask some outside supporters to continue for one more year. God has been incredibly faithful throughout the process. We've found that our offerings increase more slowly than our attendance numbers. We think it is because a majority of those who come are unchurched, so they are not used to tithing. In addition, about a third of our regular attenders are from skid row, and another 10-20 percent of us are in college or graduate school. Nonetheless, God has continued to provide for our needs, whether through unexpected offerings, giving from outside or through amazing people who have provided us with great deals on major facility expenses.

BECOMING AN INCLUSIVE GOSPEL-CENTERED COMMUNITY

From the beginning we have been as diverse as one can imagine. About a third of us are from a skid row mission or low-income housing, and about two-thirds of us are from the lofts or outside of downtown. We are 20 or 30 percent each of blacks, whites, Latinos and Asians, including many multi-racial people. We have no dominant race or group. Our people range in age from their twenties to their seventies, although their median age is probably mid-thirties. In addition, about 10-20 percent of our people identify themselves as GLBTQ. Most people who visit our church tell us that they have never been to a more diverse church. In fact, many say that they have never been to a more diverse gathering of any kind.

One of the things we do at New City, not only during our Sunday worship gathering but also during our grow-and-serve group gatherings, is share our stories with one another. This has helped create a culture of being real with one another. One of the first persons to share was a lesbian who shared how she felt more welcome at New City than at any other church she had been to. She said that this was the first church ever in which she openly shared her sexual orientation. She became a part of the fabric of the church, and she helped create a culture of inclusiveness.

So many different kinds of people have come together and experienced life transformation at New City. When one gay man in his early sixties came to New City, it was the first time he had been to church since he left as a teenager. He gave his life to Christ and was baptized. An African American woman who was addicted to drugs for decades gave her life to the Lord, was baptized and has been sober since. One of our key leaders shared that he had spent several years in jail for financial embezzlement; he is now one of our treasurers. We have a Muslim who became a Christian and got baptized. He is one of our leaders now. We have people going through healing from abuse as a child, from broken relationships and from all kinds of mental illnesses. We have a Harvard grad suffering from mental illness who goes back and forth between reality and her own world, often talking to herself during worship. We have people who have spent time in jail for all kinds of felonies and have come back to the Lord and live in accountable communities together. We have investment bankers, engineers, Harvard grads, PhDs, MBAs, and all kinds of professionals and artists, as well as people who never finished high school and are struggling with unemployment. Most of us are learning from one another and engaging in relationships that lead to a greater appreciation for people we would have never been friends with.

How did such a community come about? The foundation of our church is the belief that we are all messed-up people living in God's grace. We constantly teach that our life, worth and identity come by grace, as a gift from God and received by faith in the finished work of Jesus on the cross, and not by our performance, accomplishments or how good we are. It is only by the cross, not by our works, that we are who we are. When our identity is based on God's grace, we are all equal before God. There is no basis for judgment or hierarchy. Without this gospel foundation, people's attempt to love those the world sees as weaker (financially, socially or morally) becomes patronizing at best. We may try to respect them and not judge them, but in our heart, we can't help feeling that we are better than them. That attitude is dangerous when we do community together. It will come out in little ways. We teach that we have to reframe our identity under the gospel in order for us to be truly inclusive.

Built on this gospel-centered foundation, we are very intentional about building a diverse community of believers. As I mentioned earlier, we made diversity a critical factor when recruiting the first twenty people—the core group—into the church. The diversity of this group made growing in diversity much more natural. But without being intentional it wouldn't have happened. The staff and the worship team were diverse from the beginning. Currently, we have an Asian (me), two whites (one of whom is a woman), one Latino and one black woman. Our webpage emphasizes diversity. When things move away from diversity, we tweak the way we do things. For example, at the beginning of the church, particularly because we started at a restaurant, we had a pretty good brunch spread (10 a.m.) before our worship service (10:30 a.m.). Everyone got to chat a little and get comfortable before we started to worship together. In fact, people sat around tables to worship. This worked great when the church was small. Even after we moved to the theater for worship, we continued this format. But we discovered that people from skid row always came by 10 a.m. for the brunch, whereas loft dwellers and people outside of downtown started to come a little late—10:20 or even later. I think they tried to make it on time, but they knew in the back of their minds that the worship service didn't start until after the brunch. We also found that most newcomers came on time. So, when newcomers came their first impression of the church was that the majority of the people were from skid row. They saw the church as caring for the poor, but many of them didn't see it as a church for people like them. Our goal was to create a positive first impression, and after much discussion, we decided to move the fellowship time to after the worship service. This created some interesting discussions, but we came to realize that this was an important tweak to keep a demographic balance that accurately reflected the community. It was clear to all of us that this was not an issue of discrimination against skid row residents. If we were doing something that made us look like the church was for loft dwellers at the expense of skid row residents, we would have changed that as well.

We are also intentional about reaching out to the GLBTQs. About 25 percent of the loft dwellers identify themselves as GLBTQ, and the rest are very open and passionate about including gays. We want to be a church where people who are gay can belong and be loved and accepted, as God works in all of us. There is a tremendous hunger among gays for the gospel. Many are not satisfied in a gay church. Often, it is too much about their sexuality and feels a little watered down spiritually. They don't get the sense that the church takes a high view of the Bible. But they want to come to a church where there is spiritual vitality without condemnation. We have struggled with how to reach out to this group.

The gospel has become our answer. This is how we express the reasons for our inclusiveness: We are a church that seeks to thrive on trying to be like Jesus—both radically loving and accepting, and also taking the Word of God seriously. We are neither a conservative church nor a liberal church. We really don't feel that the gospel of Jesus fits into those categories. We believe that Christianity is not primarily about rules or morals, but about understanding that our flaws and darkness within us are bigger and darker than we think they are *and* at the same time we believe that God loves us and accepts us more than we can imagine. So, this means we are not a church that says that anything goes, but rather we are a church that says we have all screwed up and therefore have no basis for judging anyone. We accept and love all people not because we are all okay but because we are all messed up together. We believe that the dynamics of acknowledging both our brokenness on the one hand and God's unconditional love and acceptance on the other compel us to be humble, accepting and loving without being judgmental.

We have become a come-as-you-are church. We have people who have been in jail for felonies, in recovery for substance abuse, struggling with homelessness, in gangs, divorced or in codependent relationships, suicidal, mentally ill or abused as a child. We also have people who seem to have it all together, who look "normal" on the outside. They have a job, a family, a home. But, as they say, everyone is only normal until you get to know them. It is so good to be a part of a church that allows messiness to be the norm. In many ways this creates the freedom for people to be themselves and to love one another and be loved as they are.

One of my concerns in creating a multisocioeconomic community, particularly with people in desperate need, was that the people who have more financial resources would tire of helping those who are struggling. That has not been the case. We have seen people freely helping one another. But because a real relationship has developed between the loft dwellers and skid row residents, we've noticed that economic abuse is not really an issue. We help one another in a way that really helps and is always in context of a relationship. In addition, we are connected to many of the resources that are available for people in need. Our set-up team leader noticed that a certain member always came to church very early with his luggage and helped set up. He found out that this person was living on the streets and having difficulty figuring things out. The leader stopped by the street where this person hung out during the day and took him to PATH, an organization that helps homeless people. It just so happens that one of our members works there, so we were able to connect this person to housing.

Help between people of various socioeconomic classes has certainly not been one way. The faith of many in skid row is vibrant, real and powerful, and has had an amazing impact on the rest of the congregation. I think they are the most responsible for the culture of openness at our church. Some of our leaders come from skid row. They are an integral part of the body at New City.

Growing Together and Serving the City

Our vision statement says that we *grow together* and *serve the city*. Our community groups, the small groups where we did life together, learned together, shared and prayed together, were designed to be the primary place where we grew together. At one point, when the church's regular attendance was about 120, we had about ten groups. The groups were vibrant. We in-

Interview Q&A 1

Editors: Your grow-and-serve groups are engaged in serving your neighborhood. How have the voices of neighbors helped the groups see
something, shift their imagination or discern what God calls New
City to be and do?

Kevin Haah: Each grow-and-serve group determines how they reach and serve
their neighbors. Some of them are project oriented (e.g., they volunteer at a nursing home, a mission, Habitat for Humanity). Some
of them are more relational (e.g., English conversational class in the
middle of a heavy immigrant community). Our church motto for
ministry in our neighborhoods, especially in skid row, has always
been that we are not here to minister to them and come back to our
holy huddles. We are here to include them. Our ministry is not
transactional but relational. So we never see homeless people as
"them" but as "us," and they regularly inform the way we do discipleship and other ministry at New City.

We are finding that our Healing Rooms grow-and-serve group can
be a powerful outreach tool to the Latino immigrant community.
We have noticed in our Latino neighborhoods that there are numerous botanicas, which are retail stores that sell folk medicine,
candles, amulets and other products regarded as magical. We see
this as a hunger for the supernatural in the community. We are in
the process of thinking about how to bring our Healing Rooms (a
group that creates time and space where we pray for healing) to
this community.

tentionally mixed people up, not based on any affinities. Loft dwellers and
skid row residents were coming together, sharing, learning and praying together. We saw people help one another with financial needs, housing and
other needs. We saw skid row people influencing loft dwellers and vice
versa. A vast majority of our regular attenders participated in one of the
community groups, but over the years the participation rate declined. By
mid-2011, when our attendance was around 250-300, we only had five com-

munity groups left. We were trying to start up new groups but had difficulty doing so. We tried to take a more smorgasbord approach to growing together, asking people to choose between one of four ways: a community group; a discipleship group; The Current, a mid-size gathering where people came together to soak in worship and prayer; or the recovery ministry or other Bible study classes. However, this approach didn't work either. We got a lot of people involved in more activities, but there was a segment of the church that was not connecting to any of these growing together opportunities. We had to figure out another way to grow together.

Another issue we faced was in serving the city. There was a team assigned to regularly put together volunteer opportunities. Some people came out to those events, but I was not satisfied with the number of people involved, compared to the number of people in the church. Our goal was not just to transactionally minister and serve the people in need, but to include them in the community and develop relationships with them, learn from them, and seek to help them holistically. In many ways we did that because the poor were already among us. As we learned to share and help one another, we were helping the poor. Nonetheless, I felt that God was calling us to do both: include people into a Jesus-centered community of sharing *and* serve those outside of the community.

So, we were struggling to figure out how to restructure our community group system and how to get more people to serve the city. After much research and discussion, influenced by the people in the missional community movement, we started grow-and-serve groups. These groups are where we grow together *and* serve the city. We currently have fifteen vibrant grow-and-serve groups of ten to twenty people each, with different genres of service for each group: anti–human trafficking, food and clothing pantry, children at risk, financial peace, high school group, men's group serving skid row, arts, learning English conversation groups for immigrants, meals on wheels and visitations, recovery group, healing room, nursing home visitations and street prayer ministry. We've had an amazing response to the grow-and-serve groups. Even as we serve the community, the powerful element of the groups has been developing a deep community where we can share our lives with one another and become lifelong brothers and sisters in the Lord. This has been a great way to grow together *and* get the majority involved in outreach and service at the same time.

Interview Q&A 2

Editors: You indicate the amazing breadth of gifts and faithfulness among New City Church's participants. How has God used their connections, discernment and creativity to shape the church's life and mission.

Kevin Haah: I believe in communal discernment of the leading of the Holy Spirit. Since the church is a community of God's people, the direction of the church must be discerned communally. So, since the beginning of the church plant, we had two official leadership bodies that helped the church discern the movement of the Spirit. One was the management team, which held the authority of the board and was composed of outside people, and the other was transitional advisory group (TAG team), composed of about ten people from the church. Even though the TAG team was advisory in its capacity, they actually made all of the important decisions of the church. During our third year we switched the management team's and the TAG team's roles so that management team became advisory and TAG team (renamed leadership team) became the board. In addition, the staff, team leaders (leaders of various ministries) and our grow-and-serve group leaders (leaders of our small groups) have influenced every major decision of the church.

EXTENDING GOD'S KINGDOM BY PLANTING A CHURCH IN EVERY NEIGHBORHOOD IN LA

From the beginning, the vision of New City has been to start a church-planting movement in Los Angeles. Our vision is not to be a megachurch for the entire city. We want to be a church for downtown Los Angeles. We want to be a neighborhood church, to love, reach, serve and make an impact on the neighborhood. But our vision is for the entire city. We want to be a part of planting a church in every neighborhood in Los Angeles.

Los Angeles is composed of 119 distinct neighborhoods, ranging from about 10,000 to over 200,000 people in each neighborhood. If you count the neighborhoods in the cities near Los Angeles, there are more than 200 neighborhoods. Most people don't say they are from LA, unless they are outside of LA. Instead, they identify with a certain neighborhood: Downtown, Koreatown, Silver Lake, Westlake, Boyle Heights and so on. Many of these urban neighborhoods have churches with a great building but also with a significant decline in membership. When the neighborhood demographics shifted, the churches didn't change along with them. So, we see many churches with fewer than fifty elderly people who are of a different ethnic group from the neighborhood the building is in. There are also churches that have a certain demographic focus—Korean, Armenian, Ethiopian, Latino, black. They are often not focused on being a church for the neighborhood but are just located in that neighborhood, and if they do reach out, they reach out to their segment throughout the city. All of these churches may be necessary, but there are very few churches who bring people together to serve the neighborhood they are located in. That's our vision—to plant more churches that are gospel centered, bringing the various people in their neighborhood together, and not only sharing the gospel but also being the gospel to that community by serving the community.

God has sent us several couples who are passionate about church planting. I have started to mentor them, meeting with them as a group on a monthly basis. But I don't want to wait until New City is financially stable before we plant a church. So, in partnership with Stadia, we have put together the Los Angeles Church Planting Movement of about a dozen churches so far, which are coming together to pool resources to start planting a church in every neighborhood in LA (facebook.com/LACPM).

It's awesome to see how God is working to bring churches together to start a church-planting movement here in Los Angeles. As of spring 2014 we have eighteen churches involved as sponsors and five new initiatives either launched or in formation.

CREATING THIRD SPACES
THE LIGHT @ BARE BULB COFFEE

Nikki Collins MacMillan

THE LIGHT @ BARE BULB COFFEE

Location: Warner Robins, Georgia
Denomination: Presbyterian Church (USA)
Year of Foundation: 2011
Regular Participants in the Life of the Church: 75
Website: www.barebulbcoffee.org

The story of Bare Bulb Coffee is unique in the midst of this series of stories. The initial focus of visionary pastor Nikki Collins MacMillan and those that were a part of her team began not with a dream of a church but of an intentional missional embedding. Enjoy this story out of the Presbyterian Church (USA), told from a suburban context in Warner Robins, Georgia. The intentionality of the people that created Bare Bulb Coffee is an exemplary tale for those looking to plant by creating third spaces such as bookstores, art galleries and coffee shops. Bare Bulb Coffee has only existed for three years yet they have already created enormous transformation in the community, while creating a financially stable business in the midst of our tricky economy.

Beginning

Bare Bulb Coffee was borne of one congregation's hope to connect with their growing community. Good things were happening at First Presbyterian Church of Warner Robins, Georgia, and good things were also happening in the larger community. However, the traditional and timeworn measures of outreach and evangelism were not bridging the gap between the church and the community. Because people under the age of forty and without a prior relationship to a congregation were rarely taking part in church events, the leadership of First Presbyterian Church sought to go into the neighborhood. At the same time, several conversations were taking place across the broader Flint River Presbytery. Alan Roxburgh had coached the presbytery, introducing the concept of the missional church to presbytery leadership. A cohort of churches ripe for transformation joined together in the Reformation Project led by presbytery staff. The project's aim was to engage congregational leaders in an intentional and prayerful process of visioning, with the goal of shaping congregations to be active proclaimers of the gospel, makers of disciples and engagers of the larger community. In addition, a group of seven churches joined for the Unbinding the Gospel Project by Martha Grace Reese. Through small group studies focused on prayer and simple sharing of faith, participants' understanding of evangelism was transformed and their faith was deepened. First Presbyterian Church was deeply involved in each of these conversations, so the leadership was ripe for new mission in the world.

In his 1989 book *The Great Good Place*, Ray Oldenburg argues that a community finds its anchors in places that are neither home nor work, but that foster conversation and creativity. These places are accessible, often have inexpensive food and drink, and foster a community of regulars.[1] By acknowledging that church is no longer a significant "third place" in the culture and that Jesus sends us into the world to bring good news, the leaders began to experiment with ministry outside its walls. The staff started to keep office hours in local coffee shops and restaurants. Small groups meet in members' homes rather than at the church building. Neighborhood "block parties" were hosted in the church yard. These sorts of experiments led the church to wonder, What would happen if we were to be a new kind of church community—one that set aside our traditional perceptions of space and structures in order to meet people outside of our congregation?

What if we were a community sent into the world rather than gathered behind stained glass? What if we were a group of disciples whose life together was centered in public space—quietly declaring that there is no place in this world that is not holy and infused with God's presence?

Conversations began between the pastor of First Presbyterian Church and the director of youth and young adult ministries, but quickly included the church Session and the new church development committee of the presbytery. The first steering committee was convened by action of the presbytery in August 2008 and included the pastoral staff of the church, several members of the congregation, and an ex officio member who was ordained in the United Methodist Church and was worshiping in an area Episcopal congregation. In February 2009 the presbytery appointed an administrative commission to oversee the project and to assist in matters of property and finance. Its members, all ordained officers in the PC(USA), came from beyond the immediate geographic area. Church leaders allocated a large sum of money for a new project that would direct the congregation outward and forward into the neighborhood.

The church could not do this alone. Several other groups joined in on what God was doing. Flint River Presbytery had previously designated the geographic area of Houston County as a "future site of new church development" and was eager to add their resources to the project. The Synod of the South Atlantic and the General Assembly of the Presbyterian Church (USA) and other area congregations contributed finances. Each of these bodies invested financial and human resources in an emerging model of forming a faith community—one that would not rely on known paradigms of church planting or tested benchmarks for measuring success. Instead, it was fueled with the hope of transforming church and culture, forming community and new patterns of faithfulness, gathering in the midst of daily life and participating in God's ongoing work in the world.

THE STORY THAT ENCOURAGED US ON

In the fall of 2008 an initial group of leaders gathered for a day-long retreat to listen for God's leading and to catch a glimpse of God's vision of how the project might serve the world. Around pizza boxes, soft drinks, coffee pots and candy wrappers, the group prayed and laughed, brainstormed and read Scripture. The story that rose to the surface bubbled up from shared Sunday school songs. Luke 19 tells the story of Zacchaeus, a man so intent on seeing

Jesus that he climbed a tree to see over the crowd of Jesus' followers. What our group realized in that moment is that through our structures, architecture, polity, language and internal battles, we have stood in the way of others who are curious and desire to connect with Jesus. Getting out of the way became our first intention—with the hopes that we might be able to stand as witnesses to the moment when Jesus met them, perhaps overhearing Jesus calling their names, proclaiming mercy and grace, and moving into their lives.

We began to envision the ways we could be in the world that would make a way for others to meet Jesus. How could we order our lives, organize our mission and create opportunity to build real and rich relationships with the Zacchaeuses of our day? How can we attend to those who stand on the fringes straining for a chance to know who Jesus is—but are kept at bay behind the crowds of Jesus' followers?

IMAGINING A THIRD PLACE

Warner Robins, Georgia, is an Air Force town. The city came into existence at the end of World War II as a depot base for the maintenance of aircraft. The largest employer in the area by far is Robins Air Force Base, which draws some active duty personnel, but the vast majority of its employees are defense contractors who provide high tech logistics and support to the Air Force. Base employees are often retired military service members who come from all over the United States and the world, making Warner Robins a fairly cosmopolitan and quite diverse community. The average age in Warner Robins is significantly younger than the average age of members of First Presbyterian Church. Most families in the area live hundreds of miles from extended family. Other than Little League sports and the large traditional churches in the area, there are few spaces for people to meet outside of work and home. We wanted to foster a space where people could gather around common interests, conversation and the arts. Jesus did significant ministry around wells. The wells of ancient Palestine were akin to present day water coolers, pubs and coffee shops. Wells were the places people would go to quench their thirst not just for water but also for conversation and community. They may have been the third place of Jesus' day. We envisioned the modern equivalent of a well as the gathering place and launching pad for our mission—a coffee house.

How did we pay for it? The original project planners were clergy, Air Force pilots, defense contractors and stay-at-home parents. There was not a restaurateur, entrepreneur or barista in the bunch. We had no background in launching a new business or running a coffee shop. It was through the providence of God that a successful coffee shop owner was added to our pool of resources. Through this person we quickly learned what sort of financial commitment would be necessary to start a new business. An initial capital investment of approximately $250,000 would get a coffee shop up and running in our market. To fund the project, we would need grants from the presbytery and other denominational bodies, as well as contributions from First Presbyterian Church and other area congregations.

By all accounts the money invested in this project was significant for the development of a new faith community. However, the model intentionally includes a source of funding beyond the grants and the giving of the local faith community—the cash register. We projected that after a little more than a year of operation the coffee shop would generate revenue exceeding the initial capital investment. Furthermore, as the coffee business grows and becomes profitable, its proceeds will support the mission of the community.[2]

THE BUMPY ROAD, DEAD SPOTS AND SEASONALITY

This project did not consist of big leaps. Instead, it comprised two years of hard work and piecing together the specifics. In this we have seen ourselves growing from business plans, mission statements and ministry projections to a vibrant, growing mission and ministry. Our earnest planning began in the fall of 2008, and our grant applications were approved and initially funded in the spring of 2009. The original projections included opening the coffee shop in the fall of 2009. Our timeline coincided quite well with the troubles in the American (and global) economy. One of our first questions was where to locate. The impact of the economic crisis on real estate development was significant. Simply put, we could not find a location.

We were drawn to a part of our community where new schools and houses had recently been built. This area also showed promise for future development. Because of this we could easily find vacant storefronts available for lease. However, nothing fit the space and traffic pattern needs for a successful coffee shop and ministry. We drove and prayed the thoroughfares of the area. We ate lunch in restaurants, analyzed the shelves of grocery stores, scoured subdivisions and waited for God to reveal the place we would land. Ultimately, a new commercial development was announced in the middle of the area we targeted. A small strip of shops would be located between a major home improvement store and a new multiplex cinema with an anticipated draw of one million moviegoers from a forty-mile radius. Bare Bulb Coffee could occupy an end space (with a drive-thru) large enough to accommodate both the coffee business as well as space for music, art and worship events. The space was exactly what we were looking for. The downside was time. Our building would not be ready for occupancy until a year after our initial projections. What would we do in the meantime? How would we plant seeds of a ministry of hospitality and welcome people without a physical space? How would we occupy the waiting period?

This waiting time became a critical period of formation for the project. We did what all good church people do: we fought, we experimented, and we were dragged along by the Spirit, who knew far more about what we needed than we did. Our initial timeline would have resulted in an immature start. The additional months of planning, though very difficult—and expensive—led to critical leadership formation and correction of some of our initial assumptions and plans.[3] Over that time the vision of the project became more clearly focused on serving the larger community in an indigenous way rather than funneling them into already existing structures of church life. The time also provided much-needed opportunities for learning about the business model of the coffee shop itself.

Throughout our planning process, we prayed—sincerely and regularly—for the people who were not with us yet. We believed that these people—patrons of the coffee shop and people who would become a part of the community of faith—were important for our planning conversations. However, the hard reality was that when we looked around the table, we saw only one another—all with ties to existing congregations and deeply enmeshed in the life of the established church. Our commitments to the institution that was sending us out kept us busy in places we already occupied and with the people who were already a part of a Christian community.

We struggled to imagine and plan for a community shaped by people we did not know. We imagined that these people's lives were not organized around the activities of church, but that their commitments were as important to them as ours were to us. With so much unknown, we spent far too much time and energy trying to figure out how what we were doing would fit with what we already knew, and how the new thing would energize the old thing. We wanted to figure out how the old thing would transmit its values to the new people. We were being ignorant. We were so far inside the world of the traditional church that we could not understand the questions and stories, or dwell in the richness of the broader community. Our plans were formed by our needs to go coupled with the church's desire to live to see another day, rather than walking in partnership with new friends who desired Jesus. We would talk about having conversations with people who did not attend a church, and we would realize that we did not know very many people who did not attend church. We lived in a bubble with our backs against the sides and the only people we could even see were ourselves. There were moments when we would be inspired by what could be, but for the most part, until the coffee shop actually opened and we began to escape our bubble, we were never able to put wheels on what we imagined.

The doors of Bare Bulb Coffee opened in October 2010. Thanks to some great newspaper articles and good word of mouth, people in the community found us quickly. By the end of the calendar year we were exceeding our sales projections. Focused first on understanding what it means to run a coffee shop and to welcome the community into our space, we did not immediately begin with worship or Bible studies. We began with meeting people and learning to listen to their stories. Our first events in the coffee shop were intended to draw large and diverse crowds. We let stories, hopes, songs and creations of the larger community begin our conversations. The following are some of the first things we did:

- filled our walls with art from local artists and launched a series of "Meet the Artist" receptions
- invited local musicians to perform on our stage
- facilitated small conversations about recently released movies
- hosted a Harry Potter release party
- invited customers to talk about things that matter to them on our bulletin boards
- began a weekly open mic night that drew capacity crowds (and beyond) and uncovered a wealth of local talent
- built a relationship with two local elementary schools that allowed our customers, friends and the larger community to fill backpacks with weekend food for children who receive free lunch

- gathered more than one hundred blankets to share with the homeless of our area

- introduced ourselves, learned names, listened to stories and made new friends

We learned quickly that we had hit a nerve in our community. People were longing for a place to be—a venue that would welcome them to share their talent and their stories, a truly hospitable space that could serve as a living room, meeting place, reading corner and game table.

Early one Tuesday morning after we had been open for a couple of months, a mother came in for a cup of coffee on her way to work at a nearby school. She told us that due to an anxiety disorder her daughter was working with a homebound tutor. The sixteen-year-old girl could not make it through the school day in her nearby high school. Surprisingly, however, she had found a safe space in our coffee shop. The coffee shop became a place for her to study and take tests with her tutor. When we found out that she made an A on a test she took at the coffee shop, we were moved. With tearful eyes her mother thanked us for giving her child a safe place to land while she worked through a tough time in her life. We were humbled by the way the Spirit had used us—without our even knowing it—to offer a sanctuary amid the busy crossroads, steaming espresso machines and whirring blenders.

Within the first months people often expressed their gratitude for Bare Bulb Coffee. As we worked our way through the crowd on open mic night thanking the young (and not so young) people who shared their talents on our stage, our words were quickly covered by people's thanks for offering them the opportunity to perform and listen to one another. "This is exactly what the community has needed for so long. Thanks for giving us this chance." In January 2011 a middle-aged man hovered at the door to the shop on open mic night. When he was invited in to play his guitar he said he would like to but that he must confess he was "nervous as a whore in church." That night marked the first time the man had played guitar on a stage while sober in twenty years. Having given up drugs and alcohol seven months earlier, he was seeking a place to share his gifts and to make new friends. Since then he has become an active participant in many aspects of the life of the community—rarely missing Sunday evening prayer gatherings. In these gatherings he offers insight from his knowledge of biblical Greek and

Hebrew as well as nineteenth- and twentieth-century philosophers and mystics from earlier times in church history. He volunteers to help with the sound system, offers guitar lessons and teaches Bible studies. Walking with him through this transformative period in his life has also been transformative for the larger community. He challenged us to let go of labels and prejudices and allow ourselves to be stretched. We are a stronger and richer community because of this journey and because of his place among us.

BEGINNING TO WORSHIP TOGETHER

On Epiphany 2011 Bare Bulb Coffee began two new gatherings on Sundays: a morning running group and an evening prayer service. The running group's purpose was to build relationships along the lines of a mutual interest in health and fitness. The group gathers at the shop, runs through the neighborhood and then cools down at the shop over conversation and cold water. For some this is a Sunday morning run before they attend church in another community. For others it's simply a run with nice people at the beginning of the week. Still for others it is a first taste of Christian community, a safe way to explore a life of faith. The running group has hosted a road race to benefit the mission of Bare Bulb Coffee. They regularly compete in local races and travel together for competitions around the Southeast. The group aims to spawn a running group for children and youth, passing along the value of caring for one's body and encouraging others to overcome challenges and build strong habits of health and fitness.

The second group is a growing community who gather for evening prayer on Sunday nights after the coffee shop closes. This is the worship time for the community coming to know itself as The Light @ Bare Bulb Coffee. Together we have wrestled with the Gospel of Matthew as prescribed by the Revised Common Lectionary in a style of worship that blends ancient and contemporary music, simple prayer, and conversations around tables about the challenge of Scripture for our everyday lives. The prayer service is quite different from any other worship service in our larger community. Children worship alongside parents and grandparents. Teens and young adults hold conversations with men and women three times their age. We explore the passage through artistic expression, the sacraments, a shared meal, letters, creative writing and conversation. Musical leadership is drawn from the talents of the community and rotates each week in a shared and collaborative fashion.

Music styles vary from rhythm and blues to Taizé chants, to popular contemporary Christian music, to traditional hymns and house church songs, to original pieces written specifically for the community. The coffee shop is closed during the time of evening prayer, but coffee customers can choose to stay in the shop and "overhear" the service. The worshiping community has come to welcome these individuals, giving them both the grace of distance and a genuine yet gentle invitation to become a part of the faith community.

The people who participate most regularly in evening prayer count it as a formative time in their week, filling a void in otherwise harried and full lives. One interesting development centers around interdenominational worship. Many of the participants in evening prayer also worship with other area congregations, some Presbyterian, some United Methodist and Episcopalians, some Pentecostal, and some nondenominational. We did not anticipate this, but we have learned that the ethos of openness to each person who crosses our door has truly provided a meeting ground for individuals who otherwise would not have known one another. The commitment to listening, respecting and understanding beyond our traditional institutional affiliations and even deeply held theological convictions (or doubts) hints at a time when the divisions we have created for ourselves will be replaced by a joyful feast around a shared Table.

Since beginning weekly worship the community has begun additional gatherings for building disciples. Neon Light, Bare Bulb's youth group, gathers regularly to serve God in the world. These middle- and high-school-aged students are learning to follow Jesus by shedding light in dark and broken corners of the world. They feed the hungry, make blankets for the grieving and imagine a future where everyone has food, shelter, health care and clean water.

Bare Bulb Coffee's ministry with children has taken on a life outside the coffee shop environment. In 2012 we launched Little Lights, a literacy and faith formation program in partnership with Cherished Children, a private childcare center for low-income families. Every Wednesday, adult and teen volunteers from the Bare Bulb Community spend an hour reading, singing and laughing with a class of four-year-old children. The model emphasizes relationships while pairing classic children's literature with stories from Scripture. Each month, every child receives a new book for his or her library, and at the end of the year, each child is given a children's Bible with each story they read marked by our volunteers. We have learned from the center staff how important these books and Bibles have become for the families of the children. For our community, these relationships have made real the challenges of poverty and the beauty of the curiosity of children.

EAGER TO JOIN IN GOD'S WORK

Midway through our planning we set out to define the core values and practices we hoped would shape this new community of faith: prayer, hospitality, service, invitation to and practices of worship, seeking, offering, and welcoming. At the time of conception these values were both shots in the dark and also our clearest hope for what we would become—colored with openness to those who would eventually join us in our mission. Without a doubt these are the core values and practices of the community, reflecting what we hold dear and how we seek to live and move in the world. To these values have been added two significant convictions: God is in the world, and we are God's in the world—called to be in the light and sent to shed light.

When we are open to the Spirit moving in our midst, the Spirit will lead us to listen to stories and receive the grace of new relationships. The community of The Light @ Bare Bulb Coffee is composed of busy people—living and serving the world in their neighborhoods, in the metropolitan area and around the globe. They are engaged in and looking for signs of the Spirit and are eager to join in God's work. They know themselves as blessed by God and have felt the warmth of fellowship in the light of God's Son, and they want to carry the warmth and light they have known into dark corners, office cubicles and soccer complexes.

One woman tells the story of carrying light from this community into her daily routine. While her father was ill with lymphoma, she did the grocery shopping for her parents. As a young man with mental disabilities was packing her groceries one day, they chatted about her two separate orders. She told him she was shopping for her mother and father. He stopped packing and said, "Can I pray for you?" She was humbled by his invitation and said that, yes, he could pray for her and for her parents. And so he did—right at the end of the checkout counter. After he prayed, she offered to pray for him as well. At first he refused and said everything was okay, but as she pressed just a little more, the young man said she could indeed pray for his family as well. His father had died the night before, and he said, "That

Interview Q&A 1

Editors: You consistently engage your neighborhood. How have the voices of neighbors helped you see something, shifted your imagination or clarified what God calls you to?

Nikki   During the first year of our gathering as a community of faith, God sent
MacMillan: a group of young musicians to our fellowship. These young men and women would share their gifts at our open mic nights and eventually began to join us and offer their gifts for evening prayer services. Many of them are part of a music ministry launched by a local Pentecostal megachurch—a ministry intended not just to train musicians for that particular congregation but to nurture the spirits and souls of artists and musicians in order that they might go elsewhere to offer their gifts to God in the world. During the next year we are entering an intentional collaboration with this group to offer worship leadership workshops and instrumental and vocal clinics to the broader region and to provide weekly music leadership for evening prayer at Bare Bulb. It is a rare and precious gift to find Presbyterians and Pentecostals leading worship together and learning from and embracing practices unique to these seemingly disparate traditions. It is a nudging of the Spirit none of us would have ever anticipated. What we are witnessing—and calling others to witness—is God's work in all of God's world. God speaks to us in all music. Coffee and scones are elements of the Eucharist. Pastoral care is extended across the cash register.

is the only daddy I'm ever gonna have, and I'm really gonna miss him." In a dark moment of shared grief (and groceries) these two caught a glimpse of light and hope. The woman returned to share the story to the evening prayer gathering because she counts the prayerful listening we do each week as real preparation for her life outside the safety and fellowship of the coffee shop. The strength and hope she finds by dwelling in the light of the world sends her out to be the light of the world for others.

From a group of churchy people living in the bubble of church community and structures, we have become God's own in the world—aware of God's movement outside the forms we have known and in relationships we would never have experienced had we stayed inside our church walls or sought to build a new community according to old structures and expectations.

WHAT'S NEXT?

Entering our second year of business and mission, we are clearly still figuring out how things are going to work as we move forward. Though each of the leaders and many of the participants can clearly articulate who we are and what we are seeking to do when we are in one-on-one conversations, we have struggled to interpret ourselves and our mission broadly. The community knows us as a coffee shop first and foremost. Many know us as a coffee shop "run by a church," but we have been very careful *not* to describe ourselves as a "Christian coffee shop" for fear of building walls where we would like to build bridges. Our hope is that people will experience our coffee shop and our community without assumptions about who we are or how we will treat them if they do not adhere to a particular set of beliefs. We are trying to recognize the ways the church pushes away the curious, the doubtful and the afraid. We have spent a good bit of time defining ourselves in the negative. We are *not* that kind of community. You *do not* have to believe/act/dress that way to be a part of our fellowship. The consequence is that we do not say clearly enough who we are and what we hope to be in our world. It takes time and relationship to redefine a concept everyone thinks they know. One of the challenges in the year ahead will be to say clearly and succinctly, "This is who we are. This is where we are headed. You are welcome to join us."

Another challenge for the months ahead is to transition from a project driven by leadership from other area congregations and the presbytery to a community led from within. Cultivating leaders from a new community and vesting them with the power to make decisions about how the community and the business will function requires the original visionaries (and investors) to let go of their dreams for the group. Things will take new shapes. New ideas will be added. Different priorities will be identified. Although such a shift has been the stated intention all along, the realities of the transition can be different for everyone involved.

Change is hard. Forging a new path and living the vision of creating a new sort of Christian community is messy. However, the people who make up The Light @ Bare Bulb Coffee have given themselves over to the work of the

Interview Q&A 2

Editors: You note that you had lots to learn about the neighborhood. How is God shaping boundary-crossing relationships and connections for you?

Nikki MacMillan: Because our mission and faith community are housed in a coffee shop, most of the people we meet are capable of spending $4 on a latte several times a week. The boundary that we are crossing with much intentionality is the boundary between the sacred and the secular. Worship in our community provides a "big tent" for shared experiences of the grace of God. Our space fosters—and necessitates—intimacy among worshipers who come in all shapes and sizes, from children to grandparents. The primary time of proclamation is a conversation shared around tables of four to eight people that might include elementary children, teenagers, young adults and adults up through their early seventies. In addition, those gathered come from wide theological perspectives, including cradle Presbyterians and Spirit-filled Pentecostals, and from the varied lifestyles of teachers, executives, bikers and airmen. Everyone present has a voice in the conversation. Each person is a trusted listener for the Word of God. One Sunday evening a man in his sixties had a beautiful conversation with a six-year-old girl over the Scripture passage for the day. Her words became one of the summarizing thoughts of the conversation, helping everyone present to confront (in that moment) our stubbornness in the face of God's claim on our lives.

Spirit among us and in our own individual hearts. When asked how they have changed through participation in the mission of Bare Bulb Coffee, participants talk about opening their hearts to others, turning outward to the world that God loves, discovering the joy of deep relationships with people they never expected to know or to meet. Love has shaped them and healed them in ways they did not expect. They express purer love for God, broader love for others and a healing realization that they too are worthy of love.

```
┌─────────────────────────────────┐
│  GROWING ROOTS IN A             │
│  SECULARIZED CONTEXT            │
│  NORTHLAND VILLAGE CHURCH       │
└─────────────────────────────────┘
```

Nick Warnes

NORTHLAND VILLAGE CHURCH

Location: Northeast Los Angeles
Denomination: Presbyterian Church (USA)
Year of Foundation: 2010
Regular Participants in the Life of the Church: 125
Website: www.northlandvillagechurch.com

In the story of Northland Village Church expect to encounter a narrative of people engaging a neighborhood embedded within an overtly post-Christian setting. Northeast Los Angeles has been historically filled with progressive ideologies, diversity and lots of artists. Pastor Nick Warnes, from the Presbyterian Church (USA), laid out a vision for reconciliation in the midst of a dechurched people. With a decentralized approach to leadership and a heart for creativity, read about how this two-year-old church plant has grown roots in a secularized context.

IN THE BEGINNING: A POST-CHRISTENDOM ENVIRONMENT

When Whitney (my wife) and I, along with a varying group of conversation partners, were exploring planting a church in Northeast Los Angeles, we observed that very few people were connected to a church. Those few people who participated in churches found themselves at the edges of society. I had begun walking the streets of Northeast LA, praying for this place and these people, and asking God to shape my awareness and conversations. I met a parishioner who said, "I don't know what happened to our church. I have been at the same church for forty-six years and I look around and no one is there. All of my friends that used to go to our church are gone, and there are very few new people in the pews." He was right. People connected to the church were few and far between.

We estimated that fewer than 14 percent of the population in Northeast Los Angeles were connected to the church on any given weekend.[1] The church was no longer at the center but was instead functioning as an exilic people, living from the edges.[2] Some in the churches, like the man I met on my prayer walk, lament the loss of power and influence. They miss the days when a faith in Christ was assumed in the neighborhood. They lament the loss of common ideologies and worldviews. As our conversations continued, we knew that in creating Northland Village Church (NVC), we would need to embrace our exilic cultural position, just as God's people have historically done in the Scriptures, giving space for God to lead the way in our context: think Israel, think Egypt, think desert, think Babylon, think Jesus away from home, think reactions that Paul experienced in different cities. What if we found our story in these places rather than in places of perceived Utopia in the Bible?

This cultural phenomenon is increasingly common across the landscape of American communities. Darrell Guder defines Christendom as

> the functional reality of what took place specifically in the North American setting. Various churches contributed to the formation of a dominant culture that bore the deep imprint of Christian values, language, and expectations regarding moral behaviors. Other terms like "Christian culture" or "churched culture" might be used to describe this Christian influence on the shape of the broader culture.[3]

It was a time, Guder notes, when the society provided churches with "specially designated privileges."[4] It was clear in our neighborhood that this reality was of the past. Christian influence was no longer embraced or privileged among the people who were making the decisions for our part of the city. Our context, like many now in America, was not a part of Christendom. It was a post-Christendom context.

While Christendom may still be hanging on the edges in some rural and suburban communities in North America, we quickly learned that most urban centers are fully steeped in a post-Christendom context.[5] Conversations with neighbors, observations of community dynamics and research about behaviors and belonging all pointed away from Christendom. This prevalence of a post-Christendom ethos has scared many away from starting new churches in cities. We learned that many, for this reason, strategically plant churches in the suburbs. That is where the money is, where new communities are sprouting, and where the best chance for "success" in church-planting lies. We wanted to challenge this norm and follow our call to move toward the city.[6]

As this context lured us, we became engaged by the question of how and where we would begin. It was fascinating to come to understand that the best place to begin was hard to see because it was right under our noses. After spending months thinking about where to ground ourselves, Whitney and I eventually decided to begin with the church I was already working in. Glendale Presbyterian Church (GPC) was located two miles to the north of the Los Angeles city border. At first it didn't make institutional sense for this church to participate in the plant. We were without a pastor, and the elders of the church were already working overtime. Yet the Spirit of God was clear, and my wife and I began sharing the vision of a new church with our church family. The leadership humbly listened to our vision and took time praying through the implications of becoming a parent church—one that sends people, prayers and resources to the new church plant. After three months of discernment, GPC officially decided to become the parent of Northland Village Church. This meant that Whitney and I would move two miles south of GPC, into Atwater Village, a neighborhood central to Northeast LA. Here, we would begin living among the post-Christendom people around our home. With the support of GPC and the San Fernando Presbytery, we were ready to begin moving toward the public launch of Northland Village Church.

DEVELOPING A COMMUNAL IDENTITY:
AGENTS OF RECONCILIATION

Once we moved to Atwater Village, we were already inviting people into the vision of the church, which emerged out of 2 Corinthians 5:18-19. This verse was laid on our hearts and minds as a fitting theme for the context of

Northeast LA. I began reading this verse and discussing its implications with dozens of people.

I had been shaped by a jarring question that Jürgen Moltmann had addressed to Miroslav Volf, "But can you embrace a četnik?"[7] Earlier, Volf had made a convincing case in front of an impressive audience for the importance of embracing our enemies as Christ had embraced us. Moltmann was his mentor at that time, and he had responded to Volf's polished lecture with that penetrating question. Volf proclaimed a theology of embracing one's enemies. Moltmann knew that the četniks had become the ultimate other to Volf, who was Croatian. Četniks were Serbian soldiers who had been desolating cities, raping woman and murdering innocent Croatians for years. Volf answered in front of the gathered crowd, "No, I cannot—but as a follower of Christ I think I should be able to." Moltmann's question was the catalyst for Volf to write *Exclusion and Embrace: A Theological Exploration of Identity*, a major twentieth-century book on reconciliation. Volf's answer penetrated our church's initial reflections on reconciliation. We felt that a similar chasm had been developing in the relationship between the church and people not connected with the church. How might we as a new church be able to begin bridging this gap? How might we become agents of reconciliation in the midst of two groups that consider themselves as others? How might the healing power of God redeem these relationships?

The theme of reconciliation had become important to us because relationships have always been at the center of the story of Northland Village Church. Our denomination, the Presbyterian Church (USA) (PCUSA), wants to initiate new worshiping communities. We believe that we need to move from a building- and property-centered model of church planting to a focus on relationships and leadership. Our presbytery's last effort to plant a church focused on raising millions of dollars so the presbytery could buy property in the newest suburb, build on the property and place a Christian "professional" in the middle of the property to run the institution.[8] Needless to say, this church didn't grow into the vision that people had originally imagined and soon fizzled out. While this model for starting new churches may have been effective during the middle of the last century, it was clear that it was no longer working in the complex fabric of life and culture in Northeast Los Angeles. Thankful to have the stories of this previous church in our back pocket, we were fortunate to be working with a denomination that knew times had changed and relationships (among participants and neighbors) were central as we move forward as the people of God.

As I would sit over coffee with potential participants in the launch team, Paul's words often focused our attention, "All this is from God, who reconciled us to himself through Christ, and has given us the ministry of reconciliation; that is, in Christ God was reconciling the world to himself, not counting their trespasses against them, and entrusting the message of reconciliation to us" (2 Corinthians 5:18-19 NRSV). I like working with Paul's word for reconciliation, *katallassō*, which is made up of two words—*kata* and *allos*. *Kata* means "to come alongside," and *allos* means "the other." Thus *katallassō* means "to come alongside the other." Our conversations often helped us reflect on how churches try to mold others and keep them afar rather than come alongside them. This realization would then lead to the heart of why we felt called to plant NVC. We knew that the people who are no longer participating in any meaningful church activity are often dechurched for good reasons. Some had experienced sexual abuse by former pastors, and others told stories of how the church made God's story too boring. The bottom line was that so many around us had personally experienced what we came to call "otherification" by the church. A deep hope for something better began to stir. After six months of work approximately half of the eighty people that I asked to join our "launch team" accepted the offer and decided to give church another try. It has been my experience in speaking with other church planters to expect about half of people that one invites into a vision to latch on. This placed us in the category of what Stuart Murray calls a transplant congregation and has the density to immediately begin functioning as a church.[9]

Strategically, some planters will only invite unchurched people into the launch team, some will invite a racially diverse group of people, some will pull only from the parent church, and some will begin without any sort of formal launch team. As we began, we knew that we would need a humble group of people because our context was steeped in a post-Christian, urban environment that required lots of listening and learning. We assumed the work would be slow and difficult. We heard stories of other plants that had tried to go in as "the heroes" to save "the pagans" by bringing God to the "Godless" in Northeast Los Angeles. We decided to take a different approach. We began reminding people that God was already in the midst of the city and among these neighbors, so we began asking what God was already up to in our context.[10] There were so many positive things already going on in the community. We simply wanted to join in with the goodness of what was already being initiated by an immanent God.[11] Northeast Los Angeles had weekly opportunities for people to engage with their neighbors. From harvest festivals to music, to arts shows, to concerts and plays, there were many opportunities already in place for people to build relationships with the people around them. We prayed that by joining in the already-existing activities we would build trust with our neighbors and begin the process of reconciliation.[12] This was the foundational approach we invited the launch team into.

SETTLING IN THE SOIL

In the summer of 2009 our budding launch team gathered around the simple practice of eating dinner and sharing Communion with one another. This space allowed people who did not know each other within the launch team time to build relationships. Our conversations around the table would eventually move toward dreaming about our call of becoming agents of reconciliation in our context. The nudges of the Spirit were increasingly clear in the lives of the people concerning becoming church and discerning God's work among us and our neighbors. The Spirit's promptings were emerging in our conversations about creating safe spaces for people to investigate their faith. Our hope was that people would find their story in the grand narrative of God's redemption. We became aware that our presence and gifts could come alongside the lives and gifts of our neighbors, allowing us to indicate the presence of the gospel with our neighbors. We continued to feast on the bread and the wine through the summer. Communion has become one of the more important weekly rituals that we enact with one another as a community. It is a place of not only remembering God's faithfulness to the people of the church as individuals but also a place of remembering God's faithfulness to our church body.

In the first part of the autumn of 2009 our weekly table gatherings morphed into worship and the Communion Table. We would meet for two hours on Sunday evenings. The first hour would be spent in prayer, song, Bible study and feasting at the Table. The second hour continued our worshipful activities, but in a different way. The second hour was a prayerful time for learning and preparing to embody God's mission to Northeast Los Angeles together as a

Interview Q&A 1

Editors:

Among the launch team and those who have become participants with NVC there are obviously significant gifts of leadership. How does the church engage the leadership gifts of the church?

Michaela Long (NVC elder):

Engaging the diversity of gifts in our congregation has been a learning process. We are learning to respond to leadership in the following ways.

First, we use a variety of gifts assessment tools with all new members. We are very careful that these tools do not become means for labeling people or herding them into service of a particular ministry. Instead, we use the tools as a platform for similar language and an opportunity to listen to the stories of new members. From their stories we begin to think about how their leadership gifts might suit what is already going on at the church and in the neighborhood.

Second, the leadership team of NVC works to sanction experiments that arise from within the congregation. If a person or group of people gathers around an idea that fits within our understanding of God's mission, NVC does whatever we can to support it. This has been an important posture in our efforts to decentralize leadership and lean on the gifts of the larger congregation. In our community some of the greatest examples of leadership have been unexpected.

One such experiment arose when a guy said to us, "I'm not sure that I want to be a part of a church. But I do want to be part of what NVC is doing in the area. I'm really good at crafting unique beer. Would this be of any service to your church?" Open to unique expressions of the gospel, we immediately rallied energy around this gifted brewer to create an event that coupled beer drinking with gospel sharing. This event was so successful that it turned into a series of events called "Brewfest." Now, the event is held in a local bar or restaurant, affording us to connect further with neighbors in Northeast LA. People are often intrigued and excited about our willingness to talk about God and drink beer in the same space.

community. For six months we engaged extensive exercises for developing the leadership skills needed by the launch team. Through all of this we were learning who we were becoming as a church. Assessme and StrengthsFinder helped us to learn who we were as gifted individuals and also who we were as a gifted community.[13] I still remember looking at the overall collection of gifts of the launch team and standing in awe as I realized that we were a beautiful mixture of abilities and passions. From ideation to innovation to execution, all of the gifts were essential to building a solid foundation for executing our mission statement of creating spaces for reconciling relationships. After we finished this process of discerning gifts, we wanted to learn more about Northeast Los Angeles. We were blessed with extensive neighborhood exegesis from students of Mark Lau Branson at Fuller Seminary, who had given us ten pages of information based on their work in interviewing dozens of people within the context of Northeast LA. When paired with the data from Dave Olson's book *The American Church in Crisis*, we had gained an initial understanding of the sociocultural backgrounds and current perspectives of the people in our part of the city.[14] After praying through the thirty pages of info that was gathered, and living in the neighborhood, we decided to highlight five felt needs within Northeast LA. We wanted our own hearts to be engaged by whatever affects God's heart. We understood that "felt needs" are any needs that would be identified by the common person living in the everyday context of Northeast LA. The five felt needs that we identified were community beautification, youth, adequate access to resources, gangs and to be welcomed into meaningful relationships. Because we wanted to come alongside our neighbor and care for the life of the community, it was at the intersection of our gifts and these felt needs of the community that we wanted to explore opportunities for creating meaningful expressions of faith that joined God in God's already-existing work of reconciliation in the area.

Creating is one of the most joyful opportunities of being a part of a church plant. Our church never had a problem coming up with ideas for what we wanted to create. The problem that we faced was how to choose which ideas we would actually move forward into the process of creation. People began throwing around dozens of ideas, so effectively whittling down all of the ideas was going to be a challenge. To work through this challenge we combined a parable with a rubric. The parable went as follows:

There were three people who were commissioned to build a sidewalk in a grassy park. One said that the sidewalk should go on the left. The other said the sidewalk should go on the right. After much dispute between the two, the third finally recommended that they all stay patient and spend the day observing where people were already walking. "It's on the bent grass," the third man said, "that we should build the sidewalk."

With this parable in our back pocket, we then created a rubric that functioned as a basic set of perspectives and priorities that was shaped by everything we had been learning about Northeast LA, our own gifts and God's call on us to work at this intersection. For instance, if someone on the launch team were to bring forward an idea for a deer-hunting ministry, it wouldn't have survived the rubric, as this idea wouldn't have fit what we had already discerned to be our context. The rubric would have shown us that the deer-hunting idea wouldn't make sense in light of the five felt needs we were exploring or the strengths that we observed among the launch team participants.

With the rubric in hand, the launch team came up with twenty-three ideas. We then prayed, discussed and voted. After this, the six elders comprising the leadership team chose the final five ministries based on the vote, the need for diverse experiments, and the options we had for shaping each ministry team. An elder was placed on each team, which met at least once a week over the next four months. The teams prepared and began to practice the ministries that would be in place for the public launch. The following are the five ministries we decided to create.

1. A local school partnership within the Los Angeles Unified School District. We have tutors in the school during every day of the week.

2. A small groups ministry. We call them "village groups," which are formed when a leader in the church discerns an idea that fits well for the context in which they find themselves.

3. A needs ministry. This focuses on meeting the needs of both the neighborhood and of the people of NVC.

4. A worship ministry. Many on this team focus on shaping our worship gatherings in line with the community ethos.

5. A connection ministry. This team was given the task of continuing to help us connect to one another and to the people and institutions of Northeast Los Angeles.

Front and center, we held that the foundation of all of these ministries was not to build programs but to implement our mission of creating spaces for reconciling relationships.[15] This focus was important because some on our launch team were moving through significant ecclesiological shifts from a programmatic mindset to a relational mindset. With making our vision more tangible through these ministries, we were getting close to public presentation.

While heading into the public launch of the church we focused on two areas: one went well and one did not. We began preparation for the public launch by arranging three preview services to share the vision of the church with a growing number of people connected to the relationship networks of the launch team. Such preview services are a recommended strategy for building momentum, testing worship elements, growing a larger group prior to the public launch and perhaps finding some new key people. This approach, while effective in many contexts, was not effective for our post-Christian, urban context. Many people could sniff through the "manipulation" that was happening in trying to grow our launch team prior to the public launch.

While there is an advantage to having more density for the public launch, our church's vision was never to gather people for the sake of density. Any sort of top-down emphasis from the church will probably not work well in a post-Christian context. Our push to grow the launch team prior to the public launch did not feel natural to those we felt God calling us to become, nor did it feel natural to the neighborhood. A more appropriate way for us to move into the public launch would have been to continue to do what we were already doing. We were naturally good at inviting people into our vision one at a time through the work that was already beginning in the church and larger community. Keeping this pattern would have been more fitting for us.

On the other hand, the way we advertised the launch went very well. Against the advice of many church planters, our church chose to do a reverse tithe during worship on a Sunday before the public launch. We found that the money it took to send thousands of postcards was ten times as expensive and much less effective than equipping the people of NVC to speak about our movement within their networks. If we had spent $10,000 to send postcards to all of Northeast Los Angeles, we forecasted that 3 percent of the snail mail would have been read, and only 1 percent of the recipients would have given the mail serious consideration. (Many more would have been frustrated with our church for being another religious group wasting paper in the name of God!) We equipped the voices of NVC to share our story by giving people the reverse tithe in envelopes with five-, ten- or twenty-dollar bills. The purpose of using the money was to go and tell somebody about the emerging story of Northland Village Church. Some connected with local nonprofits, some took friends out for coffee and some grilled chicken in a park and gave it to all who wanted food. This move took people by surprise, both inside and outside of the church, but it gave us some unique momentum heading into the public launch. One example of the momentum that came from this venture was in the partnership that was formed with Integrated Refugee and Immigration Services (irisct.org). One of our families donated their twenty dollars to them, and this has formed a reciprocal relationship that we still enjoy today.

These prelaunch months were very important for our church and for the relationships that were deepening both inside and outside of the church. From our first dinner with one another on June 12, 2009, to our public launch on April 4, 2010, we had set the relational foundation for NVC. We intentionally worked through conflicts, we celebrated together, we mourned together, and we continued to dream about what it might mean to become a church that masters the art of becoming agents of reconciliation. The most important result of these relationships is that we had built trust with one another and with the community of Northeast Los Angeles.

ENACTING RECONCILIATION

Relationships have continued to be at the center of NVC's activity in Northeast Los Angeles. Almost two years since that original launch team meeting and sixteen months since our public launch, we have seen the church grow in three important ways: in relationship with God, in relationship with others in the church, and in relationship with the people of Northeast LA.

While the other two areas of growth are essential, the area of growing in relationship with the people of Northeast LA has been the most exciting for me. To gain such extensive connections within a community in such a short amount of time has been my favorite part of God's orchestration in our city. Two avenues are especially notable. First, we have come alongside neighbors in the context of community events and activities. We have spent hours not only networking to create opportunities for engagement but actually executing the opportunities that emerged from the engagement—from being in charge of the setup and tear down of our local centennial festival to being placed in charge of community beautification and garden projects, to the different opportunities for blessing that flow out of our partnership with the local elementary school. Through the relationships that we have built in these opportunities, we have gained a reputation for helping the neighborhood, and this has been foundational for reestablishing trust in Northeast LA. The moderator of the Atwater Village Neighborhood Council, Leonora Gershman-Pitts, said this about Northland Village Church:

> Simply put, Atwater Village is a better place because of Northland Village. As a community organizer, I spend the majority of my time working and hoping to organize volunteers to help with all our projects. It sometimes feels like the same seven people show up each time. But then the church started their work here in Atwater Village. Nick once said to me, "Whatever you need, we will be there." And they are, event after event, month after month. Whether it's organizing a neighborhood-wide simplicity sale, which gave my family the push we needed to declutter our home, setting up a fun area for kids during one of our neighborhood events, hosting a very successful art walk with local artists, or getting their hands dirty, literally, by planting an entire swath of our long median, this is a group of people who show up and *help*.

We learned that by engaging in existing events we avoid reinventing wheels. New churches often believe they need to initiate new projects, and we have done some of that, but we have learned there are advantages to coming alongside our community in numerous civic activities. My favorite example of this was our engagement at the Atwater Village Harvest Festival, the yearly gathering of all the families of Atwater Village. The families walk through all of the stores and various booths collecting candy and participating in the various activities provided. We networked with the local neighborhood council, which agreed to let us run a booth in the festival. Our booth included candy, face painting, two different carnival games and a team of people ready to answer any questions about the church. From this event we connected with a couple who have become very important to our church. Both are blind and became curious about our work with the community through the missional presence that we initiated at the harvest festival. We now regularly pray with the couple that they will again receive sight and that God will use their gifts to further bless the neighborhood. While this sort of event work is not glitzy or complex, it has gone a long way in helping us connect and build trust with the community as over a thousand people went through our Harvest Festival booth and began to connect with NVC.

Second, with the church's encouragement I became part of the local neighborhood council. Los Angeles has formed approximately ninety neighborhood councils, each electing people from the neighborhood. I was fortunate to be voted onto the council immediately upon moving to Atwater Village, thus giving me the inside scoop on many opportunities in the neighborhood. Here, I learned of the Centennial Celebration, the Harvest Festival and the Summer Movie Nights, where NVC donates money and hosts a lemonade stand throughout the summer. Here, our church pitched our Atwater Art Walk and we were given money by the council to host the event. These have all been amazing connections that not only set us up to engage in the city but have also set me up to establish meaningful relationships with my neighbors. The people that I have met on the council have become my best friends in the community. However, we need to keep in mind that the council and its members don't exist as a means to the end of the success of NVC. Instead, they exist as fellow neighbors, and we work together for the betterment of our neighborhood. I am so thankful that the neighborhood council has welcomed me and the church with such open arms.

We have also grown in relationships with one another. As a pastor, I have learned to appreciate the fact that I don't get invited to all of the social events that occur among church participants. This may sound counterintuitive, but allow me to explain. When the church began, my wife and I would often initiate dinner parties, double dates or any number of events with people from the church. We knew everybody within the church, while others in the church were just beginning to gain trust in one another. For Whitney and me this took a lot of energy, and while we enjoyed it, we now have an even greater appreciation for all of the relationship-building events within our church that do not require our energy.

I remember the first time that I heard a story of this happening. It was on a Sunday after our worship gathering, but before our public launch. We had triple dated with two of the same couples a number of times. During the car conversation on the way home after one of the dates, Whitney and

Interview Q&A 2

Editors: You consistently engage with your neighborhood, and we have heard the voices of some neighbors. How have the voices of neighbors helped you see something, shifted your imagination or clarified what God is doing or what God calls you to?

Michaela Long (NVC elder):   When NVC was first planted, we purposed ourselves to participate in God's ministry of reconciliation in Northeast Los Angeles. We envisioned God's work playing out among artists, creative professionals and those who had been hurt by the church. However, when we began to hold our centralized gathering in an elementary school gymnasium, our understanding of God's ministry of reconciliation expanded.

After we moved into the gymnasium, we decided to get involved in neighborhood events geared toward families. Through conversations at movie nights, harvest festivals and art nights, we began to realize that the Spirit was active in the lives of families in Northeast LA. Because we wanted to be a part of God's work, we formed a partnership with the school. In the beginning the school principal asked us repeatedly, "So, you just want to help us? You don't want anything in return?" When we finally convinced her that we were just there to support, she was thrilled. The initial phases of the partnership included tutoring, a chance for congregants to be in the school reading with kids who needed extra help.

The stories that come from tutoring sessions often shed light on the inadequacies of the system and the lack of financial resources the school district has to work with. Roger, a tutor, told me, "It's just really hard for me when the kids can't read or do math. They should have access to more help, but there are just too many students for the teacher to help all of them. Some kids fall through the cracks."

These stories have helped broaden our imagination of how God is working in the neighborhood. NVC is learning how to further participate in brining justice to these kids by helping support the school, teachers and families. Expanding our vision of how we participate in the community has helped us to understand that God's ministry of reconciliation is active in all corners of Northeast Los Angeles.

I speculated that the time had gone well, but we weren't sure. On this certain Sunday I heard that the two other couples had gone out on a double date with one another—without us. At first, I selfishly felt sad, but then a deeper sense of awareness emerged and I became weirdly enthralled, knowing that people who once did not know one another in the launch team were now double dating. This sort of activity has multiplied exponentially and has fostered a fitting transition as more and more people in the church spend time in fellowship with one another. Through double dates, baby showers, birthday parties, weddings and funerals, the community of NVC has grown in their appreciation and trust. This growth has naturally resulted in the decentralization of our relational networks. We are confident that this decentralized community will present us with a much more sustainable model of the church as we move forward in our vision.

While making this transition into trusting one another has been beautiful, it also has come with some challenges. We have experienced that as people have grown increasingly comfortable with one another, they naturally begin to turn inward in their priorities for the church, rather than continue to assume that our life in the neighborhood is at the essence of church life. Even though we always emphasize a missional ecclesiology, we are aware that everyone brings habits from their earlier concepts and practices concerning church. Our leadership has had to continually model and encourage our apostolic call to the church. An appropriate mutual appreciation and intimacy characterizes the atmosphere of our church, but rather than turn us inward we understand that it should move us toward hospitality with visitors and with our neighborhood. We continue to remind ourselves of a popular phrase we find throughout the Hebrew Bible: "You shall also love the stranger, for you were strangers in the land of Egypt" (Deuteronomy 10:19 NRSV). We were once on the edges as "otherified" people, and so we should keep our eyes focused on the edges. Being aware of others keeps producing stories like that of Naomi. She is from the neighborhood and had not been connected to a church in ten years. She told us,

> In my past experiences with church I have always felt like I needed to hide things about myself to be accepted. So if you ask what Northland Village Church means to me, it means no more hiding. To me Jesus is the embodiment of unconditional love and acceptance, and I feel that I have finally found a church home that embodies that as well.

Naomi's story is common at NVC and is the primary reason why we need to continue to resist the momentum to turn inward and keep focusing outward.

The final way that our church has grown in relationships since our genesis is in our relationship with God. After leaving seminary I was cynical about how churches work and how God functions in the world. From my perspective the two did not seem to be in solidarity. Much of what I had been previously taught had been deconstructed while in seminary, and I was just beginning the process of rebuilding a vision for the church and the world that is proving to be much more meaningful. I imagined a place where people could be reconciled with themselves, with their neighbors, with their enemies and with God—all through the redemptive work of Christ. To my surprise this cynicism initially had been quite helpful for reaching people in our neighborhood, as our neighbors are filled with cynicism, especially toward the church. As Paul says to become all things for all people (1 Corinthians 9:22), I held tightly to becoming a cynic for Jesus. However, my cynicism about the disparity between God and the church in the world has decreased as I have seen God's faithfulness with NVC unfold over the past two years.

FACING PERSONAL CYNICISM AND DOUBTS

Overall, I suppose that church planting does not make sense on numerous levels. The hurdles that we face in moving toward a functioning church often seem higher than most are willing to risk. Before we moved into Northeast Los Angeles, Whitney and I were visiting my family's cabin in Northern Michigan. We had just finished several days of assessment at an assessment center for church planting, and we had received a green light to proceed. We were the youngest ones to receive a green light by fifteen years, we were right out of our time at Fuller Seminary, and we felt called to plant in one of the most difficult parts of all of Los Angeles. Soon after being at the assessment center Whitney and I were beginning to count the cost with my parents at the cabin. I had heard the stories of numerous new churches across America, and the majority of the stories had ended in hurt and disappointment. What once was a vision filled with energy and imagination had often turned into an unsustainable model of church that left people worn out and tired. There were, however, a couple examples of churches that had made it and had grown to hundreds and even to thousands of people in just a few years. While at first this type of a plant seemed exciting, this example of growth also didn't seem to fit the type of movement that Whitney and I and our conversation partners envisioned. Could we create a small church that could plant churches that would multiply? My doubts and cynicism and fears seemed to collide. I was standing with my father on a frigid porch, and as I voiced my doubts I was surprised by my own tears. At this point I began to grasp the concept that my cynicism might no longer be good enough to persevere through these tricky waters. It was time to stop talking about the downfalls of the church; it was time to risk following the Spirit into a neighborhood.

One year later, when 33 percent of our outside funding was intentionally cut (based on our own plan), a similar fear enveloped my thoughts. I would wake up at 4 a.m., eyes wide open, heart pounding, asking myself, *How are we going to make it?* I remember golfing with a friend from our parent church (another reason why parent churches are important!), telling him of my worry about failing. He looked me in the face and told me that everything would be okay. He had seen the trajectory of NVC unfold, he had seen God in the movement, and he was wise enough to remind me to trust. This was another key moment for me. I realized that my cynicism was good for certain contexts, but not good for leading the overall charge of a new church. I listened to my friend, and God has proven faithful in sustaining and growing our church through year two.

Now moving into year three, I feel as if I have personally reconciled with God on numerous levels of faith. I wasn't the only cynic on the launch team, and I've confessed my role in encouraging these unhelpful affections, but we have seen how God has reconciled us to a larger and more provocative foundation of hope. God has taught us of God's faithfulness through the relationships that have been given to us, through the growth that we have experienced and through the sustainability that continues to emerge in our church. Planting in Northeast Los Angeles made very little sense, yet God nudged a group of people to plant a church in this location. While what has unfolded has been different than I think that anyone imagined, the relationships that have emerged between the church, the community and God have been rich beyond our wildest dreams.[16]

CONTINUING TO DISCERN GOD'S DREAM INTO THE FUTURE

We are very aware of the God of faithfulness as NVC moves into year three. In year one we wanted to spend lots of time listening to the community; in year two we set out goals of building relationships; and in year three we are deepening our participation in the fabric of Northeast Los Angeles by taking a more active role in the community.

For us, taking a more active role means that we are focused on creating more spaces in the neighborhood for fresh expressions of reconciliation. For example, in year two we hosted our Simplicity Sale for Atwater. Armed with a garage full of household items that had been gathered by one of our ministry teams, we distributed five hundred flyers around the neighborhood and used a Facebook event page to invite our neighbors to simplify with us. We asked a local business to allow us to borrow their outdoor porch for an afternoon in order to give people room to sell their extra stuff with us. We wanted to provide space for people to practice the spiritual discipline of simplicity by getting rid of their extra stuff. With just a bit of networking, thirteen people from the neighborhood joined us by hosting their own tables. We held the event right next to the weekly farmers' market, so we expected significant attention. We believed that the Spirit had nudged us into this innovation, and it was a success as hundreds of people came through and enjoyed the booths set up by NVC and thirteen of our neighbors. We had designed this to be more that the usual flea market—we encouraged everyone to ask what we knew were theological questions about practices related to living more simply in regard to material goods, and it worked![17]

We had previously participated in the neighborhood by creating two other spaces. We hosted our first Brewfest, which focused on helping the story of the church reconnect with the historical reality of the church and its innovation with beer. This identity has largely been lost in America, and once a person from the community offered to make us ten gallons of beer, we worked at gathering the community to remind them of the tradition. We met in a local bar, gave away one hundred beers and had a sermon right in the middle of the event. It was a perfect event for dechurched people to once again have a connection with the church. This was also a premier example for us of the biblical tradition of preaching in the marketplace, not just in the worship gathering.[18] The event was another success. People from the community interacted in a fresh and intimate way as they drank beer and heard the Word of God proclaimed.

We also hosted the Atwater Art Walk. A five-member team from our church received a $5,000 grant, then networked with eight local businesses and seventy-five local artists to put on the Atwater Art Walk. The purpose of the event was to get people to share their story through the medium of art. When any artist applied to be in the show, they needed to include with their art a paragraph about how the piece told their story. For five hours on a Saturday, over five hundred artists and walkers shared their stories along six blocks of stores and restaurants. As people heard the stories of friends and strangers, the event was ripe with potential for people to reconcile with one another and with God.

My favorite story from the art walk emerged from a local Internet messaging board. A blast of information about the art walk went out the day before the event. One person noted on the board that she was excited for the event until she heard that it was being hosted by a church. She wrote on the board that she would never support anything being hosted by a group of people that hated the gay community. Several of our neighbors reported back that our church was not like that, and that she should still go to the event. This brief interaction sparked a lengthy discussion by dozens of people in the neighborhood regarding the intersection of the church and sexuality. There were people on the left supporting gay rights, people on the right not supporting any gay rights, and people trying to function as a bridge between the right and the left. At minimum it was a lively conversation! The best part, however, came on the last post. The initial person who had said that she was not going to go to the art walk posted that she had indeed gone. She said, "We went and had a lovely time!! We even ran into some old friends we hadn't seen in a long time at 55 Degree Wine." We continue to pray for this individual as she moves on her faith journey. We are thankful that the art walk was a step for her toward reconciliation.[19]

Now moving into year three of our church plant, we plan on more experiments that will create spaces for reconciliation. This is the work required in post-Christendom, and while this exilic work can be painfully slow, the victories are extra sweet! We have begun putting together a business plan for NVC to begin its own business right in the center of town. The plan is not complete, but the team has chosen to begin an Upcycling business. We are going to take old, ugly, useless items and ask the artists from the church to turn them into beautiful and useful items. (We find this vision to be especially meaningful in light of our focus on reconciliation. We regularly embrace the story of worn-out people once again becoming beautiful through the work of Jesus [see 2 Corinthians 5:17].) The items will then be sold on consignment. The theological implications of creating new life are unending, and the opportunity to build stronger connections with the neighborhood are plentiful.

We also continue to pray for our first church to be planted out of NVC. Many will say that we are still too small to plant, but people told our parent church the same thing. The reality is similar to having a baby. Parents seem to never be fully ready to give birth. Planting is not about being mature enough to reproduce. Planting is about a church's ability to effectively discern the Spirit of God and follow courageously into where that Spirit is leading. With this is mind, we are working against temptations to turn inward, into safety and comfort, and to continue to attend to the missional impulses of the Spirit of God. It would be a lot easier right now to begin to focus on setting up better structures to maintain the people who have connected to the church. This, while important, cannot become the focus of our church. Our focus must keep us engaged with God's mission. We are almost three years into this journey, and we trust God to generously fill us with courage and energy to continue this relational work of being agents of reconciliation.

8

AN EXPRESSION OF
FAITH THAT FITS

THEOPHILUS CHURCH

AJ Swoboda

THEOPHILUS CHURCH

Location: Portland, Oregon
Denomination: Foursquare Church
Year of Foundation: 2009
Regular Participants in the Life of the Church: 200
Website: www.theophiluschurch.com

With a wealth of dynamic information regarding the people of his city, Pastor AJ Swoboda, of the Foursquare Church tradition, writes a compelling chapter on planting a church in the unique place of Portland, Oregon. Beginning in their living room, AJ's family pursued God's initiatives by meeting people in a local coffee shop. In three years they have missionally joined God in creating an expression of faith that fits the unique people of Portland. If you are interested in bivocational ministry or how your academic background can equip you for church planting, please continue to read.

STUMPTOWN JESUS: INTRODUCING OUR PORTLAND CHURCH-PLANTING STORY

It's urban legend that Portland, Oregon, boasts more nonprofit organizations and strip clubs per capita than any city in the world. If this is true, it's a city doing the breast stroke in the kiddy pool of paradox. That's where Jesus sent my family and a small group of Christians to live and lay down their lives. What follows is why and how we started a church in Portland, which we call Theophilus.

In 2003 my wife, Quinn, and I became college pastors at a Christian co-op called Onyx House on the campus of the University of Oregon (Eugene). Each Friday evening we'd gather together, worship, break bread, and I'd teach Scripture. Without fail, nearly three hundred people showed up every week to worship Jesus. Then, in 2008, our future took a screeching turn in a radically different direction. On a rainy Saturday afternoon nearly 120 miles north of our home in Eugene, Quinn and I stumbled into Stumptown Coffee Roasters in the Belmont district of Southeast Portland for a cup of coffee.[1] I remember that day in high def. Nursing their various beverages were thirty young people I'd swear to have known as spirit children in pre-earthly existence: tight jeans, dark-rimmed glasses, tattoos on their tattoos, with the palpable scent of cynicism. *I'm looking in a mirror, I thought.* God seemed to be there. Oftentimes when describing that event I resort to speaking as though I'd gotten pregnant, because it's the only way I can begin to approach the feelings I experienced. After returning from that trip to Portland, I spent the better part of the next six months waking up at 3 a.m. with a 3-D picture of Stumptown. That little coffee shop—with the tight jeans, tattoos, dark-rimmed glasses and the rich, sweet coffee scent—was our new land. It was at this time that I had one of my life's few memorable "Abraham moments"—like when God called Abraham from his hometown to a new town known as the Promised Land (Genesis 12)—and within six months we were packing our bags, with a plan to move right next to the coffee shop. After collaborating with our pastor and finding a suitable pastoral replacement, we moved to the land of the tight-jeaned people.

Despite being a lifelong Oregonian, Portland was a foreign land to me.[2] Many Christians I knew described Portland as a suburb of Sodom, complete with liberals and long-haired fascists from the Green Party living in communes and living on a steady staple of "brownies." Portland is much more complex than that. Attempts to exalt the multicultural spirit of diversity notwithstanding, Portland is one of the whitest cities in America (87 percent white).[3] Portland has one of the largest and most active LGBT communities in America. It boasts the first openly gay mayor (Sam Adams) in US history. Everyone in Portland is a nonconformist like everyone else. The beer flows like wine; thirty-eight microbreweries exist within city limits. People love and embrace the eclectic and the local. One friend calls Portland a city of "Mayberrys"—a city of little villages. You find that no one actually *lives* in the city of Portland; people live in their neighborhoods (e.g., Hawthorne, Elwood or the Mississippi). It's a very liberal city. Both Ronald Reagan and George Bush called Portland "little Beirut."

Portland is a religiously odd city. It's home to both the Church of Elvis and Our Lady of Eternal Combustion Church. Just down the road from us is where Heaven's Gate, the cult, was started. In this context Portland has staggeringly low numbers of evangelicals and Protestant Christians. Simply put, if it's organized, it's struggling. Portland Christians have a knack for being very unique: embracing questions about life and faith, living in the gray areas, and exalting ambiguity in the mystery of the gospel and their own faith expressions. Some evangelical churches have found unique ways of thriving in such eclectic environments. One such church—Imago Dei—is an influential and unique Christian community in Southeast Portland.[4] Despite some shining successes such as these, it has proven to be a difficult city to plant churches in. A few weeks prior to our move to Portland, a local pastor quietly told me that in the last ten years he'd observed eighty-nine church plants start in Southeast Portland, the very location we were planning to live. God seemed to be calling people to this city.[5] However, in the local pastor's recollection, only two of those churches still existed. Like Lewis and Clark, we started our journey with no map but with a bunch of zeal.

THE GENETIC MAKEUP OF A CHURCH CULTURE

From what I remember, I got rather bored of the womb just before birth. I was ready to go. Following the anticipated announcement of our departure, well-meaning Christians began asking Quinn and me questions about something they called *vision*. They'd ask questions about our target market, outreach strategies or discipleship models. Largely this was their way of assessing whether we were sufficiently equipped and ready to plant a church. This created a bit of a problem for us; we'd been *called* but not *trained* in the complexities and verbosities inherent in the language of church-planting culture. Initially, we tried to alleviate this problem by spending inordinate amounts of time with other church planters, brainstorming creative ways to answer these questions. We met with church planters from other cities, states, even other countries to dialogue about vision. Ultimately, I found these efforts in creating a language about vision both unhelpful and, honestly, a bit manipulative. One problem stood out to me: *How could we create a vision having never lived in Portland, eaten the food, walked the streets or even joked with our mailman?* One particular evening I was struggling to come to grips with why I was feeling frustrated about our lack of vision. Opening my Bible to the beginning of Acts, I read as Jesus tells his disciples to go into Jerusalem and "wait" (*peremenein*) just before his ascension (Acts 1:4). The word *wait* struck me. Considering that Jesus had never taught his disciples on important church-service practices—the two-fast-songs-three-slow-songs set, the greeting time, the announcements and the like—his direction to wait felt like a letdown. Jesus told them to just go and *be* in Jerusalem. Why was this? It's provocative to note that the command to "hear" and "listen" is uttered some 1,500 times in Scripture. Here in Acts 1 was Jesus' church-planting vision: wait. And listen. And hear. This made sense in the context of someone like Paul, who would enter a city not finding what he expected (e.g., Acts 16:13), but then, after being there, his task became clear.

This "wait" thing spoke profoundly to me, and in hindsight it was the most obvious thing God did in me in the whole process. Jesus did not send his disciples to Jerusalem to get assessed as potential church planters or to do vision-discernment training sessions, or to get their missional-emergent-eschatological-vision language ingrained. None of that. They went to Jerusalem to receive God's Spirit. I concluded that the only thing coming close to a church-planting assessment in the New Testament is what we call *Pentecost.* We aren't called to plant a church so much as we're called to plant the gospel by being present as Spirit-filled people.[6] When this conclusion didn't silence the *vision* seekers, I simply told them to sing "Be Thou My Vision" and then they'd know our vision.

Truthfully, the time with other church planters was irreplaceable and absolutely necessary. However, we came to believe that vision can only be birthed out of time spent with those whom the vision is for. This is humbling. Who doesn't *want* to have a profound vision that inspires everyone? Sadly, this was my pride burrowing itself into the cracks of God's calling on my life. Hidden in every calling is a seed of angst. Church planters are sanctified enough to listen to God *and* stupid enough to follow through. I must acknowledge that part of my desire to plant a church was birthed out of frustration with my current context. In one way this is holy, a righteous indignation. Without anger and frustration, Christianity and Protestantism, as well as Apple computers, wouldn't have been birthed. However, in another sense this type of frustration is diabolical. The last thing the church of Jesus Christ needs now is more churches that are "different." What is needed are more *called* churches, churches that God has specifically instigated.

On many levels I was frustrated with my church situation in Eugene. However, all of those frustrations transferred to the new church I was starting. The angst is not in the church—it's in the soul. Church planters must recognize that *they're going to be frustrated wherever they are*. It's in their nature. They're reformers. To be a church planter is to be frustrated, be it with the world, with the church, with the gospel's slow spread or all three. I still believe in reconciling all of our problems within the womb. If we can't do that, the genetic makeup of the church will turn out to be angst. When all is said and done, a church's vision will be a byproduct of how it is born. Based on the whole Acts passage, we simply believed we were called to move to Portland and *peremenein*. To go, and then to wait. The vision would come after we had eaten the food, walked the streets and tipped our mailman.

THE MOVE TO PORTLAND

On a Saturday afternoon in late August 2008, we moved to Portland in our Honda Civic, overpacked with furniture, memories and idealism. Riding into the sunset, we'd no concept of what lay ahead. Some of our packed belongings I wished we'd left behind; chief among them were idealism and some false dreams. I'd heard it said early in the process that it was easier to have babies than to raise the dead.[7] That is, church planting affords you the opportunity to sidestep many of the problems of pastoring an existing church. *This idea, I've found, is the intellectual property of Satan.* If "easy" is what someone is after, church planting isn't the best option. Despite knowing this, I was convinced of my future fame in Christendom, and convinced that our church plant was going to be "different" and "unique," and that we would woo everyone with our nonconformity and hip ecclesiology. Honestly, hiding in these idealisms is a bigger problem; it is a failure to grasp that we are not God's solution for the world. Even if our church was "different," it would still die someday. Every church will. It's humbling to acknowledge that not one of the churches Paul planted still exists. Either Paul was a really bad church planter, or he understood that a birth must always be followed, as well as preceded, by a death. Yet I was convinced of our future glories: we'd be the next Mars Hill (pick one of the two); I'd be on the cover of *Christianity Today*; everyone would invite me to speak at their conferences and write in their books. These idealisms, frustrations and false dreams couldn't pad the pain that was soon to come. We were scared to death, and, oddly enough, that was maybe one of the few things we got right.

The relationship between a church plant and its parent congregation is complex and can be messy or tenuous. We were lucky in that our sending church, Eugene Faith Center, sent us out with blessing. Eugene Faith Center is a church within the Foursquare movement, as is Theophilus. However, we are not loud about it. This is by no means because Foursquare is not a good denomination; rather, it's because we've found that in a post-Christian environment like Portland *no one is looking for a Foursquare Church*. No one is looking for church in general.

Eugene Faith Center also gave us some financial support, although it was a very modest amount in church-planting circles. Still, what we lacked in money was more than made up for in friendship and emotional and spiritual support. Oftentimes, church planters feel somewhat neglected by their mother church for various reasons. Steven Johnson writes that if you observe mother ants, you'll notice that the queen will not tell the ants what to do. *She simply births them.* This is central to understanding the loneliness and isolation church planting can bring. Conversely, it is equally important to realize it will not be the mother's job to give direction all the time.[8] In hindsight, I've come to believe that the latter bears much more importance than the former. Why? Because when everything hits the fan, money doesn't cry with you. Nickels give bad hugs. I've encountered many church plants with endless financial support but no spiritual or emotional support system. I'd trade the money for prayer and friendship any day.

INVITING OTHERS

We began inviting people.[9] We knew we would need eccentric people for this kind of journey, and Quinn and I felt well prepared in the incubator of our Eugene years, the home of the University of Oregon (quite the eccentric place in its own right). Nevertheless, this part was tricky, because the only people we invited were those we knew deeply and had a relationship with. Our initial criteria was that they had to be trustable. Another element of our invitation came via a secret we'd been told by a well-experienced church planter. He said *how* you ask people to come will be *how* they leave. If you invite people with language of frustration, they'll leave frustrated. If you invite people out of competition, they'll be apt to leave your church for the hipper one when it arrives. So on and so forth.

We asked people to have the lowest expectations possible. The preacher Clovis Chappell regularly came to mind: "The prize of eternal life is won only by those who dare to give and hazard all they have."[10] Jesus promised blessing for people who sacrificed and left things for the kingdom (Matthew 19:29). We invited with warnings of the hazards, and we told people to prepare for hell. This meant many things. First, don't expect Portland to come to our church because we're finally here. We aren't the Conquistadors. Second, don't expect positions of prominence and power. Expect to serve, bleed and die. Tithe too. Furthermore, don't expect the pastor to spend every minute feeding you deep truths of God. Expect *nothing* but eternal life. Caution signs such as these weeded out the uncalled. I believed, and still do, that if I had to convince people to join, I'd eventually have to convince them to stay. This ultimately set the tone for the group, providing a sense that if anything good did happen out of this church plant, it would be over-the-top exciting. Praying for a month, those who'd been invited decided their fate. Out of thirty, fifteen came. During this period we also created a team we named the "Dream Team." This group of financially stable families were invited to partner with us by supporting us financially for one year. The thinking behind the single year was this: we felt that if it was any longer we wouldn't be required to get off our butts and do hard work of getting jobs and reaching our neighbors. We probably should have asked for more than a year, but by God's grace we were able to be sustainable that first year.

LITURGY AND FOOD

The church was born in our living room on a hot Sunday evening in late August. Our liturgy would be annoyingly simple: we'd bookend our worship gatherings with food. We dreamed of a living room full of people, the smell of cuisine pervading everything and conversation flowing. First, we'd eat a meal together as a church. Every week. Then we'd worship, read Scripture and pray. Following this, the gathering would conclude with what we hoped would be the highest moment of the gathering: Eucharist. No one could say they didn't get fed. *Literally.*

Being a part of the Pentecostal tradition, this was a bit reactionary on our behalf. I'd found that in Pentecostalism and most forms of Protestant worship the sermon, not the Eucharist, is considered the highest moment in the service. As I did not find this to be normative either in Scripture or in the history of the church, we did it differently. One initial question we had to wrestle with was whether we would allow wine in our church gatherings. Historically speaking, grape juice in liturgy is rather new, going back only to the eighteenth century. However, in Portland, alcoholism is rampant. For this reason, we chose early on that our gatherings would include grape juice, not wine.[11]

Our first gathering primarily consisted of those who'd moved from Eugene. The reason for this was quite simple: our marketing department stunk. Because we didn't name the church for an entire year, the only means of invitation came through friendship and personal invitation. Still, in a short time our numbers grew: the seed members brought friends, and then friends brought friends. You get the picture. This relational approach, as one can imagine, proved to be incredibly important for us, and I'm still very proud of this. We never handed out a single piece of paper or business card. The people of our city, similar to those in proximity to the early church, couldn't say "Let's go to Theophilus." They could only say, "Hey, let's go to dinner at that place where they eat a lot and talk about Jesus." I should also mention we'd discovered that Portland people love all things unmarketed (e.g., people love the alternative rock concert that's the hardest to find). The best concerts are those held in a living room with only twenty people and that wasn't advertised in the paper. Portlanders eat this stuff up. For them, marketing ruins it. Hence, we followed suit.

The genetic makeup of our gatherings was centered on a few ideas, foremost of which were as follows: we would strive to practice radical hospitality and cloying honesty. People, whoever they were—gay, straight, black, white, Republican, Democrat, tongue speaker, cessationist—could come and be themselves. The caveat was that if we could come as ourselves, then God had the same permission. So while people came as they were, regardless of race, sexuality or creed, they were asked to be willing to encounter a God whose Son could change us right where we were. Doing this created space for a lot of screwed-up people who'd never otherwise go to church. We had no grand delusions that theological uniformity led to orthodoxy. Rather, we believed that as the church gathered in the presence of Jesus, he would change us all by being himself and being worshiped as himself. Because, for us, Jesus himself *is* orthodoxy. If Jesus accepted us for who we were, then we owed him the same posture.

SLOW GROWTH

We saw almost no growth for three months, aside from a few friends of friends. I called those we did draw the "young and the restless"—those either in or just out of college, the 18-25 crowd, who generally had a bone to pick with *the Man*. Frustrated, cynical, sporting tight jeans and dark-rimmed glasses—they were exactly the people at Stumptown. Because our initial thrust was with these sorts of folk, we found it very difficult to retain anyone with wrinkles, which, as it were, was not much of a surprise. I had expected to reach people ten years older and younger than myself. Yet this created a problem. First, old people did not feel like they had a place. I recall one such visitor calling us a "glorified college group." This was basically true. The second problem was I began to feel ashamed of our youthfulness, as though it was a problem to be fixed. One evening we read together as a church Paul's first letter to Timothy. In it he told his *padawan* Timothy, "Don't let anyone look down on you because you are young" (1 Timothy 4:12). Paul told him this because his was a multigenerational church and he was inordinately young. I believed that commandment not only meant that Timothy should not look down on himself, nor should he let anyone else do so, but that a church had no right to look down on itself or any other congregation for its age or youthfulness. Eventually we embraced ourselves being young as simply the way Jesus had created us.

The third problem was purely practical. In developing things like eldership, it required us to be creative. For nearly six months I studied and prayed about the biblical model of eldership found in the Pauline literature. What I found surprised me. In parallel passages (Titus 1:5-7; 1 Timothy 3:1-7), Paul gives seemingly two different lists of expectations regarding the character of elders. To one, Timothy, he instructs him to not allow elders who were new believers. However, in his list to Titus, Paul omits this commandment. This was for one reason. *The church Titus pastored was new and very young.* This gave us hope; even in Scripture there is room for still-developing and imperfect ecclesial models.

Week after week we'd meet on Sunday evenings and worship Jesus and wait. We found out very soon that church planters have to eat too. Because we began the church with very modest funding, I was required to be bivocational.[12] For a living, I taught biblical studies, theology and church history full time at five local universities and Bible colleges. Because my PhD had been completed, it afforded me an opportunity to make a living as a professor. Frankly, this was wonderful. I loved being able to go to church after a long week of work and sit down and pray with someone whose boss had been a jerk that week and be able to sympathize. Indeed, I could sympathize. It also gave me the chance to spend time with people who I didn't pastor. It is as difficult as can be to be a pastor in a city like Portland. Inform someone on the street about that line of work and you can expect the conversation to end. It's got to the point now that I don't even tell people I'm a pastor; rather, I tell them I run a nonprofit with a really well-known CEO. When they hear I run a nonprofit, they're totally into me.

There was another aspect of this that made being bivocational a holy venture for me. *I love the idea that as their pastor I have other stuff going on in my life aside from the church.* Having bigger problems than the church freed me up to have a life. This became a church mantra. We wanted to be a church where everyone had bigger problems in their life outside the church. Having another job allowed me to incarnate this mantra. I'd teach and study during the week, prepare sermons in the evenings and on breaks, and do pastoral care and evangelism all day Saturday. Though it was crazy, it was never short of excitement. In teaching I could work out my theology for a paycheck, and in pastoring I could work it out for love.

We communally decided on some principles toward finances. Since day one, our goal was to be sustainable and locally supported by those in the church. How would we do this? To begin, we never passed a plate. We had a small shoebox in the back of the room for people to put their money in. I was brutally honest with our church about money. I had to be. Again, I wanted to eat. Some churches tell guests they don't have to give anything. We told guests to give because we didn't know if they were coming back.

Finally, we made the commitment to give our first 10 percent away to social justice needs (e.g., feeding the poor, caring for widows) and the second 10 percent to our denomination to support other church plants. Sadly, I quickly learned that those who gave the least were the ones who complained the most. I resolved to not let this bother me. Some months we had enough, some we didn't, but never, at any point, did Jesus leave us hanging.

The neighborhood we moved into was as weird as our team. The Hawthorne district is known for its oddness. Our approach was be simple: we'd move into the neighborhood and spend our lives living, serving and knowing people by name. At first our gatherings on Sunday evening became a sticking point because the parking in our neighborhood was so limited. One evening we went door-to-door to meet our neighbors and ask their permission to park in front of their houses. This gave us the chance to meet many of them, and we discovered our immediate neighborhood reflected the diversity of Portland. In the immediate space next to our house were atheists, a gay couple, a Roman Catholic family and a young firefighter who was never home. As opposed to doing flyers and inviting people to church, we believed (as we still do) that our greatest impact would be twofold: first, we would be there a very long time and actually know our neighbors; second, we would never presume we are just there for them. That is, we would try to allow that maybe our neighbors have been sent by God for us, and that *we* were to be changed by *them*. On Sunday evenings we would talk specifically about one important factor in ministry: reciprocity. Not only did we come to serve and know our neighbors, but they were sent to us so that we might learn the love of Christ.

CALL US LOVER OF GOD

We still didn't have a name. An ancient tradition holds that Jews often refused to name a child for a long time because the child's character should determine his or her name. We wanted our name to come after seeing the character of our church. This, however, created a setback, in that many people, once they started showing up, found it deeply impractical to say they were going to someone's house for church. Their friends and family grew concerned they were part of a cult. Though we disliked inconveniences such as this, there were inherent benefits to not having a name. The minute you have a name, you're Google-able. People can write reviews of your church. For this reason we believed it was essential to withhold our public face. In a way, we developed a Messianic Secret approach toward church planting.[13] By that I mean we actively sought to stay out of the public light. Jesus did this all the time in the Gospels, while also instructing individuals against telling his story. Because no one could Google us, almost no one left a church to come to ours. Any of the people who were really angry at their particular church didn't leave it and then bring their anger to ours.

Eventually it was time to name our church; there's only so long that people can refer to their church as "that place where we go to eat down the street." We got our title from the books of Luke and Acts. For the entire first year of our existence we read the book of Acts to watch and see how the Holy Spirit leads the church. It's worth remembering that each of the Bible's works were penned for a particular person or community in a particular time and for a particular reason. First and Second Timothy were both written to an ill-equipped and underaged pastor on how to keep the church he led from losing its mission and heart. Revelation was written by an apostle named John while he was stranded on a distant island called Patmos; it was addressed to a number of churches for whom God had a specific message. The first letter to the Corinthians was written to a church that had got caught up in some rather awkward sexual and dietary practices that made even their idols cringe. Interestingly, the largest portion of the New Testament was written by a Gentile named Luke, who addressed it to a near-anonymous guy named Theophilus. All we know about Theophilus is his Greek name and his apparent willingness to fork up enough money to personally commission two major books in the Bible on very expensive papyrus: the Gospel of Luke and its companion Acts. Theophilus means two things: "lover of God" and "loved by God." It's a name that conveys reciprocity, like a two-way street. Other than his name, Theophilus is a mystery (see Luke 1:1-4; Acts 1:1-2). We liked the idea of the mysterious man of anonymity who loved and was loved by God, and who desperately wanted to hear more of these stories about Jesus. Thus, the name stuck.

We continued the first year in the hard but gratifying work. One week felt like Good Friday; the next like Easter. We oscillated between the hell of death and the joys of resurrection, along with everything in between. After our first year, the first couple left the church. If that experience is prescriptive of how things go in church planting, the first people to leave the church will scar you. I should have been more prepared. All the books predicted it, calling the initial team "the scaffolding people," and this metaphor accurately describes the usefulness of these people. However, it doesn't live up to either their value or how hard it is to lose them. If people are just scaffolding, we might walk all over them to get to the top, and then break them down and give them away when we are done with them. It seems to me that, in this utilitarian stance, if we think of people as scaffolding we will treat them as such. *Yet how in the world could scaffolding hurt me so much?* It can't, because people aren't scaffolding. People are people. Every single one of them counts. Which is why it *still* hurts when people leave the church. The book of Jonah got me through that particular month or so. In reading the story of Jonah, I discovered that while God does send missionaries to reach a city like Nineveh, often God sends a missionary in order to reach that specific person. God sends church planters that *they* might get saved. God sends missionaries to reach the missionaries themselves. So when the people who helped start a church leave, hopefully it is done with grace from them as much as from the church. It is a wonderful opportunity to "work out your salvation with fear and trembling" (Philippians 2:12 NIV).

Leadership must be built. After three months I asked fifteen or so of the people who appeared to be both sane and saved to serve on a small leadership team I was calling Communitas. This gave me time to devote to leadership development, assignment giving and gifting discernment. In regard to leadership I found it difficult to see how much of the church-planting literature used metaphors that I was not comfortable with. Church-planting literature often uses the metaphor of the missile and rocket: When are you *launching*? What is your *target* audience? When are you *pulling the trigger*? I think the metaphor should resemble that of the movie *Little Miss Sunshine:* we would all get in the van together with the awkward son, the loud and annoying grandpa, the aspiring girl, the balanced mother and the multilevel marketing father, and then just go. Because by being in the van long enough, we'd fall in love with each other. That is how we developed leaders. Putting opposites together, giving them assignments and telling them Jesus was in it all.

LIKE ADAM ASLEEP: THE STORIES OF A CHURCH PLANT

Too many stories came out of this journey. Three brief ones stand out. The first is a story about God's provision. In the founding of any church, people will inevitably come from other churches and, invariably, they can't *not* compare your church with their old one. A great challenge arises with those who have come to start the church because often they will have great fondness for the place they have left. These people will talk about how wonderful their old church was, and in so doing will come across as though they are judging their new situation. I remember seeing someone in our church listening to a podcast from our parent church, and I felt angry. I thought, *Aren't my sermons good enough?* Church planting is kryptonite to pride. Even though the book of Ecclesiastes warns against praising the past, we all do it (Ecclesiastes 7:10). We praise the past, bemoan the present and anticipate the future. Learning to live in the now requires people of encouragement, people who can let the now be what it is and find joy in it.

The first family from Portland that joined the church was that for us. Joe and Asena Kurkinen were bold enough to bring their two children and a healthy dose of encouragement to our community. God sent them, I believe, to us that we might find hope in the now. Sadly, it is impossible to go out and find a couple like this. They can't be found; they can only be called. I still believe the best things come when we don't look for them, like Adam sleeping and waking up with a new wife. Along the way God has done this in one form or another. The Kurkinens came from God. Every church planter will have a Kurkinen sent to them. When God does this, spend *too* much time with them. When you have a baby, it is important to be very careful about *who* you let hold your baby. If they are sick, they'll get your baby sick. God will send some healthy people like the Kurkinens so that you aren't the only one holding your newborn. Eventually, of the initial fifteen who moved from Eugene to help begin the church, six would leave—two out of frustration and four for new jobs. The rest are still with us. The Kurkinens, sent by God, created for us a sense of stability that helped us sleep at night.

Another story came early on during our first Halloween in Portland. It had been a couple of extremely rough weeks. Very few people were coming to the church, finances sucked and I was getting very discouraged. On Halloween we threw our neighborhood a huge party for the kids to come and have fun. We planned to have different rooms set up in our houses that were themed, along with great food and music for the parents, plus a culminating dance party at the end. Tons of neighborhood kids came and had a blast. Near the end of the dance party, at about nine at night, we noticed that one of the neighborhood kids of about thirteen was dancing by himself in the corner of the room. Now, it is important to understand my wife for this story to make sense. She has felt compelled since day one to know all of the kids in our neighborhood by name. Among these kids she'd gotten to know was the one dancing in the corner of the room, Alex, who lived across the street from us. Honestly, it was kind of awkward. With about thirty college students dancing, there is one thirteen-year-old kid dancing by himself in the corner of the room. Fun, but nonetheless awkward. All of a sudden Alex left, walking out of our front door. Quinn followed to see where he was going. As she went to see where he was from the front porch of our house, she could see him walking back across the street with another kid from the neighborhood to come to the party. At this point Alex was evangelizing his friends to come over to the dance party. As Alex strolled across the street, Quinn called out to him saying, "Alex, get over here and dance with us." As she did so, she could hear Alex say to his friend (Theo) as they came toward our house, "You see: here, *they know my name.*"

I resolved that day to believe that God is in the small things. Simply knowing a few names is a sign that the kingdom's water is breaking. Perhaps in Texas, when you don't go to church, people ask, "What's wrong with you?" In Portland, when you go to church, people ask, "What's wrong with you?" Because of this, we can't expect people to come to church. We must be willing to engage Jesus outside church, like Alex did in the street outside our house.

The last small story has to do with our neighborhood high school: Cleveland High. Our relationship with Cleveland began at an interesting time in the life of the church. The first year of the church we spent what I felt was an inordinate amount of time focusing on the church. In hindsight I think this is necessary. Keep in mind that one-year-olds are selfish humans, and everyone is focused on them in the earliest years of their life. As they grow up, we focus less and less attention on them. This is no different in the life of a church. A baby requires a ton of attention. As we were finishing our first year, I was feeling as though we needed to break out of our season of self-focus and find more creative ways to serve our city. Cleveland is classic Portland. I initiated a meeting with the principal to find any creative ways that we might serve their school with no strings attached. They, rightfully so, were not interested in proselytizing Christians sharing their message after serving. The principal asked if we would do some yard work for them that needed to be done for parent-teacher conferences. So we did. We

Interview Q&A 1

Editors: You consistently engage with your neighborhood. How have the voices of neighbors helped you see something, shifted your imagination or clarified what God calls you to?

AJ Swoboda: Our neighbors taught us what we know. I think of the evangelist John Wesley who was widely known for being a voracious reader. On bumpy horseback, Wesley would ride from town to town to preach the gospel of Christ to anyone who'd dare hear. Being on horseback as much as he was gave him ample time to read. And read he did. Wesley was popularly known to have read whole volumes on horseback as he prepared sermons for the next town. Often, he'd read the books of those he knew he'd be preaching to. Why? In the back of his mind Wesley knew he couldn't preach effectively without knowing intimately the different questions of each town. Without knowing it, his audience taught him what he needed to preach.

Our neighbors have taught us more about the dynamics of the gospel than I could explain. Like Jonah, the stories of the Ninevites have taught us a shocking amount about God's grace, love and power.

Two of our neighbors taught us about the beauty of hospitality and the gospel. During our first month in the house, a sweet, older couple who'd just moved from Alaska provided unsolicited hospitality one afternoon, including, food, conversation and a pack of microbrews. They taught us that the gospel is sometimes unsolicited grace. We'll never forget them.

Another set of neighbors taught us the value of covenant love. Over the period of six months, we painstakingly watched a wife across the street care compassionately for her dying husband. After his passing, our church was able to share some love and space with her. But it was her love for her husband that taught us a beautiful lesson of God's love for the church and our calling to covenant love in marriage.

brought nearly seventy-five people, rakes and gloves, and made the place sparkling. They were so happy and have asked if we would be open to doing mentoring in their school. I think Jesus is in this.

I'LL FOLLOW YOU INTO THE DARK: OUR FUTURE

It's been nearly four years. Whew. I feel as though we have been led into the dark. That said, we will keep following Jesus into the dark. What is important for Theophilus as we move forward? I would suggest that three core theological convictions remain that we believe will carry us into the future. First, we cling to a very strong and pronounced theology of Pentecost. We believe that Acts 2 doesn't expire. The Spirit, which fell on the gathered postresurrection followers of Christ, keeps on falling. For us, this means women are anointed and have not only permission but encouragement to speak in the church. The gifts of the Spirit (e.g., tongues, prophecy, love) are all central points of importance for those endowed with God's Spirit. This is the presence of Christ in his church: the *Christus praesans*.

Second, we hold to a unique conviction that the Spirit is not only alive today in our midst but *has been* alive in the history of the church for centuries past. We call ourselves Anglicostals: Pentecostals swimming in the history and tradition of Anglicanism. Sadly, Pentecostal and charismatic spirituality can often lead to a spiritual framework that garners little or no respect toward all the wonderful stuff that comes out of the Christian tradition. Our approach is to hold to and respect both the historical movements and the movement of the Spirit in the life of the community. I want people to be a part of our community and to be infected with a desire to live the Spirit-filled life *and* see the role of the Spirit in the beautiful history of the church. In this way we are restorationist and nonrestorationist, holding both in tension. The Spirit is restoring us all into the now by helping us understand our place in the history and family of the church.

Third, we desire to practice a missional approach based on "faithful presence."[14] We are not going anywhere until told otherwise. We are called to our neighborhood, to Stumptown, to Cleveland High and to Alex. There are various expressions of this commitment in our midst. First, I don't conceive of this church as my steppingstone; I am not using it to move higher in the Christian ladder of success. If that were the case, I have every confidence

Interview Q&A 2

Editors: Your Communitas group, along with others, are your leadership. Tell us how God has used their connections, perspectives and creativity to shape your life in the Stumptown.

AJ Swoboda: In the course of three years after the church's founding, we've attempted to flatten our leadership as best as possible. Church planting naturally makes this difficult—especially if the church planters are an individual or a couple. We refused the CEO model. Through tedious research, prayer and contemplation, we constructed a communal ecclesial model that makes room for the voices and perspectives of the Jesus-loving people in our church, voices that are sometimes very prophetic. Today, this includes deacons (service oriented) and elders (leadership oriented) who lead alongside myself and the staff. Our lay leadership team, Communitas, consists of any leader currently serving and helping shape the genetic makeup of our community.

While this flattening has been integral, I've quickly discovered a looming challenge remains in being a visionary who can prophetically create space for the vision of those around you. Single-minded visions never capture more than one mind. As hard as it may be, bringing others alongside myself to make decisions, shape vision and dream theologically is paramount within the participatory culture or our time. While many leaders have vision, few are visionaries. The first sees things. The second gives others a pair of glasses.

Communitas has beautifully undermined my own personal leadership ignorance.

One leader, Katie, in the middle of a Communitas meeting raised her shaking hand to share she feared our community had forgotten to pray for our city. In response, I asked her if she'd lead us into a fuller prayer life. She's now the deacon of prayer life in our church.

Another leader, Luke, has perpetually reminded me of his frustration with our liturgical shallowness. He's been able to do so because there is an open-door policy to share thoughts, frustrations and encouragements with me. Because of his voice, we now have a deacon of liturgical life who's job is to create communal sacred spaces.

in the people in the church, who are too smart and would call me out on it. Even more so, we are called to our neighborhoods for a very long time. What keeps a church missional? What keeps it from moving to a realm of something else? In the words of Seth Godin, it seems clear to me that church planters, like lizards, get hungry, scared, angry and horny.[15] When things get tough, we all want to flee. We go into protective mode when we're afraid, hiding under rocks. I am committed to stay.

I remember that in the story of the *Odyssey*, when the ship is passing the Sirens' island, Odysseus commands the sailors to tie him to the mast so he can hear their enchanting song without leading the ship to crash into the rocks. He tells them that no matter what he might utter when he hears the song, they must *not listen to him*. After pouring beeswax in the sailors ears, he is tied to the mast and they sail by. He hears the Sirens' song and they survive. I was listening to this guy talk about how psychologists call the mast a "commitment device," something you tie yourself to when you have a cool head so that you make good decisions when you have a hot head.[16] Locking a credit card away. Putting your credit card in ice. Canceling your Internet account to be free from porn. We do these because there are two heads in all people. We all have two selves. The present self is Odysseus wanting to just live in the moment, hearing the song. The other self wants to retire with his wife Penelope in Ithaca, what we might call the future self. Why do we need commitment devices? Because we are all tempted. Resisting the temptation to flee to brighter pastures or the suburbs is hard; there is more money and better buildings there. We, however, feel called to the city. God's mission is our commitment device. We are convinced that Jesus needs us and wants us in this beautiful city. Alex is our commitment device. Cleveland High is our commitment device. Stumptown is our commitment device. Our neighborhood is our commitment device. Because love is what church planting is all about.

We have many commas in our story, and much unfinished business. In the next few months we are initiating deacons and elders in the life of the church. We are continuing to eat together and will know we have outgrown our place if there is no room around the table. We are working to serve with Cleveland High in any way they desire. All of these will come and go. Yet at the end of the day, we love our city. This strange little kiddy pool called Portland is where we are learning to swim.

CREATING GLOCAL DISCIPLES OF JESUS

LIFE COVENANT CHURCH

Tim Morey

LIFE COVENANT CHURCH

Location: Torrance, California
Denomination: Evangelical Covenant Church
Year of Foundation: 2003
Regular Participants in the Life of the Church: 200
Website: www.life-covenant.com

For a story of a church disciplined in creating disciples of Jesus continue reading. Pastor Tim Morey, a denominational leader within the Evangelical Covenant Church, continues to lead a new church that has already planted eleven other new churches. Life Covenant is also leading the charge on what it means to be glocally missional. With an early focus on the neighborhood, Life Covenant has now also expanded into meaningful ministry in Africa. The simple recipe of intentional discipleship, church parenting and glocal mission has created a moving story of God's faithfulness for the people of Torrance, California.

COMPELLED

"If you can do anything else, do that instead."

He was not particularly intent on discouraging me, but he did want me to understand that planting a church was not a calling to be entered into lightly, and that I shouldn't start down this path unless I truly felt compelled. I poked at my lunch but didn't reply. Paul Kaak knew what he was talking about. He and Dieter Zander had planted a church called New Song in San Dimas. New Song was one of the first so-called Gen X churches, and at that time it was one of the very few models for those wanting to start the types of churches that might reach the emerging generations.

Just twelve months previous I didn't even know what church planting was. Strange as that may sound, I was still fairly young in my faith, no one around me was talking about church planting, and I had never stopped to think that someone must have started all these churches that reside on so many street corners. In truth, I was halfway through seminary and two years into a role as a (very) junior staff pastor before I ever heard the words *church* and *plant* used in the same sentence.

That being said, it won't come as a surprise that my passion for church planting started as a passion for something else. I had begun to follow Jesus in earnest in college, and I deeply wanted to see my peers connect with Jesus. The church I was a part of was an amazing place, but I sensed a cultural disconnect that was difficult to overcome. What's more, I found that I was not particularly gifted in convincing the church to reinvent itself to better reach the university students down the street. When I heard about church planting, something clicked, and I knew almost at once that God would be leading me down that path.

My friends and I were convinced that there had to be a way to be the church—faithfully biblical, perhaps even radically biblical—in a way that resonated more naturally with the culture we were ministering in. Though we didn't have the verbiage, we were longing to see the church engage in the same sort of critical contextualization that it managed so well on the mission field. We wanted to see the gospel take root in a specific soil and grow into churches that resonated with the heart language of those living there.[1]

Several months before graduation from seminary, my wife and I attended a church planter assessment center, where, to our tearful surprise, they recommended we plant a church. This was a huge and much-needed confirmation. In spite of our eagerness to get started, in the months that followed we felt the Holy Spirit telling us it wasn't time. We were in our mid-twenties, had only been married a year and had no idea how little we knew. God, in manifest grace and wisdom, led me to take a position as college pastor at a church in Los Angeles where we spent five years serving and learning.

CHALLENGES

At the time I was going through the hiring process for the college pastor job, I hoped that I might serve there for the next five years or so and then be sent by them to plant a church. I raised this possibility during the interview with the search committee, and the room went very silent. Finally one of the members spoke up and said, "Tim, if you come here, you need to let go of that hope. We don't plant churches; we build bigger ones." I didn't expect it at the time, but over the next few years the church's attitude toward church planting would change, and they would eventually send me out to plant a church.

During this time God was forging in me some values that would shape our church. My experience of meeting Jesus and growing in relationship with him had happened within the context of personal, thoroughly accountable relationships, or what I like to refer to as *deep community*. Small groups, mentoring relationships, even living in the same house with a bunch of men who were committed to sharpening one another and reaching out to our neighborhood—these were my earliest experiences of faith. I brought these aspects of mutual discipleship with me to this church experience, and though we employed them liberally in our college ministry, I always felt a little dissonance between what we were doing and the overall thrust of the church. Serving at a large, multistaff church had many perks, but was a much different animal than the deep community that had so markedly formed the foundation for my faith.

During that time my philosophy of ministry was subtly but steadily changing. While I appreciated the resources available in a megachurch and the scope of ministry such an entity could have, I knew that mode was ultimately not for me. In that context we continued to reflect on theological and ministry perspectives that would lead us toward church planting. These reflections seemed to confirm the call that we had investigated earlier.

At this large church I struggled with the fact that the vast majority of worshipers on a given weekend were content to be anonymous to one another. *How does it affect our spiritual formation,* I wondered, *if we don't know the names or the stories of those with whom we worship?* In what ways are we diminished by the inherent lack of community in such an arrangement? Is God's worship itself diminished in any way? It was a given, for us in that context, that success was to a large extent defined numerically. I began to wonder, *Is our size the best metric of success that we could utilize?*

Many people were serving in worthy capacities in the church, but as a percentage it was a low number relative to worship attendance. The same was true of giving. How is the call to discipleship affected if the invitation to salvation is an anonymous one, where a decision to follow Jesus happens while every head is bowed and every eye is closed, and a raised hand is celebrated as a conversion whether or not we ever see that person again? I began to wonder, *Is a setting of this kind the healthiest environment to make men and women into disciples of Jesus?* I love to teach the Bible, and the thrill of speaking to a big crowd had an undeniable appeal, but increasingly I envisioned myself leading a congregation of two hundred or less—small enough that we could know one another and anonymity would be difficult. I had a growing hunger to be part of a body where we truly did life together.

I didn't realize it at the time, but through conversations, reading and ministry experiences God was slowly forging in us the values that would become foundational for us as a church.

Church as mission. The church is the community of the worshiping, sojourning people of God. It is a group of people on mission. The church exists for the good of the world—God's precious children called out of the world and sent back into it. As modern mystic Thomas Kelly put it, "He plucks the world out of our hearts, loosening the chains of attachment. And He hurls the world into our hearts, where we and He together carry it in infinitely tender love."[2] We saw biblical mission as encompassing a range of endeavors, from evangelism to compassion to justice. We wouldn't want to be a church that focused only on one to the exclusion of the others.[3]

Disciplemaking. Jesus called his church to make disciples. It was no longer adequate to invite people to a salvation experience that was divorced from apprenticeship to Jesus. Our aim had to be to learn how to live what Jesus commanded while teaching others to do the same.

Transformation. While the gospel of the kingdom carried with it a message of personal salvation, getting to heaven after death was far from the totality of Jesus' message. To become his disciple was to be changed, to enter the process of being transformed from the inside out and to be made into his likeness.[4]

Authentic community. Anonymous Christianity wasn't going to be an option for us. To know and be known, to do life together deeply—this became our emphasis and passion.

Church planting. We wanted to be a church who planted churches. We weren't opposed to large churches, but knew our call was to be something different. We found ourselves praying things like, "God, if you bless us with growth, we'd rather be ten churches of two hundred than one church of two thousand."

Leading as a team. That part of me that craved recognition, that wanted to stand as a lone heroic figure and be praised as the pastor who built a great church needed to die. If we believed the Holy Spirit empowered all believers—that there were going to be multiple people in the church who were gifted to lead, to teach and to shepherd—then I needed God to chasten my ego and teach me how to lead as part of a team.

Contextualization. Cultural relevance could not be optional. We needed to practice critical contextualization, not in the sense of marketing ourselves to the public or of capitulating to culture, but in the missiological sense. We wanted to bring an articulation and embodiment of the gospel to our culture in a way that connected with the heart-language of our hearers, and that allowed the church to spring up in ways that were authentic to the soil in which it was planted.

Courage. The God who was calling us to plant was calling us into his great adventure. We needed to trust God to give us brave hearts to live into all that God might have for us. I am somewhat timid by nature, and I knew this part of the call would mostly mean that God needed to do a work in me. We had no idea how soon or how often this courage would be needed.

Grace. If there is one word that we hope marks our community, it is *grace.* We pray that this uniquely Christian quality will permeate all that we say and do.

BEGINNINGS

The church where I served as college pastor eventually decided to send me out as a church planter, but three months before our launch we lost the funding they had intended to give us. To us and the small team we had gathered around us, it felt like a punch in the gut. We didn't know it at the time, but this would be one of the best things to happen to us along our church-planting journey.

Painful as it was, this was a good decision on their part. The church had undergone a leadership crisis that left the congregation reeling and the budget decimated. Staff members were being laid off, and funding a church plant would have been irresponsible. "We're sorry, Tim," the leadership told me. "If you want to hang on we might have enough money to send you out next year."

I spent that weekend praying with my wife and a couple of close brothers and came back feeling more certain than ever that we needed to plant. I swallowed hard, went to the elders and asked, "Will you send us out anyway? If you give your blessing and let us invite a few others to come with us, that will be enough. We will trust God to provide the money."

I was a ball of anxiety the next few months. Was this going to work? How would I provide for my family? Was Starbucks hiring? Slowly, a community emerged around us. Ten, then fifteen, then twenty-five. God provided a core of people who shared our vision and felt called to make that vision happen. People gave. They sacrificed in big ways to make the dream happen. At the eleventh hour, just a couple of weeks before our official launch, we got word that another church in our denomination shared our vision too. It was a graying church in California farm country that none of us had ever heard of, but they carried a burden to reach the younger generation. They were not positioned to do so themselves, but when they heard our story they felt called to be part of seeing the younger generation reached through us. A check arrived in the mail for the impossible sum of $30,000. We wept for joy.

It's hard to describe the effect this had on us. We were primarily a bunch of young adults, meeting in our living room and praying for a miracle. None of us had ever trusted God for something like this, and we were blown away when it happened. To trust in God, step out in faith and see God come through— God planted this experience deeply in our narrative so that we could always recall how tangible and specific God's graces are. This made certain values even more important and embedded them firmly in our DNA. Faith. Sacrifice. Courage. These traits became part of our ethos, reaching far beyond the core group in our living room to affect those who would join our community in the years to come. Had we thought to pray for these traits, we would have, but we would never have guessed the means by which God would bring them about.

The whole experience seemed surreal. For the first four months we intentionally met as a launch team only, without public worship services of any kind. This idea was part of the training we received from our denomination (the Evangelical Covenant Church), and it resonated well with who we wanted to be. We valued worship and looked forward to a worship gathering being part of our church life, but we were wary of the danger of church being reduced to the worship gathering. We had it in our hearts to be a Monday to Saturday church, not just a Sunday one.

So for four months we met as a launch team, praying, sharing meals, worshiping, reflecting on what the Bible says a church is and what it meant for us in particular to be the church in a particular context. We forged our values and sought God for a more detailed vision. We served one another and served our city. We practiced those things that we wanted to be sure would become part of our DNA. It was important to us that we would be a blessing to our community before we had the public presence churches were most known for—Sunday worship. These were rich times of bonding, and Life's founding members still reflect on them fondly.

Following that season we incorporated worship gatherings into our life together, but only once a month. We spent another four months continuing to meet weekly as a launch team, living together as a church family, only now we had another venue (worship) where we could include our friends.

Eventually we began gathering for worship on a weekly basis. It felt organic. God had forged deep bonds between us, we had grown together, and we were doing the things we believed a church should do. Having a long incubation period gave us the sense that a foundation had been laid, one that we hoped would help guard us from a reductionistic approach to church.

APPRENTICES AND MISSIONARIES

My biggest fear as we started the church was that we would be unchanged, and that we would leave the world around us unchanged as well. We were convinced that our city needed this church, but not if we simply became the flavor of the month for religious consumers. At the root of what we were attempting was an understanding of the gospel that majored on transformation. To know Jesus was to apprentice ourselves to him as rabbi, to follow him and in so doing be changed into his likeness. We wanted to learn from Jesus how to live our lives as he would live our lives.

To that end we decided to take a "high bar" approach to membership. This was a big shift for me. In earlier days I had wanted to dispense with church membership all together. *What's the point?* I wondered. *God knows I'm committed—what benefit is there in attending a class that somehow makes it official?*

Yet the more we reflected on the population we were reaching, the more we began to see membership as a valuable tool for our spiritual formation. Women and men of our generation are notorious nonjoiners. We hesitate on a Wednesday to make plans for Friday in case something better comes up on Thursday. In terms of church allegiance, this fickleness works in concert with our consumeristic approach to church to undermine our capacity for true community. Living deeply together takes time and commitment, and we realized we were not serving our church if we didn't call them to a robust commitment to one another.

So we let it be known that all were welcome in our fellowship, but we would challenge those people who felt called by God to be at Life to make it a real commitment. In saying yes to membership, people were acknowledging the call of Jesus to live out their apprenticeship to him in this particular time and place, with this particular community of people. A person was making a commitment not to run when it got hard, and to live in a way that contributed to the good of the community as a whole. We developed a rule of life, based on those utilized by the early monastic communities, that detailed the practices, experiences and relationships we saw as critical for growth in Christ in our context.[5]

Our rule of life paired this concern for spiritual formation with a desire to live as a community on mission. Again, the twofold fear was that we would be unchanged and leave the world unchanged. Why bother starting a church if we become little more than religious consumers? What good was church if it was only going to be about ourselves?

We determined that one of the best ways we could keep both outreach and spiritual formation in front of us was to build each into our primary ministry structures so people wouldn't pick and choose between the two. To participate in one was to participate in both. We settled on three communal disciplines we wanted everyone to be involved in: worship gatherings, a small

Interview Q&A 1

Editors: You are obviously engaging your neighbors. How have their voices shifted your imagination, caused you to rethink your plans or even helped you become different people?

Tim Morey: *Local homeless children.* These three words gripped us as a neighbor told us about children in our city who were being put into foster care, not because their parents were incapable of raising them but because these parents had lost their jobs and then their homes.

Life has always ministered to the local homeless and working poor (some of whom were families with children), but primarily in ways that met an immediate need (a hot meal, haircut, giving blankets, doing laundry, etc.). While we see these efforts as meaningful, we have felt a real burden for those homeless friends who we see could come off the street if they received the right help. Our hearts were there, but we didn't have the knowledge or resources to move forward.

But this same neighbor who made us aware of the problem had a solution as well. She was looking for partners who could help develop a sort of co-op shelter and job-training center for homeless families, where congregations would take turns in week-long shifts housing and feeding a handful of families while their kids went to school and a social worker guided the parents through the process of acquiring work and permanent housing. We are still young in this new aspect of local ministry, but already we are seeing it cause our people to come alive in Christ in fresh ways, and we trust that the impact on our community will be a beautiful expression of the kingdom of heaven.

---

group or a mentoring relationship, and ministries of compassion and justice. We saw these as crucial to how God forms us, but also structured each in such a way that mission was built-in. We taught our church that these three ministries correspond to the needs of our unchurched friends and represent the primary ways our friends will connect to this body. We discerned these needs as follows: the need for transcendence, the need for community, and the need for purpose. For those friends who are longing to experience the transcendent spiritual reality they suspect is out there, the worship gathering might be the best place for them to connect. For friends who would value an environment with more dialogical interaction and a closer connection to others, our small groups would be the place to start. For friends who long for their lives to make a difference, there would be ample opportunities to bring them to serve with us in ministries of compassion.[6]

The deep change God's grace brings in these settings is beautiful. I think of Anna, a self-proclaimed "proud atheist," who first encountered God through our worship gatherings, and over the next year came to faith with others in a small group and served alongside church members in ministering to the poor. I think of another young couple whose marriage was all but over, and how the community continuously loved them, prayed for them and nurtured the embers of that relationship until life reemerged. Now that couple has a powerful ministry to other young couples. I think of the many dechurched individuals who had long since abandoned faith (at least in any communal form) and who have now found that God's grace not only brings forgiveness but allows them to stop pretending they are whole and simply be real about their brokenness as well.

And this grace deeply changes those already in the church too. Sometimes grace is expressed in forms as simple as human touch. In our ministry of providing hot meals for the homeless and working poor, we try to always make a point to learn and remember people's names, to hear their stories and especially to touch them—a hand on the shoulder, a handshake, a hug when appropriate. We regularly hear from them how much this means to them, how it humanizes them. As we were cleaning up one night, one of our young men was trying to articulate what many of us have said or felt, and said this: "I always come away from serving at these events feeling like I'm the one who's been fed." Serving the less fortunate humanizes us as well.

Out of these related desires for spiritual formation and mission came a document that articulated our values and dreams. While I served as the primary architect, rehearsing and then further shaping this document became part of what happened each time we gathered. People would share insights gained from reflecting on Scripture, past experience (both good and bad) and from books that were influencing us.[7] What emerged was more manifesto than vision, and it arose from the specific experiences we were having with God, with each other and with our neighbors.

To be and make disciples: We envision men, women, and children who live as deeply devoted students of Jesus. They are becoming real—transformed from the inside out. They live in this world, but belong to another. They are learning to live their lives as Jesus would live them, and are free from legalistic rule-keeping, phony posturing, plastic spirituality, attempts to earn the favor of God and people, and from bashing themselves and others. Their lives result in others becoming followers of Jesus as well.

In authentic community: We envision a loving, authentic community of people who want to come closer to God. They do life deeply together. They have been immersed in the reality of the Trinity, and are part of the great family of saints that transcends the bounds of race, gender, age, social status, culture, and time. They journey together, encouraging, challenging, carrying, and pushing one another. They are deeply aware that they have received compassion from God, and they give it generously to everyone they encounter.

For the good of the world: We envision an outward-focused community, eagerly looking to share what they have received. Their lives overflow in compassionate service and in the proclamation of the good news of Jesus: that the Kingdom of God is available to all! They are ambassadors of God's Kingdom, placed in society as students, teachers, laborers, and professionals. They carry Christ with them into every area of life. Their unique giftedness is used to carry out God's mission in the local church, and in numerous churches planted, from the South Bay to the farthest corners of the planet.

In the presence and power of Jesus: We envision people who live an authentic spirituality, intimately connected to Jesus. The real and present life of Christ alive in them is transforming them into the people God always envisioned them to be. They move in the strength of the Spirit, carrying out God's purposes for them and growing in love with God and with people. They live with grateful hearts, as those who have learned how to receive a gift. Their thankfulness spills out in awe-filled lives of passionate worship and an outflowing of God's grace.[8]

core values:

- *biblical (up)—God has revealed himself through the Scriptures, which are our source of authority for life and worship*
- *devotional—(in) nothing is more important than a love relationship with Jesus*
- *missional—(out) mission is why the church exists*
- *connectional—(together) authentic, loving community is the context for mission*
- *bravehearts—courageous faith*

- *contextualization—cultural relevance is not optional*
- *grace-full—we will live in the abundant grace of God, freely receiving it and freely giving it away*

PLANTING CHURCHES

Life was about two years old when we planted our first church, but I'm told that we were about ten minutes old when the topic of planting the next church first came up. It's been in our DNA from the beginning, and more than any other single characteristic, being a church that plants churches has probably been the defining mark of our young church. In eight years we have been blessed to grow to eleven churches on two continents, and as I write this we are making plans for subsequent plants as well.

One of our early commitments was to start planting churches before it was comfortable to do so. We knew of too many churches who said they would plant a church when they could afford it or when they grew to several hundred people or when the time was right, but they never seemed to reach that right time. Like having biological children, who can ever afford it? Who is ever ready? If we waited for the time to be right, we feared it never would be.

God opened the door for us to plant our first church when one of our members invited a pastor friend who was in between churches. He and his wife came looking for a place where they could simply regain their bearings and let the bruises incurred in ministry heal. Instead of facilitating their extended respite, we quickly discovered that God was calling this gifted pastor to be a church planter, and he came on our staff part time as a "church planter in residence." For a year he and his wife underwent training by immersion and were involved with everything from budgets to preaching, children's ministry to church discipline, and then we sent them out.

Part of our commitment to this new church was to provide appropriate financial support as well. The amount we needed to raise was hefty enough that it kept me up at night. It represented about 20 percent of our annual budget. But when it came time to plant, our church joyfully and sacrificially gave to see this new church planted. The money was raised in six weeks.

In that same time period God brought us a second gifted church planter, and he began a year of residency as well. Twelve months after birthing our first daughter church, our people again gave above and beyond to see a new church planted. This time the money was raised in three weeks. I'll never forget how on that final night a woman came up to me, having just written a faith-stretching check, and with tears in her eyes asked, "So we're doing this again next year, right?"

This was a time of huge lessons for us. We discovered that the residency we had intended for the planters' benefit had a huge benefit for our congregation as well. We owned these plants deeply and personally. We weren't just planting churches in the abstract; we were sending Doug and Angelina, Jon and Lindsey—beloved family members—to continue the mission in a new locale.

Equally important, we learned the importance of church planting for spiritual formation. We were motivated to be a church that plants churches because of mission, but were caught off guard by the dramatic effect participation in this venture had on people's spiritual formation. People were stretched in their faith, challenged in their giving and lifestyle, forced into prayer, and all eyes were on God as we waited to see how God would work. I'm convinced that nothing we have done as a church has helped people grow more than planting churches.

Church planting has helped to keep us outward focused. It is difficult to pray, give and rejoice with the successes of a daughter church and give no thought to what God is doing in our own neighborhood. We have been challenged in ways both joyous and convicting as we see the evangelistic fervor of one of our recent church plants. They are prayerful and intentional in their evangelism, and they began baptizing new believers months before they ever held a public worship gathering.

Similarly, as we see our daughter and granddaughter churches in Africa, we are humbled by their example. Having severely limited material resources, they rely so deeply on prayer and trust so fervently in God's provision that at times we collectively blush at the example they set for us. We praise God for the good work God is doing through them, and we pray that God might make us (the parent!) as beautiful a church as they.

Global Ministry

We knew from the beginning that we were going to be a smaller church and thus would have limited resources. We wondered what this status might mean for our global ministry efforts. Most of our people who were passionate about global missions came from churches with large mission programs that sent short-term teams around the world every summer. As we prayed about the shape of our global efforts, we sensed God leading us in a different direction. What if we prayerfully picked one place in the world to minister—a dramatically different approach from our more wealthy counterparts—and committed to that place for twenty years? We would be more laser beam than shotgun. If we were focused, what kind of impact could we have, even as a small church?

God led us to make that commitment to the underserved African nation of Mozambique. Our strategy was to begin by addressing issues of poverty, and out of those efforts we prayed and hoped that God would open the doors for us to eventually see indigenous churches planted there. As God would have it, an amazing organization called Opportunity International, which specializes in microfinance development, was looking for partners to start a bank for impoverished people in Mozambique.[9] For our first two years we invested ourselves heavily in this ministry and saw tremendous fruit. When we sent a team to see in person what was happening there, we met AIDS widows who had started businesses and were now able to feed their families. In a nation with 75 percent unemployment, these women were doing well enough to adopt other children who had lost their parents to AIDS, and some were already at a point where they could hire employees as well. Far better than merely supplying them with food, we were giving them a means of supporting themselves, investing in their local economies and helping in a way that gave them hope and dignity. In a nation riddled with shame and self-loathing, we saw these women hold their heads high as they made a way for their families and provided education for their children.

Prior to that first trip we prayed that God would lead us into key relationships, and we were not disappointed. We developed a friendship with one Mozambican pastor named John, who at the time was working for a relief agency. Our team stayed in touch, and when he told us of his vision to start an orphanage and community center, we knew God was calling us to partner with him. Our team's second trip to Mozambique was scheduled to coincide with the dedication of the community center. As our group arrived, the entire town came out to surprise them with a greeting of music and dancing. Pastor John had another surprise for them as well—the dedication of a church that was birthed in the community center. "Would it be all right," he asked, "if our church took your name, and we could be your daughter?" Our

Interview Q&A 2

Editors: You often use the pronoun *we* to describe initiatives and decision making. Tell us how God has used other leaders and participants in your church—how their connections, perspectives and creativity help the church attend to God's initiatives around you.

Tim Morey: Life has tried to build ministry around the interconnected ideas of giftedness, team and empowerment. The assumption we work with is that everyone has something to contribute, that those contributions will ordinarily be accomplished in partnership with others and that those closest to the actual work (in whatever area) need to be empowered to make decisions for that work. Consequently, many of our best ideas and most fruitful ministry has come from congregants as they simply try to live out their calling.

One example of this has been our work in Mozambique, Africa. Our global ministry team has served as a great example of believers empowering one another to serve in their giftedness, and the result has been beautiful. At a pivotal crossroads in our work, a Mozambican couple we were in relationship with contacted our church in hopes that we would help them start an orphanage and community center. Life was not yet at a place where we could partner, but one couple on our global team sensed God's hand in this and quietly nurtured and supported the work until the church as a whole was ready to participate. Those with medical gifts have been drawn to this team, and their expertise has proved indispensible time and again in addressing serious health issues our Mozambican friends face. Others with entrepreneurial gifts have served to move our Mozambican partners toward self-sustainability, those with engineering gifts have helped bring them clean water and other appropriate technologies, those with theological gifts have helped launch a pastors' training program. Our global work has been birthed and nurtured through the insights and efforts of a team of "ordinary" church members who each simply brought to this work the gifts God has given them.

team wept. At the time of this writing, Life in Mozambique has grown to seven churches, with others on the way.

DIFFICULTIES

I don't remember if it was during church planter training or in a book I read, but I remember being told to expect that in three years we would have lost all of our original core team members. We were blessed. At the five-year mark we had seen only a handful move on. I think I figured we had dodged the bullet and that our story would be different from the norm. I was wrong, and when we did begin to lose people I was totally unprepared for it.

We were in year five when the recession hit, and the impact it had on us was pronounced. For a two-year period we averaged one family *per month* moving out of town or out of state to find more affordable places to work and live. We were blessed to add close to the same number of people, but the effect these moves had on the church in general and on me in particular was dramatic. I found myself frequently discouraged—frustrated because it felt as if we were running full speed just to stand still.

We felt even worse concerning those who didn't move away but simply left the church. We had been blessed to experience this so infrequently in our early years that I was totally unprepared for it. Where it seemed like other pastor friends had developed calluses for this type of thing, I had not, and it wrecked me. There were those whose faith faltered and who washed out of church altogether. With others, my impression was that they simply got tired and wanted to return to a church where it was acceptable to be spectators and less would be demanded of them. A few of those who left were trusted allies—men and women I thought would be with us for the long haul. My discouragement deepened, frustration flirted with anger, and I found myself deeply fatigued.

Though it was a season I wouldn't care to revisit, God met me in it. I learned in that time just how much of my faith was not in God but in people. I was embarrassed to find that even as the leader of a missional congregation so much of my security was wrapped up in attendance, giving and on having strong leaders (as if God couldn't develop more). It was hard for me to admit that so much of my self-worth was caught up in these things, but that was reality. This painful pruning God did in me—it too was a grace.

FUTURE

Life Covenant Church had begun in 2003 as a community of people committed to learning from Jesus what it would mean to live our lives the way he would live them. We have named the values of grace, authenticity, community, and love for God and neighbor. We have begun to live out a commitment to an existence that brings good to our city, especially among those less fortunate. Our initial connections to Mozambique, Africa, have become a long-term commitment to bringing sustainable change. We have been blessed to help several thousand impoverished families start small businesses to support their families. And we have begun starting churches with similar visions, and have grown to twelve churches in the last ten years.

As we look ahead to the next chapter in God's story for us, we anticipate a season of doing many of the same things, but better. We feel like we are essentially on the right track, but we long to carry out our mission more effectively.

Currently we are revisiting what it means for us to be God's missionary people in our city. Are we still passionate about unchurched and dechurched people? Somewhat, but we need to continue to refine how we equip ourselves to reach out. Are we serving well those less fortunate than ourselves? In some areas yes, but our efforts here have ebbed and are in need of fresh vision. Our demographic is changing as well. Young singles have become young marrieds, and young marrieds are becoming young parents. The ways we minister to our children and the importance of this in reaching out to our friends is taking on more prominence.

In church planting we are exploring ways to both partner with and mentor our daughter churches into becoming parent churches themselves. Our last two church plants were approached in this way, with three churches forming a network to launch the new church. These new churches are now part of this network, and they will be part of planting the next churches (likely before their second birthday). We want to see reproduction become normative and hope to provide a road map for new churches to get there.

In Mozambique we are exploring ways to strengthen the work we have started. We feel it is in this mission field that we have the potential to see the most churches planted. Truly, the harvest is plentiful but the workers are few. Our Mozambican brothers and sisters are asking above all else for theological education, and we are exploring ways to bring this to them. Our initial efforts are to start a pastors' library in our main Mozambican church plant and community center. We are equipping them with basic study tools, and hope in the future to train up Mozambican mentor-teachers to equip the pastors as the local church-planting movement expands. We envision a hub-and-spoke approach, where in each city we start a community center and then plant churches around it that help bring the resources to the different corners of the community. We are integrating the microfinance development with the churches as well. The pastors are starting small businesses to help support themselves, and their participation helps encourage their congregants (many of whom are still very suspicious of microfinance) to pursue small business development as well. We dream of a day when the church in Mozambique is known as the fountain where one goes to find spiritual, physical and financial vitality.

CONCLUSION

When Life Covenant was first starting I had the opportunity to spend a little time with one of my biggest influences, Dallas Willard. I asked him what words of counsel he would have for a young pastor starting a church. Dallas leaned back in his chair, closed his eyes and laced his fingers behind his neck as he thought. Then he opened his Bible and read me these words Jesus spoke to Paul: *"Do not be afraid; keep on speaking; do not be silent. For I am with you and no one is going to attack and harm you, because I have many people in this city"* (Acts 18:9-10 NIV). "Remember," Dallas added, "Jesus is already at work in this city. And he has many people here—some of whom already know they are his, some who do not know it yet. Try to remember that when things get difficult."

As we follow God's call into this work of planting churches, may God the Father grant each of us the grace to know that Jesus is there in our city, going before us, making his grace and love known, and may we know the power of the Spirit at work in us as we seek to carry out God's will.

10

REFLECTIONS, FRAMEWORKS AND PRIORITIES

Mark Lau Branson
and Nick Warnes

Over the last few years we have had numerous conversations with the leaders of new churches. Nick has frequently tracked with initiatives from different denominations as he began the work described in his chapter, and Mark has followed his former students and others in the Los Angeles region. When we began exploring how these stories could serve other church planters we presented the idea of a book to about fifteen potential contributors. All of their stories are worth hearing, and they have helped us consider how to shape this collection. We read some preliminary outlines, visited websites and deepened our conversations. Eventually we had to make some choices, based on diverse regions, traditions, approaches, lessons learned and (more mundane) the availability of the authors to write while doing the challenging work of missional engagement.

We were committed to letting the authors tell their stories *and* we wanted to give readers some frameworks for perceiving, analyzing and understanding these initiatives in light of the missional church conversation. We were already aware that some earlier approaches to church planting—summarized by our acronym SPEC—were inadequate for many settings throughout the United States and for keeping up with the US population growth. These stories diverge from the SPEC prioritizations, assumptions and models. The churches in this book did not begin with the vision of planting churches in strategic locations of suburban sprawl. They did not begin out of a protest that led to a church split. They did not begin with experts and their strategies. And they did not begin because a charismatic leader wanted to gather a crowd of followers. We know that none of us completely escape the assumptions and habits of those approaches—but the stories we presented profoundly diverge from the practices and beliefs of SPEC.

We have previously noted various problems of SPEC approaches, and we want to reemphasize two. First, SPEC tends to emphasize human agency with programmatic models, while missional ecclesiology emphasizes that God's agency is primary. Denominational structures and many church-planting agencies shaped by modernity face significant challenges because of the frameworks they inhabit concerning decision making, procedures, expectations, training and evaluation. The shift from "doing church mission" to "discerning and participating in God's mission" is profound, requiring different leadership competencies and activities. There are numerous writers who even use the word *missional* to mean various ways that Christians obey the Great Commission or do "incarnational ministry" or connect evangelism with social concerns, all of which are traditional modes of mission and have their own contributions to make but which also fail to engage what is genuinely new and generative in the missional church conversation. God's agency, on the ground, in real time, ahead of us and around us, is the primary conviction that impinges on everything.

Second, SPEC deemphasizes the work of everyday people in everyday churches—the parent churches and the new church. SPEC tends to leave decision making in the meetings of denominations and agencies, and the chosen leader determines the on-the-ground activities. We believe that men and women in the pews of our churches can discern God's prompts regarding one church planting another church, and we believe that the best means of presence and engagement for a new church arises in the imaginations of the men and women who are living in the daily happenings of the new context as a church is planted.

We believe that new churches are needed in many US contexts. We also believe that SPEC approaches are inadequate for fully discerning and participating with God's initiatives in these contexts. Leading into the twenty-first century, mainline denominations and agencies, with their vision for planting churches in new suburban areas, have found disappointing results, and have often pulled back. Even though churches continue to split in protest of local or national decisions, those experiences seldom provide healthy foundations for missional discernment. The cultural complexities of many US contexts are not suitable for the formulas and strategies that have been previously promoted by experts. And charismatic figures are few and far between—and they often present a sustainability challenge when they move on. Overall, these four common approaches for how churches are planted tend to proceed without the involvement of everyday people in everyday churches.

We set out four priorities and asked readers to examine the various stories with these missional lenses, instead of through the lenses of SPEC. We believe this will be a positive step in the direction of encouraging everyday people in everyday churches to become engaged in church planting. We will review those priorities, with examples from the chapters, but first we will walk through some practical ways a group can do the needed attending, listening, researching and storytelling that leads to discernment and experiments.

SOME PRACTICAL STEPS

In chapter two Mark introduced a basic picture of praxis that shapes a rhythm between action and reflection (see fig. 10.1). A church, as a whole and in various groups, is continually engaging their neighborhoods and networks by listening, conversing, sharing meals and work and recreation, and sometimes engaging in activities of mercy and justice. Throughout this book numerous stories have been told of how these churches have engaged their contexts. As these activities continue, the church, again as a whole and in various groups, reflects on their engagements in light of what they know about God (from Scripture, tradition and previous experiences). This is *theological* reflection. As Craig Van Gelder writes, "The church is called and sent to participate in God's mission in the world. The responsibility of the church is to discern where and how this mission is unfolding."[1] He proposes two primary questions: "What is God doing?" and "What does God want to do?"[2] These questions lead to the church's work of then asking how they might more faithfully participate in God's initiatives.

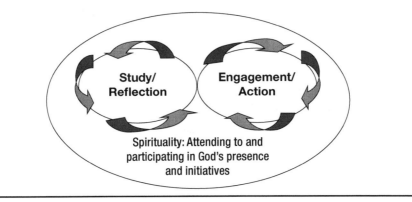

Figure 10.1. Praxis

Mark also explained the steps that are needed for reflective change. There are times when we decide to meet a challenge with a bright idea or quick fix, and that may even be appropriate. But frequently we need *reflection*—a more thorough process that engages more people and devotes more energy and time. The five steps of Alan Roxburgh's Missional Change Process (MCP) make clear what this looks like (see fig. 10.2). Our *awareness* needs to include information about the situation and ourselves in order to move us away from blindness and unreflective opinions and habits. The work of *understanding* requires research, conversations and thinking, all in service of deepening our comprehension of the situations dynamics, causes, consequences, opportunities and challenges. As we gain understanding we can reflect on our current and future role in the situation; this is *evaluation*. Then, by using a discernment process, we can try some *experiments* that on occasion lead to *commitments*.[3]

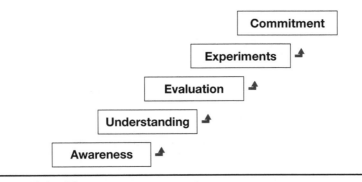

Figure 10.2. Missional change process

These steps are evident, in various forms and sequences, in the stories of this collection. For example, Kevin Doi writes of how Epic became increasingly aware of their context. Fullerton, like many cities, has significant racial and economic disparities. This awareness led to increased understanding as they met neighbors such as Meg, Jim and Valeria. Epic was able to evaluate how their values for hospitality and justice had made these relationships possible, and that they would be changed by these neighbors. For example, after hearing Valeria's story and her longing for a college education, their understanding of their context increased. Epic members experimented by gathering some members and exploring ways to participate in the Garnet Neighborhood's educational goals. Their initial involvement in a scholarship program expanded to other forms of partnerships, including tutoring, college prep and coming alongside families as more kids began to imagine that they could pursue further education.

A praxis-theory-praxis process, with the MCP elements, may be done fairly quickly and informally, with clear insights that result in obvious new activities. As AJ Swoboda writes, this was what happened when they became aware of the lack of parking around their new meeting space, so they knocked on their neighbors' doors and asked for permission to park in front of their homes, and that provided an initial way to connect with these neighbors. There are also times when this work requires a more thorough process, with attention to specific forms of input and a well-designed series of steps. Doi writes about the long process that Epic engaged as they learned that geography mattered, and this process drew on experiences, personal stories, on-the-ground realities and theology. This kind of reflection on praxis is also called *practical theology*, a process that begins with a particular ministry situation and the way the church is engaged. That experience becomes the topic of reflective conversation with specific resources from research and study, then discernment leads to new actions. It will become obvious how these steps of practical theology are a means for engaging Roxburgh's Missional Change Process.

Before going through the steps, though, some theological assumptions need to be noted. Theological assumptions have been at play throughout the book. Sometimes these have been explicit, like Swoboda's explanation that their Portland church is "Anglicostal," drawing on Pentecostal beliefs and practices concerning the Spirit and gifts while also embodying practices they find life giving from the Anglican heritage. And sometimes theology is implied, such as Tim Morey's explanation that their church focuses on being apprenticed to Jesus (an *imitatio Christi* theology), while the Spirit's role is limited to that of gifting and giving power. However, there are indications that they actually may have a more full belief in the Spirit's initiatives ahead of them and the Spirit's guiding them to people and opportunities. This may align with Tim's citing a conversation he had with Dallas Willard that "Jesus is already at work in this city."

There are three explicit theological statements in figure 10.3. First, God is ahead of us in our neighborhoods and world, engaging people and powers, and invites us to join those holy initiatives. This is about the Trinity, the entire Godhead as well as the active persons, Father, Son and Spirit. This theological assumption is behind our first priority concerning a church's work of discerning God's initiatives. Second, the church is a sign, foretaste, witness and instrument of the in-breaking reign of God. These Newbigin words describe how the church's agency is related to God's agency. Third, the Holy Spirit gifts the church with perception, wisdom, resources, courage and work so we can participate in God's initiatives.

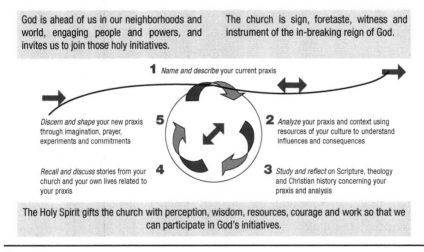

Figure 10.3.

There are other assumptions that lie behind the specified steps. For example, step 2 assumes that human cultures provide numerous resources that can aid our discernment. Step 3 assumes that the Bible is an authoritative source of stories and guidance, and that our theological traditions also provide important narratives and teachings. Step 4 assumes that the stories of our neighbors and the stories within our churches provide important clues to what God is up to, what graces are already apparent, and what deficits and challenges call for attention. These steps are modeled in the preceding stories.

Step 1: Name and describe current praxis. Discernment begins with an awareness of a situation, and that set of circumstances and activities needs to be described. This may be an energizing and hopeful situation, or it may be social challenge of some kind. In either case a team or church has encountered a situation that requires discernment. *Current praxis* means that the participants are engaged with each other and their context, and their engagement is already informed by theology (what they believe about God) and other theories (about the life of their neighborhood and what might serve justice and goodness). This initial awareness calls them to conversational reflection about God, the situation and the church/team. Each chapter provided some initial description of a particular church's context prior to their own engagement, then as they began to live and participate in the community, some specific experiences required further reflection. For example, Doi tells how Epic became aware of how their patterns of gathering for restaurant meals embodied an economic disparity with new participants who had less money. Nikki Collins MacMillan described how the Bare Bulb participants were increasingly aware that they lived in a bubble, hardly aware of the lives, commitments and gifts of their neighbors. In these cases a more comprehensive analysis and new approaches to engagement followed.

Step 2: Analyze using cultural resources. The situation or challenge that was described in step 1 now needs deeper awareness and understanding. If the church's context has an abundance of artists or schools or small businesses, what can be learned about them and from them? If the neighborhood has economic challenges or there are racial tensions, what are some of the important causes? Our culture has numerous resources that can help a group understand causes and opportunities. Step 2, in which the church *analyzes* their praxis and context using resources of their culture to understand influences and consequences, draws on the knowledge, skills and research capacities of the team. Our culture has numerous ways to do this analysis: history, sociology, economics, media studies, adolescent development, demographics, urban planning, migration and immigration, ethnic studies, organizational development, group dynamics, cultural studies and so on. Sometimes a team member will quickly formulate some initial questions and perspectives; at other times those with certain professions, college majors or other training can be called on to bring specific skills (too often ignored) into the conversation.

There are two cautions here. First, the discovery of important information and factors does not necessarily forecast some magic answers; the information discovered feeds into the larger discernment process. Second, we already noted that neighbors are not objects but human subjects, and it is very common for expert analysts to turn people into things. So the research and discussions of step 2 need to avoid objectifying people. In Los Angeles, New City Church became aware that their informal gathering time had more participation from skid row, so when loft dwellers arrived just before the worship service began the social dynamics were awkward. Kevin Haah explains that they are constantly attentive to sociocultural factors that arise because of their demographic realities. This helps the church explore how to make the dynamics of gathering (and other activities) more appropriate for all of their neighbors. A thorough practical theology process will encourage the contributions of those who see through these different lenses or who provide research than can deepen understanding.

Step 3: Study and reflect on Scripture and Christian tradition. The description (step 1) and analysis (step 2) are then brought into the group's reading of Scripture and tradition. This continues to deepen both awareness and understanding; it also might begin the church's evaluation of its own practices. Our four priorities came from this kind of biblical and theological reflection in a number of churches that were involved in transformation and planting. This is not the work of a preacher who provides the relevant truths for the team or church. Rather, perhaps with preaching as one element, the team or church immerses itself in the narratives and literature of the Bible, holding those texts and their own discernment process together as they look for connections and perspectives. For example, a *lectio* exercise with Luke 4:14-30 or Luke 10:1-12 may shape a group to see how God engages a context. Similarly Jeremiah 29:1-7 provides God's instructions for those who were exiled to Babylon, and Acts 11:19-26 and Acts 13:1-3 narrates attention to cultural diversity, leadership and continued church planting in Antioch. If a leadership team or even the whole church were to spend weeks dwelling in one of these passages, the discernment process gets reshaped by the Word. When an initial group of leaders from Warner Robins, Georgia, spent time reflecting on the story of Zacchaeus (Luke 19), Nikki MacMillan writes that "through our structures, architecture, polity, language and internal battles, we have stood in the way of others who are curious and desire to connect with Jesus."

Churches can also draw on church history and their own theological tradition. For example, Northland Village Church, with its focus on reconciliation rooted in 2 Corinthians 5:18-19, could meditate on this passage from the "Confession of 1967" in the PCUSA *Book of Confessions:* "To be reconciled to God is to be sent into the world as his reconciling community. This community . . . is entrusted with God's message of reconciliation and shares his labor of healing the enmities which separate men from God and from each other. Christ has called the church to this mission and given it the gift of the Holy Spirit."

Depending on the presenting issue, various theological statements or historical episodes can open the imagination and creativity of the group. For example, at City Church of East Nashville, Craig Brown notes how their leaders learned from authors who engage Reformed traditions of worship.

Several theological topics require ongoing reflection, study and discussion in our churches. These resources come from current engagement with systematic theology. For example, our *ecclesiologies* (beliefs about church) are being developed in the stories we have included. One way to deepen our reflections is to distinguish between our *formal* ecclesiology (what we say we believe, usually rooted in our tradition's formal doctrinal statements) and our *functional* or practiced ecclesiology (what our actions reveal regarding what we actually believe). Swoboda describes the realization that they were called to plant the *gospel* in a Portland neighborhood rather than plant a church, a realization that in fact shaped their ecclesiology. Similarly, at various times we need to attend to our theology concerning other topics: Jesus Christ (Christology), living in and engaging the world (missiology), the Holy Spirit (pneumatology), and salvation or rectification (soteriology). Swoboda notes a number of ways that Theophilus draws on Pentecostal heritage and theology as they seek to attend to the gifts and movements of the Holy Spirit. All of these beliefs will not be re-considered every time we engage a discernment process, but they can either serve as the originating focus (beginning at step 1) or they can be brought into the reflective process when the particular topic would be well served (at step 3).

Step 4: Recall and discuss church and personal stories. At all stages of exploring, experimenting and ministering, our own stories matter. Step 4— *recall and discuss*—means that we give significant time and attention to *listening.* This step of telling and listening continues to contribute to our awareness and understanding, and may include some initial sense of evaluation. Our own experiences and memories on any topic have shaped what we see, what we are alert to and how we imagine.

In the early stages of assembling a team, we believe that it is important for participants to share their church autobiographies: what happened in their spiritual, congregational and missional experiences. These experiences—the blessings and the wounds—are "in the room," so shaping space and conversations is critical. This attention to stories can then be an expected and normal practice. If the theme of the group discernment is about intergenerational life, the church can reflect on the relationships they have experienced or witnessed. For example, hearing from the church's youth about important adults in their lives can give the adults (and other youth) new perceptions.

We can also deepen our relational connections by creating times and spaces to share stories with neighbors. Brief conversations in shops or parks, or perhaps at block parties or art fairs, can allow us to hear the narratives, interests and hopes of those we share a place with. As a general practice, churches can request and learn from stories, like MacMillan describes their priorities at Bare Bulb Café, and Nick Warnes provides other accounts from Atwater Village. All of the chapters here have some neighbor stories—so the challenge is to bring the most important stories into a church's reflective work when a particular theme warrants. Perhaps during steps 2 and 3 there were already some stories arising from research and Bible studies. This step also gives time to connect personal stories with that research, such as reflecting on how commuter lives (a dynamic that would have surfaced in step 2) shape our schedules and habits so that we tend toward less hospitality with our neighbors.

Step 5: Discern and shape new praxis. All of the descriptions, reflections, research, texts, analysis and stories of steps 1-4 are brought into a prayerful space of continued conversational discernment. Leaders need to shape this space to welcome the Holy Spirit's agency. Again, the primary questions are "What is God doing?" "What does God want to do?" and "How do we participate in God's initiatives?" This is a process of imagination, rooted in the concrete, specific situation and location.

When possible, a group can be authorized to work through these steps and then shape experiments in order to explore next steps. The process should encourage risk; failure should actually be frequent as the group continues to walk into the future. Feedback loops will keep participants informed. Sometimes experiments get dropped; sometimes they are altered and reengaged; sometimes they become longer-term commitments. Both Haah and Warnes note experiments with small groups that were stopped because the participation or the activities were not suitable for their goals and values. Several authors noted how their ministry praxis led to new understanding, which altered how they engaged their context. For example, Craig Brown explains how their Nashville church benefited from various approaches to engaging the needs of their neighborhood—mercy, community development and community organizing. Each approach is based on different frameworks concerning the situation and the desired outcomes. Mercy ministries, though sometimes appropriate, are usually top-down (which means church people have all the power). Community organizing shapes peer relationships so voices and activities are more equal—which makes neighborly relationships more likely.

These practical theology steps can be useful in whole-church discernment or in smaller ministry groups. When any set of participants has the responsibility of discernment concerning a specific topic or theme, just asking these questions will make wisdom more likely. These are abbreviated questions, so the more thorough explanations already given should be considered in any given situation. (1) What do we know about our current practices concerning this ministry? (2) If we analyzed this situation using our own knowledge about social dynamics, economics, ethnicity or aesthetics, what can we learn? If we took some time for more research, what would we like to pursue? (3) What biblical and theological convictions do we have that are related to this ministry? What biblical text(s) could center our reflections? Who can provide some research into the Bible, church history or theology concerning this ministry? (4) In our church and in our own lives, what are the most important stories that have formed us? When have we been most aware of God's grace regarding this topic? (5) How should we structure a space for gathering this input, clarifying our questions and options, listening to God, voicing our imaginations, and testing experiments? While this explanation is linear, it is more common for a discernment process to be less sequential. A theme may arise because of a Bible study, a word from a neighbor, a sense of discomfort or a prompt of the Holy Spirit. The work on one step, like step 3 (biblical and theological study), might raise new questions for step 2 (social and cultural analysis), so the process loops in reverse. Or cultural analysis (step 2) may prompt a specific time for storytelling (step 4). It is important to notice, however, that this full spectrum of input is needed for a robust process of reflection and discernment.

THE PRAXIS OF PRIORITIES

When Mark described four priorities that are influenced by the missional church framework, he wrote that we did not want these to form a grade card for the chapters. While none of these churches articulated all of these priorities when they began, it seems that God has shaped them, in the midst of their contexts, toward these characteristics. We want to indicate some examples of where we saw these priorities embodied. Each of our missional priorities will be restated, with a briefer explanation and then quotations from the preceding chapters will give witness to these practices.

Priority 1: Discerning God's initiatives. "God is the primary agent, and our agency is to be that of participating with the Trinity. These theological affirmations lead us to place a priority on discernment—that a church, continually shaped and resourced by leaders, gains the needed capacities and courage to discern what God is doing in their context and in their own lives, and then to participate in those initiatives (graces) of God."

Doi. What we are learning from our neighbors is that God is here and that there are wonderful assets and dreams in the community already present in the lives of its people. This guards us from taking the stance of doing something *for* others and instead being there *with* others, where we are moving toward increasing levels of mutuality.

Warnes. "We heard stories of other plants that had tried to go in as 'the heroes' to save 'the pagans' by bringing God to the 'Godless' in Northeast Los Angeles. We decided to take a different approach. We began reminding people that God was already in the midst of the city and among these neighbors, so we began asking what God was already up to in our context. There were so many positive things already going on in the community. We simply wanted to join in with the goodness of what was already being initialed by an immanent God."

Priority 2: The neighbor as subject. *Our first priority, to discern what God is doing, helps us remember that God creates our neighbors and us as subjects or actors, rather than as objects. In this way we dispense with our tendencies to maintain power and to treat neighbors as those to whom we deliver our products, programs and truths. Rather, we come alongside our neighbors—we pay attention, we work, we eat, we cry, we laugh, we hope. These genuine human encounters, which are always life-on-life, are the times when we find ourselves engaged in God's initiatives that bring new healing, love, beauty, justice and salvation.*

MacMillan. "From a group of churchy people living in the bubble of church community and structures, we have become God's own in the world—aware of God's movement outside the forms we have known and in relationships we would never have experienced had we stayed inside our church walls or sought to build a new community according to old structures and expectations. . . . We learned quickly that we had hit a nerve in our community. People were longing for a place to be—a venue that would welcome them to share their talent and their stories, a truly hospitable space that could serve as a living room, meeting place, reading corner and game table."

Swoboda. "As opposed to doing flyers and inviting people to church, we believed (as we still do) that our greatest impact would be twofold: first, we would be there a very long time and actually know our neighbors; second, we would never presume we are just there for them. That is, we would try to allow that maybe our neighbors have been sent by God for us, and that *we* were to be changed by *them.* On Sunday evenings we would talk specifically about one important factor in ministry: reciprocity. Not only did we come to serve and know our neighbors, but they were sent to us so that we might learn the love of Christ."

Priority 3: Boundary crossing. Most humans have a tendency toward security that favors what is familiar. But the border-crossing love of God doesn't give us that kind of consumer option. If we are to know God's love for the world, we need to be carried by that love, and that means we will be changed by those who are different. We need to be especially alert to our own provincial habits, and we get the privilege and work of engaging neighbors who are different, who may give us eyes that we don't want, and who actually reshape us in the encounter.

Brown. "This [relational] connection has been Noah's experience. He has found that his life has become richer by being in relationship with the 'poorest of these.'"

> "City Church sends us out every week to enjoy and display Christ in our neighborhood. We are a people on a mission to bring the hope of Jesus and his kingdom to the people around us. I have found power and courage to begin genuine friendships with people who are not like me. The Burchas, a family of Congolese refugees, live in a housing project down the street from my house. I met their three sons at soccer game in the park and soon I was invited to their home for dinner."

Haah. "As I thought about it the multiethnic element was a slam dunk. Downtown was already multiethnic; people worked and went to school in a multiethnic context. The question then became, Would a multisocioeconomic church work? . . . We had to discern whether it was God's call to be multisocioeconomic. And given the demographic data and the vision that God had given us, it was very clear that he was calling us to plant a church that was not only multiethnic but also multisocioeconomic. Maybe our posture simply was to obey and leave the results to God."

Doi. "One of the lessons we are learning in our context about boundary crossing is simply the importance of being aware of ourselves. We have to understand that everything is interpreted, that we can only see the world through our own lenses. At best we see only partially. In a multicultural setting this has meant being cognizant of our own biases and assumptions, aware of existing power dynamics, aware of our own agendas. Sustaining such a posture is not easy, but it is central to maintaining openness to others, to valuing difference and creating the possibility for change—beginning with ourselves."

Priority 4: Plural leadership that shapes an environment. We want to emphasize that as God is shaping a people (a church), the Spirit is inspiring, forming, motivating and teaching a cluster of people who are to provide lead-ership on the ground. So, within the planting group, while one individual may be aware of his or her personal inspiration, ideas and observations, we need to be aware that others are also having such experiences. God will prompt and inform and provide hope though various people. The overall dynamic of wisdom and faithfulness is strengthened when a group surfaces, articulates and works with all of these voices and experiences.

Warnes. "I still remember looking at the overall collection of gifts of the launch team and standing in awe as I realized that we were a beautiful mixture of abilities and passions. From ideation to innovation to execution, all of the gifts were essential to building a solid foundation for executing our mission statement of creating spaces for reconciling relationships."

Morey. "That part of me that craved recognition, that wanted to stand as a lone heroic figure and be praised as the pastor who built a great church needed to die. If we believed the Holy Spirit empowered all believers—that there were going to be multiple people in the church who were gifted to lead, to teach and to shepherd—then I needed God to chasten my ego and teach me how to lead as part of a team."

Doi. "Certainly one of the things we have learned in this season was how to better discern the movement of the Spirit among the entire congregation, believing assets already present in our church community were waiting to be recognized, encouraged and empowered. This has meant affirming, re-leasing and supporting the passions and convictions of the body. This has been especially important when individuals or groups of individuals discern God's movement in the needs and opportunities around them and want to do something about it. The result has been that the church is no longer simply my vision but *our* vision."

EXPANDING PARTICIPATION

Everyone can pray and place priority on discerning God's initiatives in the midst of their neighborhood or city. Everyone can make the shift to seeing neighbors as subjects and not as objects. Everyone can actively follow the Spirit in doing the work of boundary crossing. And everyone can press against our individualistic tendencies and place priority on a plural lead-ership that is being formed in the midst of community.

These churches have also given common witness to some other tendencies. Some repeated characteristics include a focus on a geographic place, shaping worship that is participatory for neighbors, learning from and participating with churches in other countries, and fostering continued church planting. The priorities we list and these additional characteristics seem to arise from a broad set of participants. The preconceived notions of SPEC would not shape such practices. A transition from SPEC toward missional priorities makes it more likely that everyday people, in everyday churches, will believe that they too can participate in God's mission by starting new churches.

We are all shaped by stories. Our own personal stories, which intersect with those of friends and acquaintances, are enriched by other stories that we read and hear. The Holy Spirit has provided a deep and varied, sometimes confusing and often convicting collection that we claim as authoritative Scripture. We have centuries of stories from our traditions. The collection in this book is offered not as a manual but more like a collection of parables. When Jesus wanted to shift the perceptions, desires and actions of listeners, he told stories that were, actually, grace—an initiative of God to bring new life. With thanks to the churches, neighbors and leaders of these narratives, we hope our writing inserts grace into the imaginations and practices of readers so that the gospel is more visible and accessible in our neighborhoods.

AFTERWORD

This has been a book filled with hope! The stories in *Starting Missional Churches* are about the multitudinous ways God's Spirit is ahead of us in our neighborhoods and communities. Instead of packaged formulas shaped by demographics and denomination-centered "how-to" binders, you have read about creative people choosing to join with God in places of profound ordinariness. The people in these stories have ventured on journeys of discernment and experimentation in their local contexts.

What I read in Nick and Mark's framing of this book and the stories that inform its pages are thoughtful theological reflection and good scholarship. These on-the-ground stories are shaped by theological engagement and well-informed praxis. If we are to be a people of discernment, learning again to be open to what the Spirit is doing ahead of us, then we will need the kinds of reflective practices demonstrated here. The great need is for practitioners skilled in theological praxis. This book offers these kinds of frameworks and has the potential to give leaders some of these critical skills. For those teaching church planting, the book is a unique and essential tool for forming others.

Lesslie Newbigin described the church as the hermeneutic of the gospel (as the sign, foretaste and witness of the kingdom), but over the past thirty years most initiatives, books and proposals using Newbigin's name have been thoroughly ecclesiocentric. They turn God's agency into a useful tool for ecclesio- and clergy-centric proposals for fixing and making the church "work" again in North American culture. While *Starting Missional Churches* is about the church (planting), it's not ecclesiocentric. A different imagination pervades this book. The scholarship and attention to theology turns us in a more hopeful direction. Here you've read about God's people "planting" witness and presence in the neighborhood because they are convinced that is where the Spirit of God is out ahead of them. Like detectives of divinity they are convinced that the shape of being God's people is to be formed by this dwelling with, in, for and among the people of their neighborhood.

In my neighborhood, just a few houses down the street, Andy, Jolene and their four children have spent seven or so years "dwelling." They have quietly planted a "church" in their home that is outgrowing its walls. I sat with Andy this week on our front porch listening to him share stories of the street and the simple, ordinary ways the Spirit is shaping something new. God is out ahead of us in our neighborhoods and communities. Here in *Starting Missional Churches* are stories of those who, sensing this movement, are dwelling with God in the neighborhood.

Alan Roxburgh

NOTES

Chapter 1: Shifting Perceptions on How We Plant Churches

[1]David Olson, *The American Church in Crisis* (Grand Rapids: Zondervan, 2008), p. 36.

[2]Ibid., p. 35.

[3]There are estimates as low as 3,500 churches close in America and as high as 4,500 churches close in America per year. Olson's number of 3,700 is a fitting place to begin. Ibid., p. 120.

[4]United States Census 2010, www.census.gov.

[5]Olson, *American Church in Crisis*, p. 146. Estimates, according to the Harford Institute for Religion Research (hartsem.edu), place the number of churches in America at 322,000. Therefore, to keep up with population growth, churches will have to shift from planting 4,000 churches a year to planting 6,440 churches per year. This will allow us to keep up. To extend beyond population growth, we will have to plant more.

[6]This is according to Benton Johnson, professor of sociology at the University of Oregon. See Benton Johnson, Dean R. Hoge and Donald A. Luidens, "Mainline Churches: The Real Reason for Decline," *First Thing* 31 (March 1993): 13-18, www.leaderu.com/ftissues/ft9303/articles/johnson.html.

[7]Leigh Gallagher, "The End of the Suburbs," *Time,* July 30, 2013, http://ideas.time.com/2013/07/31/the-end-of-the-suburbs. This article was adapted from the author's book *The End of the Suburbs: Where the American Dream Is Moving* (New York: Port folio/Penguin, 2013).

[8]Craig Van Gelder, "Denominational Church Life and Congregational Life Cycles," parts 1 and 2, http://themissionalnetwork.com/index.php/resources/video-gallery/player/8/43 and http://themissionalnetwork.com/index.php/resources/video-gallery/player/8/42; see also Alan Roxburgh, *Structures for Mission-Shaped Formation* (Downers Grove, IL: InterVarsity Press, 2015), forthcoming.

[9]Churches always need to be careful when inviting members from other congregations to begin new churches. They are often disgruntled and leave their already-existing churches as disgruntled people. While there is space for disgruntled people to begin new churches, an excessive ratio of such people can create great problems for new churches.

[10]See David B. Barrett, George T. Kurian and Todd M. Johnson, *World Christian Encyclopedia: A Comparative Survey of Churches and Religions in the Modern World* (New York: Oxford University Press, 2001), p. 16.

[11]Alan Roxburgh, *Missional Map-Making* (San Francisco: Jossey-Bass, 2010), p. 24.

[12]This phrase is borrowed: see Anthony Giddens, *The Consequences of Modernity*

(Stanford, CA: Stanford University Press, 1990).

[13]See Alan Roxburgh's work on changing modes of leadership in *Missional Map-Making*; regarding experts see ibid., pp. 64-67, 107-8.

[14]We highly recommend regular neighborhood exegesis for all churches. Neighborhood exegesis is an exercise that includes walking, listening and asking specific questions about the neighborhood. For a thoughtful document of how to do this exercise visit the Presbyterian Centers for New Church Innovation website (www.presbyinnovate.com/resources /documents-forms; click the Neighborhood Exegesis file).

[15]Bob Logan, *Missional Journey* (St. Charles, IL: ChurchSmart Resources, 2013), p. 30.

[16]See the introduction of Ori Brafman and Rod Beckstrum, *The Starfish and the Spider: The Unstoppable Power of Leaderless Organizations* (New York: Penguin Group, 2006).

[17]Dan Steigerwald and Kelly Crull, *Grow Where You're Planted: Collecting Stories on the Hallmarks of Maturing Church* (Portland, OR: Christian Associates Press, 2013), p. xxxv.

[18]See Everett Rogers, *Diffusion of Innovations*, 4th ed. (New York: The Free Press, 1995), pp. 294-304.

[19]Lesslie Newbigin, *A Word in Season* (Grand Rapids: Eerdmans, 1994), pp. 60-63; *The Gospel in a Pluralist Society* (Grand Rapids: Eerdmans, 1989), p. 136.

[20]Craig Van Gelder does well to remind us that these contextual experiments should "mine [missiology's] rich heritage and draw on its multiple resources in order to develop substantive theological foundations and focused strategies as it helps congregations understand and engage the contexts." We hope to add to this work with the tools and stories that we are creating in this book. See his "How Missiology Can Help Inform the Conversation About the Missional Church in Context," in *The Missional Church in Context: Helping Congregations Develop Contextual Ministry*, ed. Craig Van Gelder (Grand Rapids: Eerdmans, 2007), p. 43.

Chapter 2: Perspectives from the Missional Conversation

[1]The most valuable books on planting from the perspectives that we want to front are Stuart Murray, *Planting Churches in the Twenty-First Century* (Scottdale, PA: Herald, 2010); and Martin Robinson and Dwight Smith, *Invading Secular Space* (London: Monarch, 2003). Several authors who have not written specifically on planting but whose work we find most relevant include Lesslie Newbigin, Alan Roxburgh, Craig Van Gelder and Darrell Guder. Recently we have also noted a new collection by Mary Sue Dehmlow Drier, ed., *Created and Led by the Spirit: Planting Missional Congregations* (Grand Rapids: Eerdmans, 2013).

[2]See especially Lesslie Newbigin, *The Open Secret* (Grand Rapids: Eerdmans, 1978), *Foolishness to the Greeks* (Grand Rapids, Eerdmans, 1986), and *The Gospel in a Pluralist Society* (Grand Rapids: Eerdmans, 1989); see Alan Roxburgh's comments on Newbigin and these books in *Missional: Joining God in the Neighborhood* (Grand Rapids: Baker, 2011), pp. 34-46.

[3]Roxburgh, *Missional*, pp. 73-74.

[4]Alan Roxburgh and Fred Romanuk, *The Missional Leader* (San Francisco: Jossey-Bass, 2006), p. 9.

[5]For the kinds of processes and resources needed to move a church toward missional

transformation, see Alan Roxburgh and M. Scott Boren, *Introducing the Missional Church* (Grand Rapids: Baker, 2009).

[6]See especially Craig Van Gelder, *The Ministry of the Missional Church* (Grand Rapids: Baker, 2007), pp. 59-67.

[7]On important practices see Roxburgh, *Missional*, pp. 165-78.

[8]This constant work of the church—of doing theology and engaging a missional context—is modeled and explained by Craig Van Gelder. See especially chapter one in *The Missional Church in Context*, ed. Craig Van Gelder (Grand Rapids: Eerdmans, 2007), pp. 12-43, and his method in *Ministry of the Missional Church*, pp. 95-120. See also Robert Schreiter, *Constructing Local Theologies* (Maryknoll, NY: Orbis, 1985).

[9]Mark Lau Branson and Juan Martínez, *Churches, Cultures and Leadership* (Downers Grove, IL: InterVarsity, 2011), pp. 39-47

[10]Mark Lau Branson, "Ecclesiology and Leadership for the Missional Church," in Van Gelder, *Missional Church in Context*, pp. 110-12.

[11]Roxburgh and Romanuk, *Missional Leader*, pp. 79-103; and Roxburgh and Boren, *Introducing the Missional Church*, pp. 133-46. In some writings this is called the "Missional Change Model," but that was misleading because it does not propose a model of church but a process for a people to learn and experiment their way into a local expression of gospel life. The process is rooted in Everett Rogers, *Diffusion of Innovations*, 5th ed. (New York: Free Press, 2003).

[12]Ibid., p. 141.

[13]On the shaping of a "language house," see Roxburgh, *Missional*, pp. 57-62.

[14]Roxburgh and Boren, *Introducing the Missional Church*, p. 143.

[15]Roxburgh and Romanuk, *Missional Leader*, pp. 93-94.

[16]Van Gelder, *Ministry*, pp. 59-67.

[17]Roxburgh and Boren, *Introducing the Missional Church*, p. 144.

[18]Ibid.

[19]Ibid., p. 145.

[20]Jürgen Moltmann, *The Church in the Power of the Spirit*, trans. Margaret Kohl (New York: Harper & Row, 1977), p. 64.

[21]See Mary Sue Dehmlow Drier, "Planting Missional Congregations: Imagining Together," in Drier, *Created and Led by the Spirit*, pp. 3-26.

[22]This is the core affirmation of *missio Dei*, noted in David Bosch, *Transforming Mission* (Maryknoll, NY: Orbis, 1991), p. 390. See also Darrell Guder, ed., *Missional Church* (Grand Rapids: Eerdmans, 1998), pp. 4-7, 81-3; and especially for the Holy Spirit's initiatives, see Craig Van Gelder, *Ministry of the Missional Church*, pp. 23-46; and on church discernment, pp. 95-120.

[23]See the Missional Network website (themissionalnetwork.com); see also Roxburgh and Romanuk, *Missional Leader*, esp. chaps. 6-7.

[24]Roxburgh, *Map-Making*, p. 151.

[25]Daniel Anderson, "Church Emerging: A Missional View," in Drier, *Created and Led by the Spirit*, p. 128.

[26]This parallels Paulo Freire's emphasis that particular power arrangements dehumanize

persons, and both existing oppressors and revolutionaries make people into objects for their own objectives. Instead, Freire calls for processes that humanize, so all participants are culture-creators. He even claims that leaders need to be converted, and calls this conversion a "profound rebirth." See his *Pedagogy of the Oppressed*, trans. Myra Bergman Ramos (New York: Seabury, 1970), p. 47; see also 33-34; 130-31 n. 10.

[27]Roxburgh, *Missional*, p. 134.

[28]The common emphasis on quick growth and the priority of creating a larger congregation tend to undermine the belief that neighbors and participants are subjects. A priority on multiplying churches—in which churches of about 150 send out new planting initiatives—can more easily maintain the conviction that neighbors and participants are subjects. The assumption that a church will keep planting new churches needs to be articulated from the beginning, otherwise growth toward 200 will create expectations about adding staff for the benefit of the members.

[29]Alan Roxburgh, *Missional Map-Making* (San Francisco: Jossey-Bass, 2010), p. 155.

[30]Roxburgh, *Missional*, p. 113.

[31]Dwight Zscheile, "A Missional Theology of Spiritual Formation," in *Cultivating Sent Communities*, ed. Dwight Zscheile (Grand Rapids: Eerdmans, 2012), p. 19.

[32]See Branson and Martínez, *Churches, Cultures and Leadership*.

[33]Craig Van Gelder and Dwight J. Zscheile, *Missional Church in Perspective: Mapping Trends and Shaping the Conversation* (Grand Rapids: Baker Academic, 2011), p. 156.

[34]Roxburgh and Romanuk, *Missional Leader*, p. 29.

[35]Roxburgh, *Missional*, pp. 129-30.

[36]I like much of what JR Woodward does in regard to plural leadership and the importance of gifts, though I am shaping my emphases somewhat differently. See JR Woodward, *Creating a Missional Culture* (Downers Grove, IL: IVP Books, 2012).

[37]The focus here is on Ephesians 4:11-13; this list is often referred to by an acronym APEST, for apostles, prophets, evangelists, shepherds, teachers. As noted previously, I believe the content of this text is important, but I am not confident about Bible lists becoming standardized as transferable norms and models.

[38]In Everett Rogers's work on diffusion (how new processes and products spread) he notes research that shows how innovative opinion leaders (like some pastors) can tend to slow innovation because people around them learn that only the leader's innovations deserve a hearing. Also since rapid change can create anxieties, a leader often needs to focus on creating a trusting environment of conversation and permission among participants (rather than add to anxieties by voicing more ideas). See Rogers, *Diffusion of Innovations*, 4th ed. (New York: The Free Press, 1995), pp. 294-304.

[39]For some practical matters regarding team leadership, see Stuart Murray, *Planting Churches in the Twenty-First Century*, pp. 170-83.

[40]Roxburgh, *Missional Map-Making*, p. 170.

[41]Ibid.

[42]For an overview of the various ways that "missional church" is being described, see Van Gelder and Zscheile, *Missional Church in Perspective*.

[43]Roxburgh and Romanuk, *Missional Leader*, p. 24.

Chapter 3: Balancing Location and Relationships

[1]Stanley Hauerwas, *A Community of Character* (Notre Dame, IN: University of Notre Dame Press, 1981), p. 10.

[2]Before planting Epic, I had been influenced and shaped by Margaret Wheatley's perspectives on organizations as organic, quantum, living systems in which assumptions of control do not apply and where prediction and replication are impossible. Not only does this make our world more interesting but also more surprising. See Margaret J. Wheatley, *Leadership and the New Science* (San Francisco: Berrett-Koehler, 1999).

[3]Ray S. Anderson, *An Emergent Theology for Emerging Churches* (Downers Grove, IL: InterVarsity Press, 2006), p. 186.

[4]Hauerwas, *Community of Character*, p. 150. Hauerwas argues that the body of Christ is the apologetic for faith: "What is crucial is not that Christians know the truth, but that they be the truth."

[5]Ray S. Anderson, *The Shape of Practical Theology* (Downers Grove, IL: InterVarsity Press, 2001), p. 236.

[6]I have recently discovered a more accurate articulation of a missional approach is to say that "God's church does not have a mission; God's mission has a church" (Craig Van Gelder, "God's Mission Has a Church," lecture, Northern Seminary, Lombard, IL, June 19, 2012).

[7]In those early days we seemed to always be looking for a new place to gather—relocating a handful of times over three years.

[8]For a decision this big we were able to reach a consensus on our staff and board. With the congregation we used Sunday morning worship times, congregational meetings and smaller town-hall gatherings to discuss and pray over the potential changes. Though I wish it were different, at this point in our community's life many of the important decisions felt more top-down than truly participatory. Much of the blame I place on myself for not trusting the process and the congregation with the direction and shape of our church.

[9]"Groundswell" would years later morph into our partnership class called "Epiconnections"—a course we now consider our catechism. As an American Baptist Church practicing a congregational polity, we have used our requirement for membership to encourage a covenant of embodied discipleship lived in community.

[10]"The church does not drive the kingdom into the world through its own institutional and pragmatic strategies. Rather, it is drawn into the world as it follows the mission of the Spirit" (Anderson, *Emergent Theology*, pp. 109-10).

[11]Peter Block, *Community: The Structure of Belonging* (San Francisco: Berrett-Koehler, 2009), pp. 10-11.

[12]At one point after he had been on staff with us for several years, I advocated for a formal recognition of Erin as copastor. Pragmatically this is how we operated, mutually sharing the vision and duties of the pastorate. After some consideration, however, Erin (an Anglo) declined. Instead, he insisted that I remain as the senior pastor because he believed it was important symbolically for Epic and for the rest of

the world that the Asian American (or minority person) be the lead—thus modeling a different ordering than what is often expected in the dominant US culture.

[13]Darrell Guder speaks of the role of place in mission, "A missional ecclesiology takes the context seriously, as it explores how God's Spirit forms and sends the mission community in a particular setting" (Darrell L. Guder, ed., *Missional Church: A Vision for the Sending of the Church in North America* [Grand Rapids: Eerdmans, 1998], p. 69). Ray Anderson adds, "Mission is 'being there,' not simply going there" (Anderson, *Emergent Theology*, p. 194).

[14]Andy Matheson, *In His Image: Understanding and Embracing the Poor* (London: Authentic Media, 2010), p. 42.

[15]Ethnically, we are a 60 percent mix of Asian American (Chinese, Taiwanese, Korean, Japanese, Filipino, Thai, Vietnamese) and 40 percent mix of white, Latino, and African American. As of this writing, ages range from sixty years old to college students, with a majority of adults in their twenties and thirties. Children span from infant to high school, with a bulk of our kids in elementary and middle school.

[16]Gert Jan Hofstede, Paul B. Peterson and Geert Hofstede, *Exploring Culture* (Boston: Intercultural, 2002). See interviews at churchescultureleadership.com.

[17]"Hospitality is not optional for Christians, nor is it limited to those who are especially gifted for it. It is, instead, a necessary practice in the community of faith. One of the key Greek words for hospitality, *philoxenia*, combines the general word for love or affection who are connected by kinship or faith (*phileo*), and the word for stranger (*xenos*)" (Christine D. Pohl, *Making Room: Recovering Hospitality as a Christian Tradition* [Grand Rapids: Eerdmans, 1999], p. 31).

[18]"Rather than asking, 'How do we attract people to what we are doing?' we need to ask, 'What is God up to in this neighborhood, and how do we need to change in order to engage the people who no longer consider church a part of their lives?'" (Alan Roxburgh and M. Scott Boren, *Introducing the Missional Church* [Grand Rapids: Baker, 2009], p. 130).

[19]John McKnight and Peter Block, *The Abundant Community* (San Francisco: Berrett-Koehler, 2010).

[20]"Mission is not just what the church does; it is what the church is" (Guder, *Missional Church*, p. 128).

[21]Our house churches are not to be mistaken as part of the house church movement. We have simply called our groups "house churches" because that best represents for us how we think about our biweekly gatherings in homes—as being the church. All of our house churches are unique, but eating often lies at the heart of those gatherings. As John Howard Yoder describes, sharing a meal becomes a sign of the kingdom as tangible partaking of economic solidarity with one another (John Howard Yoder, *Body Politics* [Scottdale, PA: Herald, 1992]).

[22]We are influenced by Ray Anderson's interpretation of missiologist Paul Hiebert's work on *centered sets* and *bounded sets* as applied to the Lord's Table. Anderson argues that if in the Lord's Supper the real presence of Jesus mysteriously stands before us, all ought to have access to Jesus (centered set). Therefore, at Epic we practice a Communion in which we

proclaim the risen Christ as Savior and Lord, the meaning of the bread and cup, and the table that belongs to Jesus—and invite all to partake and encounter Christ through the meal.

Chapter 4: Gathering Neighbors

[1]I first heard this phrasing from Jack Miller and have been ruined by it ever since!

[2]James Montgomery Boice offered such insight in *Two Cities, Two Loves* (Downers Grove, IL: InterVarsity Press, 1996).

[3]Michael E. Fleenor, *East Nashville: Images of America* (Charleston: Arcadia, 1998).

[4]Jana and I gathered the information in this paragraph in 2003, based on the 2000 US Census. An excellent source for finding such data is www.perceptgroup.com.

[5]*The People of Nashville: Exploring the Religions and Cultures of the People Groups of Nashville* (Nashville: Nashville Baptist Association, 2011).

[6]Christ Community Church, Franklin, Tennessee, and the Nashville Presbytery are a part of the Presbyterian Church in America (PCA). For more information about the PCA visit www.pcanet.org.

[7]World Harvest Mission is a missions sending agency that has over 150 missionaries in 14 countries. For more information about WHM visit www.whm.org.

[8]The concepts of *incarnational* and *missional* (which have now become strongly and wrongly overused) began bringing together the theology of gospel, kingdom, church and culture for me through the original writings of Lesslie Newbigin, and later by the Gospel and Culture Network. See George R. Hunsberger and Craig Van Gelder, eds., *The Church Between Gospel and Culture: The Emerging Mission in North America* (Grand Rapids: Eerdmans, 1997).

[9]The word *evangelism* comes from the Greek *euangelion*. The term referred to an act or decree of a ruler with continuing good news to be proclaimed or acted upon. Heralds would typically travel throughout the region announcing the good news. For followers of Jesus the good news was the historical reality and teaching surrounding the life, death, resurrection and ascension of Jesus. In fact, the word *gospel* is often the English rendering for *euangelion*. When used as a verb, we can properly call evangelism "gospeling." See Millar Burrows, "The Origin of the Term 'Gospel,'" *Journal of Biblical Literature* 44, nos. 1-2 (1925): 21-33.

[10]Tom Wood, the founder and president of Church Multiplication Ministries and at this point a consultant-coach for us, led a group of church planters through various exercises to help us determine what would be "essential elements" to have in place in order to launch public worship. I have been told that more church plants fail for lack of quality coaching than for any other reason! For more information about Church Multiplication Ministries or Tom Wood visit www.cmmnet.org.

[11]Through previous research related to being asked to recommend a model of discipleship for a church of several thousand in a previous calling, I realized the viability, stability and sustainability such groups had the potential to provide. Redeemer Presbyterian Church's Home Fellowship Group Manual was instrumental in forming our vision for Neighborhood Groups. For more information about Redeemer Presbyterian Church visit www.redeemer.com.

[12]The YMCA Community Action Project (Y-CAP) was and continues to be a mutually

beneficial partnership for City Church.

[13]Alan Hirsch summarizes, "We seem to make church complex and discipleship too easy." Hirsch's work has been foundational for my continual growth in attempting to understand the nuances of discipleship in the emerging cultural milieu of North America. See Alan Hirsch, *The Forgotten Ways: Reactivating the Missional Church* (Grand Rapids: Brazos, 2006), p. 104.

[14]Hirsch uses the term *simplex* to describe the gospel: "It is so simple that even the most uneducated peasant can understand it, but so complex that even the most educated scholar can never plumb its depths" (Alan Hirsch, presentation at the Church Planting Leadership Fellowship, Nashville, November 16, 2011). The concept of "simple church" to deal with complex people and communities is also addressed in Thom Rainer and Eric Geiger, *Simple Church* (Nashville: B&H, 2006); and Tim Chester and Steve Timmis, *Total Church* (Wheaton, IL: Crossway, 2008).

[15]Cornelius Plantinga, *Not the Way It's Supposed to Be* (Grand Rapids: Eerdmans, 1995), p. 10.

[16]Bob Dylan, "Everything's Broken," Special Rider Music, 1989.

[17]Lesslie Newbigin, quoted in N. T. Wright, *Surprised by Hope* (New York: HarperCollins, 2008), pp. 107-8.

[18]C. S. Lewis, *Prince Caspian* (New York: HarperCollins, 1951), p. 218.

[19]See David Kinnaman and Gabe Lyons, *unChristian: What a New Generation Really Thinks About Christianity . . . and Why It Matters* (Grand Rapids: Baker, 2007).

[20]See Timothy J. Keller, "Reformed Worship in the Global City," in *Worship by the Book*, ed. D. A. Carson (Grand Rapids: Zondervan, 2002).

[21]For more on the elements of worship, see John M. Frame, *Worship in Spirit and Truth: A Refreshing Study of the Principles and Practice of Biblical Worship* (Phillipsburg, NJ: P&R, 1996), esp. chap. 5; and Ralph P. Martin, *Worship in the Early Church* (Grand Rapids: Eerdmans, 1974).

[22]Gospel reenactment follows a pattern such as creation, fall, redemption, consummation; or law, gospel, new creation; or praise, renewal, commitment. See Frame, *Worship in Spirit and Truth;* and Keller, "Reformed Worship in the Global City."

[23]David Peterson, *Engaging with God: A Biblical Theology of Worship* (Downers Grove, IL: IVP Academic, 2002), p. 289.

[24]Emperor Julian, quoted in Rodney Stark, *The Rise of Christianity* (San Francisco: HarperCollins, 1997), p. 84.

[25]See Christine Pohl, *Making Room: Recovering Hospitality As a Christian Tradition* (Grand Rapids: Eerdmans, 1999); and Brian Fikkert and Steve Corbett, *When Helping Hurts: How to Alleviate Poverty without Hurting the Poor . . . and Yourself* (Chicago: Moody Press, 2009).

[26]Fikkert and Corbett, *When Helping Hurts*, p. 104.

[27]Ibid.

[28]People of God Organized is based on the principles of the Industrial Areas Foundation (IAF) model of community organizing. For more information about IAF visit www.industrialareasfoundation.org.

[29]Richard Lovelace, *Renewal as a Way of Life* (Downers Grove, IL: InterVarsity Press, 1985), p. 1.

Chapter 5: A Beautiful Community of Diversity

[1]"Downtown Dude" is a quick reference, sort of like the "Saddleback Sam" in Rick Warren, *Purpose Driven Church* (Grand Rapids: Zondervan, 1995).

[2]The name of the seminar is "Church Planter's Toolkit" by Bob Logan. This was considered a classic, must-hear seminar among the older planters.

[3]Ralph Winter, "Ralph Winter Auto Biography Part #2," Pioneer Senders, www.pioneersenders.org/ralph-winter-auto-biography-part-2.

[4]I adopted this strategy after reading Stephen Gray's book, *Planting Fast-Growing Churches*. His research on hundreds of church plants shows that those that launch with at least fifty people on the core group grow significantly faster. See Stephen Gray, *Planting Fast-Growing Churches* (St. Charles, IL: ChurchSmart Resources, 2007).

Chapter 6: Creating Third Spaces

[1]Ray Oldenburg, *The Great Good Place* (New York: Marlowe, 1989).

[2]Though at the time of writing the project is only in its fourteenth month of full operation, it is projected that even with conservative growth, the coffee shop will be contributing financial resources to the ministry by the end of the second year.

[3]We had a part-time staff person whose salary was funded through our grants for a year before the project began to generate revenue. This was not part of our funding projections and has necessitated restructuring our financial model and additional funding from Flint River Presbytery.

Chapter 7: Growing Roots in a Secularized Context

[1]In Dave Olson's research from his website, "The American Church Research Project," people can buy information on churches in metropolitan areas. The research here is helpful. See www.theamericanchurch.org/ppmain.htm.

[2]Walter Brueggemann, *Theology of the Old Testament: Testimony, Dispute, Advocacy* (Minneapolis: Fortress Press, 1997), pp. 614-15.

[3]Darrell L. Guder, ed., *Missional Church: A Vision for the Sending of the Church in North America* (Grand Rapids, Eerdmans, 1998), p. 48.

[4]Ibid.

[5]I have a friend who has planted a church in South Carolina where a presupposed Christendom identity was important to the mission of the church.

[6]Following God's eschatological movement toward the city as seen in Revelation 22.

[7]Miroslav Volf, *Exclusion and Embrace: A Theological Exploration of Identity* (Nashville: Abingdon, 1996), p. 9.

[8]A perfect example of the suburban sprawl strategy, the *S* in SPEC (see chap. 1).

[9]Stuart Murray, *Planting Churches in the Twenty-First Century* (Scottdale, PA: Herald, 2008), p. 173.

[10]Alan J. Roxburgh, *Missional: Joining God in the Neighborhood* (Grand Rapids: Baker, 2011), p. 44.

[11]See George G. Hunter III, *The Celtic Way of Evangelism: How Christianity Can Reach the West . . . Again* (Nashville: Abingdon, 2000), p. 26.

[12]As Martin Robinson and Dwight Smith suggest, we didn't begin with the gifts of the pastor, but instead we began with the gifts that God is already giving to the neighborhood and joined in that activity. See Martin Robinson and Dwight Smith, *Invading Secular Space: Strategies for Tomorrow's Church* (Grand Rapids: Kregel, 2004), p. 129.

[13]Assessme (assessme.org) offers four tests: (1) a test similar to the Myers-Briggs, (2) a spiritual gifts assessment, (3) a leadership style analysis, and (4) a spot to write in already-existing assets. StrengthsFinder (strengthsfinder.com) was the most important test for us concerning how to equip our people for using their gifts in the context of our mission. It also allowed us to "get on the balcony" and look at the whole set of gifts that God had brought together as a new church. I recommend all of these assessment tools.

[14]Dave Olson's book is foundational for understanding the shifting landscape of people connected to churches in North America and why church planting is essential for this shifting landscape. See Dave Olson, *The American Church in Crisis* (Grand Rapids: Zondervan, 2008).

[15]Colin Greene and Martin Robinson, *Metavista: Bible, Church and Mission in an Age of Imagination* (Colorado Springs: Authentic Media, 2008), p. 168.

[16]Many of us imagined appealing to the young, up-and-coming hipster crowd that is prevalent in Northeast LA. Instead, we have connected with a much more diverse group of people from the area. See Alan J. Roxburgh and M. Scott Boren, *Introducing the Missional Church* (Grand Rapids: Baker, 2009), p. 87.

[17]Richard Foster has a great chapter on the discipline of simplicity. See Richard Foster, *Celebration of Discipline: The Path to Spiritual Growth* (San Francisco: HarperSan-Francisco, 1988), pp. 79-95.

[18]Examples of preaching in the marketplace continue to press us at NVC. The marketplace is where most of the preaching and teaching was done in the New Testament.

[19]The conversation was posted on the forum at http://forum.atwatervillage.org /forum/threads.php?id=3382_0_13_0_C. Requires login.

CHAPTER 8: AN EXPRESSION OF FAITH THAT FITS

[1]Stumptown will change your life. Visit when you are next in Portland. See the Stumptown website at stumptowncoffee.com.

[2]Portland captivated me in earlier college years when reading Donald Miller's iconic *Blue Like Jazz*. Miller's gut-wrenchingly honest account depicts his attempts to embody the message of Jesus on the campus of Reed College in urban Portland. See Donald Miller, *Blue Like Jazz: Non-Religious Thoughts on Christian Spirituality* (Nashville: Thomas Nelson, 2003).

[3]For three blogs that give depictions of the city of Portland, see www.news4neighbors .net, www.platypuscomix.cartoonsdammit.com/fpo/ and www.portlandonline.com/oni.

[4]Visit Imago Dei's website at www.imagodeicommunity.com. Other great examples of churches doing similar work are Door of Hope (doorofhopepdx.org), Evergreen (ever-greenlife.org) and the Oregon Community (theoregoncommunity.com).

[5]While making the case that God calls God's people to the city would admittedly require some hermeneutical leaps, it is nevertheless interesting that cities are mentioned something like 1,250 times in Scripture.

[6]Thanks to Alan Hirsh for giving me this insight during a conversation.

[7]Stuart Murray, *Church Planting: Laying Foundations* (Scottdale, PA: Herald, 2001), p. 21.

[8]Steven Berlin Johnson, *Emergence* (New York: Touchstone, 2001), p. 31.

[9]One aspect of being sent by our parent church is that it was very important for us to ask for permission to begin inviting people. Paul talks in Ephesians 6 about honoring one's mother and father, and how it comes with a promise of blessing. We thought this applied to our mother church as well.

[10]Clovis G. Chappell, *Sermons on Simon Peter* (Nashville: Abingdon, 1969), p. 37.

[11]In no way shape or form is this universal, nor should it be. Each church must wrestle with this in their own context.

[12]Interestingly, most of the earliest Pentecostals and charismatics were bivocational, due to the fact that the people they served were incredibly poor. It would seem to me that the need for bivocational ministry entirely depends on the context of the church plant. For more on this see Mickey Crews, *The Church of God: A Social History* (Knoxville: University of Tennessee Press, 1990), p. 5.

[13]The "Messianic Secret," found in Mark 1:43-45, 4:11, and 8:29-30, refers to Jesus' choice at times to avoid public recognition.

[14]This phrase is borrowed from the masterpiece by James Davidson Hunter, *To Change the World: The Irony, Tragedy, and Possibility of Christianity in the Late Modern World* (New York: Oxford University Press, 2010), pp. 238-54.

[15]Seth Godin, *Linchpin: Are You Indispensable?* (New York: Penguin, 2010), p. 106.

[16]See the TED talk by Daniel Goldstein, "The Battle Between Your Present and Future Self," *TED*, November 2011, www.ted.com/talks/daniel_goldstein_the_battle_between _your_present_and_future_self.html.

CHAPTER 9: CREATING GLOCAL DISCIPLES OF JESUS

[1]Darrell Guder's and Lesslie Newbigin's writings were particularly influential in this. See Darrell L. Guder, ed., *Missional Church: A Vision for the Sending of the Church in North America* (Grand Rapids: Eerdmans, 1998); and Lesslie Newbigin, *The Gospel in a Pluralist Society* (Grand Rapids: Eerdmans, 1989).

[2]Thomas Kelly, *A Testament of Devotion* (San Francisco: HarperCollins, 1941), pp. 19-20.

[3]For a thorough treatment of this subject see Christopher J. H. Wright, *The Mission of God* (Downers Grove, IL: InterVarsity, 2006).

[4]We were deeply helped in this by Dallas Willard, *The Divine Conspiracy* (San Francisco: HarperSanFrancisco, 1998).

[5]Dietrich Bonhoeffer's *Life Together* is a key text for us in this area. See Dietrich Bonhoeffer, *Life Together* (New York: Harper & Row, 1954).

[6]For more on how we developed this and the undergirding theology see Tim Morey, *Embodying Our Faith* (Downers Grove, IL: InterVarsity, 2009), chaps. 3-4.

[7]Dallas Willard and Eddie Gibbs influenced us. For example, see Dallas Willard. *The Divine Conspiracy* (San Francisco: HarperCollins, 1998), and *Renovation of the Heart* (Colorado Springs: NavPress, 2002); and Eddie Gibbs, *ChurchNext* (Downers Grove, IL:

InterVarsity, 2000), and *LeadershipNext* (Downers Grove, IL, 2005).

[8]I'm indebted to my friend Keith Matthews of Azusa Pacific University for providing the bones of this vision statement out of his own church's vision.

[9]Check out Opportunity International's website at www.opportunity.org.

CHAPTER 10: REFLECTIONS, FRAMEWORKS AND PRIORITIES

[1]Craig Van Gelder, *The Ministry of the Missional Church* (Grand Rapids: Baker, 2007), pp. 59-61.

[2]Ibid.

[3]See Alan Roxburgh and Fred Romanuk, *The Missional Leader* (San Francisco: Jossey-Bass, 2006), pp. 79-103; and Alan Roxburgh and M. Scott Boren, *Introducing the Missional Church* (Grand Rapids: Baker, 2009), pp. 133-46.

ABOUT THE
CONTRIBUTORS

Mark Lau Branson (MA, Claremont School of Theology; EdD, University of San Francisco) is the Homer Goddard Professor of Ministry of the Laity at Fuller Theological Seminary, and a consultant with The Missional Network. Mark and his wife, Nina Lau-Branson (who also works with The Missional Network), live in Pasadena and are on the core team of a new Free Methodist church initiative. They have two adult sons, Noah and Nathan. Mark's recent work in consulting has mainly been with already-existing congregations that want to reshape their lives in missional directions. His book *Memories, Hopes, and Conversations: Appreciative Inquiry and Congregational Change* has led hundreds of churches through a healthy process for discerning God in their own stories as well as in their neighborhoods. With coauthor Juan Martínez he also wrote *Churches, Cultures and Leadership: A Practical Theology of Congregations and Ethnicities* in order to provide frameworks, stories and resources for those who know that church leaders need to attend to the cultural diversity of our contexts. Through staying connected with many of his students who have gone on to plant new churches, Mark has found new parallels between church transformation and church planting. This book is an extension of these findings.

Nick Warnes (MDiv, Fuller Theological Seminary, emphasis in worship, theology and art) is a husband and founding pastor of Northland Village Church in Los Angeles, California. He enjoys the regular pattern and rhythm of being a local pastor in Los Angeles and loves to spend his extra time supporting others to start new churches. He does this as a coach and church-planting assessor for the Presbyterian Church USA, as a coach and trainer for Bridges (a nonprofit focused on creating Christ-following communities in Southern California) and as a cocreator of a regular cohort for people discerning church planting. Nick also sits on the board of Bridges and is an adviser for the Fuller Theological Seminary Church Planting Certificate. Nick loves his time with his wife, Whitney, with his dog, Bella, and riding his bike through Griffith Park while admiring the diverse waterfowl on the Los Angeles River.

Craig Brown serves as the church multiplication catalyst for CMM, Inc. (www .cmmnet.org), providing gospel-centered coaching for church planters and network leaders. Before joining CMM, Craig was the founding and lead pastor of City Church of East Nashville since planting it in 2004. While planting City Church, Craig helped found the Nashville Church Planting Network, which helps cultivate the soil that supports the multiplication of city-focused church plants. He received his education from Vanderbilt University and Covenant Theological Seminary. He enjoys songwriting, golf, good food and drink, and running (which he says is needed if you enjoy good food and drink!). Craig and his wife, Jana, live in East Nashville and have four children—Travis, Clark, Annalise and Simon.

Nikki Collins MacMillan holds a degree in psychology and religion from Wesleyan College in Macon, Georgia, and master of divinity from Union Presbyterian Seminary in Richmond, Virginia, but she has learned the most important things she knows about life and ministry while sitting at tables with cups of coffee, good books and real friends. Nikki makes her home in Macon, Georgia, where she lives with her husband, Doug, and their two sons.

Kevin Doi is founding pastor of Epic Church in downtown Fullerton, California, and a cofounder of JOYA Scholars, a nonprofit organization that inspires and prepares economically disadvantaged students from the Garnet Neighborhood in Fullerton for higher education. Kevin earned a MDiv from Fuller Seminary and is completing a DMin in missional leadership at Northern Seminary. He enjoys meeting people for coffee around town and spending time with his wife, Dorene, and his two teenage children, Jarron and Charis.

Kevin Haah went from being a young urban single out of Cornell Law School to getting married (Grace), having three kids (Kaetlyn and twins Eliana and Bennett), making partner at a prestigious law firm, giving up law to pursue a master in divinity at Fuller Theological Seminary, and becoming a pastor and a church planter. In 2008, Kevin and Grace planted New City Church of LA, an inclusive gospel-centered community in downtown Los Angeles, where he is currently the lead pastor. Kevin also initiated and currently coleads a church planting movement to plant gospel-driven churches in every neighborhood in Los Angeles (stadia.cc/la-movement). In addition, he is a church planting coach and teaches church planting at Fuller Theological Seminary.

Tim Morey (DMin, Fuller Theological Seminary) is founding and lead pastor at Life Covenant Church, a wonderful, messy, missional church plant in Torrance, California. He also serves on the National Church Planting Team of the Evangelical Covenant Church and is the author of *Embodying Our Faith: Becoming a Living, Sharing, Practicing Church* (InterVarsity Press). Tim is the proud father of Abby and Hannah, whose beauty and charm prove that his wife, Samantha, has strong genes.

AJ Swoboda is a professor, author and pastor of Theophilus (theophiluschurch .com) in urban Portland, Oregon. He teaches theology, biblical studies and Christian history at George Fox Evangelical Seminary and a number of other universities and Bible colleges. Previous to this, AJ served as a campus pastor at the University of Oregon. His doctoral research at the University of Birmingham (UK) explored the never-ending relationship between the Holy Spirit and ecology. AJ is the author of *Messy: God Likes It That Way* (Kregel) and *Tongues and Trees: Toward a Pentecostal Ecological Theology* (JPTSup, Deo). You can find his website and blog at www .ajswoboda.com, or follow him on Twitter @mrajswoboda.